Guide to
AMERICAN POETRY EXPLICATION
Volume 1

Colonial and Nineteenth-Century

A
Reference
Publication
in
Literature

Nancy Martinez
Editor

Guide to
AMERICAN POETRY EXPLICATION
Volume 1

Colonial and Nineteenth-Century

JAMES RUPPERT

G.K.HALL &CO.
70 LINCOLN STREET, BOSTON, MASS.

Library of Congress Cataloging-in-Publication Data

Ruppert, James.
      Colonial and nineteenth-century / James Ruppert.
         p. cm. -- (Guide to American poetry explication: v. 1)
    (A Reference publication in literature)
      ISBN 0-8161-8919-6
      1. American poetry--19th century--History and criticism-
-Bibliography. 2. American poetry--Colonial period, ca. 1600-
-1775--History and criticism--Bibliography. 3. American poetry-
-Explication--Bibliography. I. Title. II. Series. III. Series:
A Reference publication in literature.
Z1231.P7R66 1989
[PS201]
016.811'009--dc20   89-2196
                                         CIP

For Terry

Contents

The Author

James Ruppert received his degrees from S.U.N.Y. Buffalo, Purdue, and the University of New Mexico. He has taught for Navajo Community College, U.N.M. and New Mexico Tech. He has also taught at the University of Munich as a Fulbright lecturer. His research centers on American literature, Native American literature, and literary theory. He presently enjoys a joint appointment in English and Alaska Native Studies at the University of Alaska in Fairbanks.

Preface

This book on pre-twentieth-century American poetry is part of a newly expanded and completely revised series that lists extensive bibliographic sources for the explication of both American and British poetry. An expansion of the successful *Poetry Explication: A Checklist*, especially the third edition (1980), these volumes retain many of the features of the previous editions, but with significant changes both in the scope of references and the works explicated.

In revising *Poetry Explication,* the compilers have sought to make it not only a tool for specialists but also a wide-ranging reference instrument for students and professionals who are not specialists, and thus suitable for home and small-school libraries.

This volume is intended first of all to update the third edition of *Poetry Explication*, which listed citations through 1977. Coverage now extends through December 1987. In those ten years the number of English-language explications on all areas of American and British poetry has grown exponentially. In addition to updating the third edition, coverage has been made more inclusive and comprehensive by including explications found in books covering individual authors and works of more than five hundred lines. Because the original editors believed that a scholar of poetry would be aware of the main sources on any individual poet, the earlier editions of the checklist included only those works that might be obscure and difficult to find.

As in *Poetry Explication*, poets are listed alphabetically by last name. Under the author headings, poetical works are listed alphabetically by the title of the work (excluding the articles *a*, *an*, and *the*). Citations of explications are then listed alphabetically by last name of the critic. Titles of frequently cited journals are abbreviated; there is a list of corresponding abbreviations at the front of this volume. Full publication data for books cited with shortened titles will be found in the Main Sources Consulted at the back of the volume.

The division of citations on American poets into the two volumes, this one on pre-twentieth-century poets and its companion volume on twentieth-century poets, follows the period designations established by standard literary histories and anthologies. In the case of Edwin Arlington Robinson, a decision was made to include him in this volume.

For anyone interested in looking at explication of the work of a poet, the Main Sources is a good place to start. Books listed there contain either numerous explications or particularly detailed and illustrative explications. For example, if one wishes to find explications of Whitman's poetry, specifically "Song of Myself," one might start with the citations under Whitman and then under "Song of Myself" in the Checklist of Interpretation. But there are more than six pages of citations in this section. Skimming over the Main Sources, however, would bring the reader to a number of titles such as Edwin Haviland Miller's *Walt Whitman's Poetry: A Psychological Journey* or Howard Waskow's *Whitman: Explorations in Form*, both of which are excellent places to begin looking for explication. Of course, in using the volume, citations for *The Explicator* magazine guarantee an emphasis on explication.

The selection of explications was governed by the definition given in the first edition of *Poetry Explication*: "an examination of a work of literature for a knowledge of each part, for the relations of these parts to each other, and for their relations to the whole." At times it was difficult to identify exactly what constituted an explication. When there was any doubt as to the appropriateness of including a citation, it was retained. In some situations, one person's explication is another's paraphrase.

I have included explications of major parts of poems where it was clear that the author was working toward illuminating the intrinsic meaning of specific lines or sections and their relation to the whole of the work, rather than toward a theoretical point outside the work. I admit that this is a subjective and delicate decision. Most scholarly research is published to illustrate theoretical insights; but to be included here, an explication had to be a serious attempt to illuminate a the work as a whole. I have omitted references to critical analyses that seek to elaborate a theory by a series of references to three- or four-line quotes from numerous poems. However, no citation was omitted solely because the author took a theoretical approach. Whether Marxist or phenomenologist, feminist or deconstructionist, if the author presented an analysis that demonstrated a knowledge of the parts of a poem and their relation to the whole, the work is cited.

Though the essential principles of explication have not changed, their uses may have. Today explication is less a goal (if it ever was purely that), and more a tool. While it is often associated with New Criticism, a brief look at the many scholars listed here will be enough to convince anyone that almost every noted scholar in the last fifty years has done critical work that has made use of explication. The list at times looked to me like an honor roll of American poetic criticism. It seems clear that almost all theoretical speculations now must be grounded on close readings, so that Cleanth Brooks's insight that "we are all New Critics now" is appropriate on a number of levels: while critical theories such as hermeneutics and structuralism may deemphasize explication, many, perhaps most, theoretical approaches--even reader response, deconstructionism, speech act, and dialogics--make use of it.

It seems clear that the valuable tool of explication is too infrequently applied to some pre-twentieth-century American poetry. This underuse might rest on the bias of critics who think of explication as appropriate only to the modern era, though this attitude may not be quite as prevalent in British literary criticism, where poetry from Anglo-Saxon through modern is heavily explicated. Too many critics of early American poetry may feel that the work is valuable primarily for its historical or biographical significance rather than as literary artifact. Also, even less explication exists of the work of minority poets and minor pre-twentieth-century poets. That is perhaps understandable, since the demands of the traditional canon have discouraged research in these areas in general. Much criticism of these writers seems to project an interest in historical and biographical analysis. There is significant explication yet to be done for poets such as Paul Lawrence Dunbar, James Weldon Johnson, Paula Johnson, James Russell Lowell, and Philip Freneau, to name but a few. I have been able to add a number of poets to the checklist who were not included in the previous editions, such authors as Phillis Wheatley and John Trumbull. Also I have been able to significantly expand the number of citations for some underrepresented poets like William Cullen Bryant and Anne Bradstreet. I hope that this will complement efforts by other critics and anthologists to create a more open literary canon.

A great deal of explication exists for the work of Whitman and Dickinson, perhaps because of our appreciation of their connections to modern sensibilities and techniques. Clearly, the best explication in the last ten years has been done on the work of these two poets. But it is a shame that the poetry of other major writers such as Melville, Thoreau, and Emerson is not more fully explicated. While there is significant explication of the poetry of Poe and Longfellow, there is still much work to be done on these writers, too.

Perhaps explication is no longer sufficiently novel to be encouraged as an end or goal by contemporary scholarly journals, or perhaps journals discourage explication for explication's sake because they assume potential contributors have mastered it as a tool; whatever the reasons, explication does not enjoy the publication support it once did. Yet, as we enter the nineties, explication may once again receive renewed interest; as we proceed with a redefinition of the humanities and we reemphasize the importance of literary appreciation and understanding, we can not fail to reevaluate our use of explication; as the foundation of literary understanding, it holds a place of importance, implicit in our teaching. Explication's greatest contributions are yet to come. While composition enjoyed revitalized interest in the seventies and eighties, the teaching of literature did not. New strategies in literary education will require that we highlight our most basic mode of understanding--explication.

I would like to acknowledge the support of many people in the preparation of this volume. Nancy Martinez, general editor of the series and organizing genius behind these volumes, supplied invaluable advice and encouragement. The staff of the Inter-library Loan Department at the University of Alaska--Fairbanks did a fantastic job. My thanks to Terry Boren for all her help.

Abbreviations

AI   American Imago

AL   American Literature

AmerS   American Studies

AN&Q   American Notes and Queries (New Haven)

AQ   American Quarterly

ArQ   Arizona Quarterly

BuR   Bucknell Review

CentR   The Centennial Review

ConnR   Connecticut Review

CE   College English

CEA   CEA Critic

CLS   Comparative Literature Studies (University of
             Illinois)

CLQ   Colby Library Quarterly

CP   Concerning Poetry (West Washington State College)

CritI   Critical Inquiry

DicS   Dickinson Studies (formerly Emily Dickinson
             Bulletin)

EAL   Early American Literature

EIC   Essays in Criticism (Oxford)

EJ   The English Journal

ELH   Journal of English Literary History

ELN   English Language Notes

ELWIU   Essays in Literature (Western Illinois
             University)

ES	English Studies
ESQ	ESQ: Journal of the American Renaissance
Expl	Explicator
GaR	The Georgia Review
HudR	The Hudson Review
IEY	Iowa English Bulletin: Yearbook
JEGP	Journal of English and Germanic Philology
KR	The Kenyon Review
L&P	Literature and Psychology
Lang&S	Language and Style
LitR	Literary Review: An International Journal of Contemporary Writing (Fairleigh Dickinson University)
MinnR	The Minnesota Review
MissQ	Mississippi Quarterly: The Journal of Southern Culture
MLN	Modern Language Notes

MLQ	Modern Language Quarterly
MLS	Modern Language Studies
MP	Modern Philology
MQ	Midwest Quarterly: A Journal of Contemporary Thought
MR	Massachusetts Review: A Quarterly of Literature, The Arts, and Public Affairs (University of Massachusetts)
MSE	Massachusetts Studies in English
N&Q	Notes and Queries
NEQ	The New England Quarterly: A Historical Review of New England Life and Letters
PLL	Papers on Language and Literature: A Journal for Scholars and Critics of Language and Literature
PMLA	Publications of the Modern Language Association of America
PQ	Philological Quarterly
PR	Partisan Review
PrS	Prairie Schooner

QJS	The Quarterly Journal of Speech
RS	Research Studies (Washington State University)
SAQ	South Atlantic Quarterly
SCN	Seventeenth-Century News
SHR	Southern Humanities Review
SIR	Studies in Romanticism
SJS	San Jose Studies
SoQ	The Southern Quarterly: A Journal for Arts in the South (University of Southern Mississippi)
SoR	Southern Review (Louisiana State University)
SoRA	Southern Review: Literary and Interdisciplinary Essays (Adelaide, Australia)
SP	Studies in Philology
SR	Sewanee Review
SWR	Southwest Review
TLS	[London] Times Literary Supplement

ABBREVIATIONS

TSE   Tulane Studies in English

TSL   Tennessee Studies in Literature

TSLL   Texas Studies in Literature and Language:
           A Journal of the Humanities

UDR   University of Dayton Review

WHR   Western Humanities Review

WVUPP   West Virginia University Philological Papers

WWR   Walt Whitman Quarterly Review

Checklist of Interpretation

ALDRICH, THOMAS BAILEY

"At a Reading"

Charles Samuels, *Thomas Bailey Aldrich* (New York: Twayne, 1965), 49.

"The Moorland"

Charles Samuels, *Thomas Bailey Aldrich* (New York: Twayne, 1965), 45-46.

"Proem"

Charles Samuels, *Thomas Bailey Aldrich* (New York: Twayne, 1965), 113-14.

BARLOW, JOEL

"Advice to a Raven in Russia"

Robert D. Arner, "Joel Barlow's Poetics: 'Advice to a Raven in Russia,'" *ConnR* 5 (Apr. 1972): 38-43.

Arthur Ford, *Joel Barlow* (New York: Twayne, 1971), 102-6.

James T.F. Tanner, "The 'Triple Ban' in Joel Barlow's 'Advice to a Raven in Russia,'" *EAL* 12 (Winter 1977/1978): 294-95.

"Columbiad"

Elliot, *Revolutionary Writers*, 119-24.

Arthur Ford, *Joel Barlow* (New York: Twayne, 1971), 74-84.

Leon Howard, *The Connecticut Wits* (Chicago: University of Chicago Press, 1943), 312-22.

Cecelia Tichi, *New World, New Earth: Environmental Reform in American Literature from the Puritans through Whitman* (New Haven: Yale University Press, 1979), 128-34.

James Woodress, *A Yankee's Odyssey: The Life of Joel Barlow* (Philadephia: J.B. Lippincott, 1958), 248-50.

"The Commencement Poem"

Theodore Zunder, *The Early Days of Joel Barlow: A Connecticut Wit* (New Haven: Yale University Press, 1934), 131-34.

"The Conspiracy of Kings"

Arthur Ford, *Joel Barlow* (New York: Twayne, 1971), 93-94.

"The Hasty Pudding"

Robert D. Arner, "The Smooth and Emblematic Song: Joel Barlow's *The Hasty Pudding*," *EAL* 7 (Spring 1972): 76-91.

Arthur Ford, *Joel Barlow* (New York: Twayne, 1971), 94-102.

"The Vision of Columbus"

Elliot, *Revolutionary Writers*, 95-109.

Arthur Ford, *Joel Barlow* (New York: Twayne, 1971), 46-67.

Leon Howard, *The Connecticut Wits* (Chicago: University of Chicago Press, 1943), 144-59.

Cecelia Tichi, *New World, New Earth: Environmental Reform in American Literature from the Puritans through Whitman* (New Haven: Yale University Press, 1979), 118-20.

Theodore Zunder, *The Early Days of Joel Barlow: A Connecticut Wit* (New Haven: Yale University Press, 1934), 131-34.

BRACKENRIDGE, HUGH HENRY

"Epistle to Walter Scott"

Daniel Marder, *Hugh Henry Brackenridge* (New York: Twayne, 1967), 127-29.

"The Modern Chevalier"

Daniel Marder, *Hugh Henry Brackenridge* (New York: Twayne, 1967), 83-85.

"Poem on the Divine Revelation"

Thomas Haviland, "The Miltonic Quality of Brackenridge's Poem on Divine Revelation," *PMLA* 56 (June 1941): 588-92.

Daniel Marder, *Hugh Henry Brackenridge* (New York: Twayne, 1967), 67-68.

"Rising Glory of America"

Daniel Marder, *Hugh Henry Brackenridge* (New York: Twayne, 1967), 64-67.

BRADSTREET, ANNE

"Before the Birth of One of Her Children"

Randall Mawer, "'Farewel Dear Babe': Bradstreet's Elegy for Elizabeth," *EAL* 15 (Spring 1980): 31-32.

Stanford, *Anne Bradstreet: The Worldly Puritan*, 24-25.

"The Burning of Our House, July 10th, 1666"

Daly, *God's Altar*, 100-101.

Martin, *An American Triptych*, 74-75.

Randall Mawer, "'Farewel Dear Babe': Bradstreet's Elegy for Elizabeth," *EAL* 15 (Spring 1980): 30-31.

Rosamund R. Rosenmeier, "'Divine Translation': A Contribution to the Study of Anne Bradstreet's Method in the Marriage Poems," *EAL* 12 (Fall 1977): 131-33.

"Contemplations"

Daly, *God's Altar*, 117-26.

Anne Hildebrand, "Anne Bradstreet's Quaternions and 'Contemplations,'" *EAL* 8 (Fall 1973): 117-25.

William J. Irvin, "Allegory and Typology 'Imbrace and Greet': Anne Bradstreet's 'Contemplations,'" *EAL* 10 (Spring 1975): 30-46.

Piercy, *Anne Bradstreet*, 96-101.

Stanford, *Anne Bradstreet: The Worldly Puritan*, 93-106.

White, *Anne Bradstreet: The Tenth Muse*, 329-37.

"Davids Lamentation for Saul and Jonathan"

Piercy, *Anne Bradstreet*, 68-70.

White, *Anne Bradstreet: The Tenth Muse*, 246-48.

"A Dialogue between Old England and New"

Piercy, *Anne Bradstreet*, 51-54.

Stanford, *Anne Bradstreet: The Worldly Puritan*, 53-61.

White, *Anne Bradstreet: The Tenth Muse*, 159-72.

"Farewel Dear Babe"

Daly, *God's Altar*, 110-12.

Randall Mawer, "'Farewel Dear Babe': Bradstreet's Elegy for Elizabeth," *EAL* 15 (Spring 1980): 29-41.

Piercy, *Anne Bradstreet*, 94-96.

"The Flesh and the Spirit"

Martin, *An American Triptych*, 50-52.

Piercy, *Anne Bradstreet*, 88-90.

Stanford, *Anne Bradstreet: The Worldly Puritan*, 85-89.

White, *Anne Bradstreet: The Tenth Muse*, 338-42.

"The Four Elements"

Martin, *An American Triptych*, 44-45.

White, *Anne Bradstreet: The Tenth Muse*, 185-89.

"The Four Humours"

Martin, *An American Triptych*, 45-46.

Piercy, *Anne Bradstreet*, 43-47.

White, *Anne Bradstreet: The Tenth Muse*, 189-92.

"The Four Monarchies"

Piercy, *Anne Bradstreet*, 56-59.

Stanford, *Anne Bradstreet: The Worldly Puritan*, 66-70.

White, *Anne Bradstreet: The Tenth Muse*, 228-37.

"The Four Seasons"

Martin, *An American Triptych*, 46-47.

Piercy, *Anne Bradstreet*, 55-56.

White, *Anne Bradstreet: The Tenth Muse*, 215-17.

"I Had Eight Birds Hatch'd in One Nest"

Piercy, *Anne Bradstreet*, 82-83.

Stanford, *Anne Bradstreet: The Worldly Puritan*, 26-28.

White, *Anne Bradstreet: The Tenth Muse*, 310-14.

"In Honour of Du Bartas, 1641"

White, *Anne Bradstreet: The Tenth Muse*, 149-55.

"In Honor of That High and Mighty Princess Queen Elizabeth of Happy Memory"

Martin, *An American Triptych*, 40-42.

"A Letter to Her Husband Absent upon Public Employment"

Daly, *God's Altar*, 106-8.

John Donahue Eberwein, "The 'Unrefined Ore' of Anne Bradstreet's Quaternions," *EAL* 9 (Spring 1974): 24-25.

Martin, *An American Triptych*, 68-69.

Piercy, *Anne Bradstreet*, 84-86.

Rosamund Rosenmeier, "'Divine Translation': A Contribution to the Study of Anne Bradstreet's Method in the Marriage Poems," *EAL* 12 (Fall 1977): 125-27.

Stanford, *Anne Bradstreet: The Worldly Puritan*, 20-23.

"Of the Four Ages of Man"

Piercy, *Anne Bradstreet*, 54-55.

White, *Anne Bradstreet: The Tenth Muse*, 208-15.

"Of the Vanity of Worldly Things"

Daly, *God's Altar*, 96-100.

White, *Anne Bradstreet: The Tenth Muse*, 241-44.

"Phoebus Make Haste, the Day's Too Long . . ."

Rosamund Rosenmeier, "'Divine Translation': A Contribution to the Study of Anne Bradstreet's Method in the Marriage Poems," *EAL* 12 (Fall 1977): 124-25.

"A Pilgrim"

Stanford, *Anne Bradstreet: The Worldly Puritan*, 115-19.

"The Prologue"

Martin, *An American Triptych*, 31-32.

Stanford, *Anne Bradstreet: The Worldly Puritan*, 63-65.

White, *Anne Bradstreet: The Tenth Muse*, 238-41.

"The Quaternions"

Stanford, *Anne Bradstreet: The Worldly Puritan*, 29-51.

"Upon My Son Samuel His Going for England"

White, *Anne Bradstreet: The Tenth Muse*, 309-10.

BRYANT, WILLIAM CULLEN

"After a Tempest"

Peach, *British Influence*, 33-34.

"The Antiquity of Freedom"

McLean, *William Cullen Bryant*, 102-6.

"Earth"

McLean, *William Cullen Bryant*, 44-46.

"The Embargo"

McLean, *William Cullen Bryant*, 91-93.

"The Evening Wind"

George Arms, "William Cullen Bryant," *University of Kansas City Review* 15 (Spring 1949): 222-23. Reprinted in Arms, *The Fields Were Green*, 18.

"A Forest Hymn"

McLean, *William Cullen Bryant*, 58-60.

"The Fountain"

McLean, *William Cullen Bryant*, 99-102.

"The Greek Boy"

McLean, *William Cullen Bryant*, 97-99.

"Green River"

George Arms, "William Cullen Bryant," *University of Kansas City Review* 15 (Spring 1949): 219. Reprinted in Arms, *The Fields Were Green*, 13.

"Hymn to Death"

George Arms, "William Cullen Bryant," *University of Kansas City Review* 15 (Spring 1949): 220-21. Reprinted in Arms, *The Fields Were Green*, 15-16.

"An Indian at the Burial Place of His Fathers"

William Bradley, *William Cullen Bryant* (London: Macmillian, 1926), 80-81.

"Inscription for the Entrance to a Wood"

William Bradley, *William Cullen Bryant* (London: Macmillian, 1926), 46-48.

G. Giovannini and Walter Gierasch, *Expl* 4 (Apr. 1946): 40. Reprinted in *The Explicator Cyclopedia* 2:66-67.

"Lines on Revisiting the Country"

Peach, *British Influence*, 34-37.

"The Painted Cup"

McLean, *William Cullen Bryant*, 128-30.

"The Planting of the Apple-Tree"

Joan Berbrich, *Three Voices from Paumanok* (Port Washington: Ira J. Friedman, 1969), 85-87.

"The Poet"

Graham Clarke, "Imaging America: Paintings, Pictures and Poetics of Nineteenth-century American Landscape," in Lee, *Nineteenth-Century American Poetry*, 201-2.

"The Prairies"

George Arms, "William Cullen Bryant," *University of Kansas City Review* 15 (Spring 1949): 221. Reprinted in Arms, *The Fields Were Green*, 16.

McLean, *William Cullen Bryant*, 40-44.

Ralph N. Miller, "Nationalism in Bryant's 'The Prairies,'" *AL* 21 (May 1949): 227-32.

Peach, *British Influence*, 40-41.

"A Rain-Dream"

Joan Berbrich, *Three Voices from Paumanok* (Port Washington: Ira J. Friedman, 1969), 77-78.

"The Song of the Sower"

Baker, *Syntax in English Poetry, 1870-1930*, 38-40.

"A Summer Ramble"

Peach, *British Influence*, 38-39.

"Thanatopsis"

George Arms, "William Cullen Bryant," *University of Kansas City Review* 15 (Spring 1949): 220. Reprinted in Arms, *The Fields Were Green*, 14-15.

William Bradley, *William Cullen Bryant* (London: Macmillian, 1926), 28-33.

Charles H. Brown, *William Cullen Bryant* (New York: Scribner's, 1971), 58-63, 102-4.

E. Miller Budick, "'Visible' Images and the 'Still Voice': Transcendental Vision in Bryant's 'Thanatopsis,'" *ESQ* 22 (Second Quarter 1976): 71-77.

Thomas O. Mabbot, *Expl* 11 (Dec. 1952): 15. Reprinted in *The Explicator Cyclopedia* 2:67-68.

Albert F. McLean, Jr., "Bryant's 'Thanatopsis': A Sermon in Stone," *AL* 31 (Jan. 1960): 474-79.

McLean, *William Cullen Bryant*, 65-81.

"To a Fringed Gentian"

McLean, *William Cullen Bryant*, 48-49.

"To a Waterfowl"

George Arms, "William Cullen Bryant," *University of Kansas City Review* 15 (Spring 1949): 221-22. Reprinted in Arms, *The Fields Were Green*, 17-18.

Vince Clemente, "Bryant's 'To a Waterfowl' and the Painter W.S. Mount," in *Under Open Sky: Poets on William Cullen Bryant*, ed. Norbert Krapf (New York: Fordham University Press, 1986), 25-28.

Donald Davie, in Wain, *Interpretations*, 130-37.

McLean, *William Cullen Bryant*, 31-33.

"To Cole, the Painter Departing for Europe"

Graham Clarke, "Imaging America: Paintings, Pictures and Poetics of Nineteenth-century American Landscape," in Lee, *Nineteenth-Century American Poetry*, 202-5.

"The Two Graves"

McLean, *William Cullen Bryant*, 82-83.

"A Winter Piece"

Peach, *British Influence*, 37-38.

"The Yellow Violet"

McLean, *William Cullen Bryant*, 46-48.

COOKE, EBENEZER

"An Elegy on the Death of the Honourable Nicholas Lowe"

Cohen, *Ebenezer Cooke*, 36-41.

"An Elegy on the Death of the Honourable William Lock"

Cohen, *Ebenezer Cooke*, 87-90.

"An Elegy on the Death of Thomas Bordley"

Cohen, *Ebenezer Cooke*, 34-36.

"The History of Colonel Nathaniel Bacon's
Rebellion in Virginia"

Cohen, *Ebenezer Cooke*, 70-83.

"A Poem in Memory of the Hon. Benedict Leonard Calvert"

Cohen, *Ebenezer Cooke*, 90-93.

"The Sot-weed Factor"

Cohen, *Ebenezer Cooke*, 6-27.

"Sotweed Redivivus"

Cohen, *Ebenezer Cooke*, 60-69.

CRANE, STEPHEN

"The Battle Hymn"

Hoffman, *The Poetry of Stephen Crane*, 158-63.

"Behold, From the Land of the Farther Sun"

Frank Bergon, *Stephen Crane's Artistry* (New York: Columbia University Press, 1975), 93-94.

"Black Riders Came from the Sea"

John Berryman, *Stephen Crane* (New York: Octagon Books, 1975), 320-21.

Bettina Knapp, *Stephen Crane* (New York: Ungar, 1987), 130-31.

Marston La France, *A Reading of Stephen Crane* (Oxford: Clarendon Press, 1971), 161-62.

"The Blue Battalions"

Hoffman, *The Poetry of Stephen Crane*, 163-74.

"Blustering God"

Bettina Knapp, *Stephen Crane* (New York: Ungar, 1987), 133-35.

"Bottles and Bottles and Bottles"

Hoffman, *The Poetry of Stephen Crane*, 184-86.

"The Chatter of a Death-Demon from Tree-top"

Hoffman, *The Poetry of Stephen Crane*, 131-36.

"Do Not Weep, Maiden, for War Is Kind"

John Berryman, *Stephen Crane* (New York: Octagon Books, 1975), 271-73. Reprinted in *Stephen Crane: A Collection of Critical Essays*, ed. Maurice Bassan (Englewood Cliffs: Prentice-Hall), 33-35.

Hoffman, *The Poetry of Stephen Crane*, 188-91.

Bettina Knapp, *Stephen Crane* (New York: Ungar, 1987), 136-39.

"God Fashioned the Ship of the World Carefully"

Bettina Knapp, *Stephen Crane* (New York: Ungar, 1987), 132-33.

"God Lay Dead in Heaven"

Hoffman, *The Poetry of Stephen Crane*, 139-40.

"I Explain the Silvered Passing of a Ship at Night"

Robert Basye, "Color Imagery in Stephen Crane's Poetry," *ALR* 13 (Spring 1980): 127-28.

"In the Desert"

Marston La France, *A Reading of Stephen Crane* (Oxford: Clarendon Press, 1971), 137-38.

"In the Night"

Hoffman, *The Poetry of Stephen Crane*, 85-86.

"I Saw a Man Pursuing the Horizon"

John Berryman, *Stephen Crane* (New York: Octagon Books, 1975), 269-70. Reprinted in *Stephen Crane: A Collection of Critical Essays*, ed. Maurice Bassan (Englewood Cliffs: Prentice-Hall), 32-33.

"I Walked in a Desert"

Marston La France, *A Reading of Stephen Crane* (Oxford: Clarendon Press, 1971), 135-36.

"I Was in Darkness"

Clarence Johnson, *Expl* 34 (Sept. 1975): 6.

"A Little Ink More or Less"

Hoffman, *The Poetry of Stephen Crane*, 78-79.

"The Livid Lightnings Flashed in the Clouds"

Daniel Hoffman, "Stephen Crane and the Poetic Tradition," in *Stephen Crane's Career: Perspectives and Evaluations*, ed. Thomas Gullason (New York: New York University Press, 1972), 300-301.

"A Man Adrift on a Slim Spar"

John Berryman, *Stephen Crane* (New York: Octagon Books, 1975), 276-77.

Hoffman, *The Poetry of Stephen Crane*, 94-99.

Marston La France, *A Reading of Stephen Crane* (Oxford: Clarendon Press, 1971), 140-43.

George Monteiro, *Expl* 32 (Oct. 1973): 14.

"A Man Saw a Ball of Gold in the Sky"

Daniel Hoffman, "Stephen Crane and the Poetic Tradition," in *Stephen Crane's Career: Perspectives and Evaluations*, ed. Thomas Gullason (New York: New York University Press, 1972), 299-300.

"Once I Saw Mountains Angry"

Marston La France, *A Reading of Stephen Crane* (Oxford: Clarendon Press, 1971), 138-39.

"Once There Was a Man--"

Marston La France, *A Reading of Stephen Crane* (Oxford: Clarendon Press, 1971), 167-68.

"Should the Wide World Roll Away"

Hoffman, *The Poetry of Stephen Crane*, 124-26.

"A Slant of Sun on Dull Brown Walls"

Frank Bergon, *Stephen Crane's Artistry* (New York: Columbia University Press, 1975), 94.

Hoffman, *The Poetry of Stephen Crane*, 86-88.

"There Exists the Eternal Fact of Conflict"

Hoffman, *The Poetry of Stephen Crane*, 156-58.

"There Was a Man and Woman"

Hoffman, *The Poetry of Stephen Crane*, 137-38.

"To the Maiden"

Marston La France, *A Reading of Stephen Crane* (Oxford: Clarendon Press, 1971), 133-34.

"'Truth,' Said a Traveller"

Daniel Hoffman, "Stephen Crane and the Poetic Tradition," in *Stephen Crane's Career: Perspectives and Evaluations*, ed. Thomas Gullason (New York: New York University Press, 1972), 297-98.

"The Wayfarer"

Daniel Hoffman, "Stephen Crane and the Poetic Tradition," in *Stephen Crane's Career: Perspectives and Evaluations*, ed. Thomas Gullason (New York: New York University Press, 1972), 285-86.

"A Youth in Apparel that Glittered"

Daniel Hoffman, "Stephen Crane and the Poetic Tradition," in *Stephen Crane's Career: Perspectives and Evaluations*, ed. Thomas Gullason (New York: New York University Press, 1972), 286.

DICKINSON, EMILY

"Abraham to Kill Him"

George Monteiro, *Expl* 45 (Winter 1987): 32-33.

"Absent Place--an April Day--"

Porter, *Dickinson: The Modern Idiom*, 90.

"The Admirations--and--Contempt-of--Time"

Ford, *Heaven Beguiles the Tired*, 106-7.

Roland Hagenbuchle, "Precision and Indeterminacy in the Poetry of Emily Dickinson," *ESQ*, no. 20 (First Quarter 1974): 45.

James Hughes, "Dickinson as 'Time's Sublimest Target,'" *DicS,* no. 34 (Second Half 1978): 32-34.

Sherwood, *Circumference and Circumstance*, 187-88.

Wolosky, *Emily Dickinson: A Voice of War*, 18-20.

"After a Hundred Years"

Diehl, *Emily Dickinson and The Romantic Imagination*, 61-62.

"After Great Pain, a Formal Feeling Comes"

Anderson, *Emily Dickinson's Poetry*, 210-11.

Beaty and Matchett, *Poetry: From Statement to Meaning*, 28-34. Brooks and Warren, *Understanding Poetry*, 468-71; rev. ed., 325-27.

Brooks and Warren, *Understanding Poetry*, 469-71.

Cameron, *Lyric Time*, 167-69.

Cody, *After Great Pain*, 328-30.

Denis Donoghue, *Emily Dickinson*, University of Minnesota Pamphlets on American Writers, no. 81 (Minneapolis: University of Minnesota Press, 1969), 29-31.

Drew, *Poetry: A Modern Guide*, 124-25.

Juhasz, *The Undiscovered Continent*, 78-82.

Lucas, *Emily Dickinson and Riddle*, 14-17.

Francis Manley, "An Explication of Dickinson's 'After Great Pain,'" *MLN* 78 (Apr. 1958): 260-64.

Mordecai Marcus, "Dickinson and Frost: Walking Out on One's Grief," *DicS* no. 63 (Second Half 1987): 16-29.

Robinson, *Emily Dickinson: Looking to Canaan*, 114-16.

Sherwood, *Circumference and Circumstance*, 111-14.

William Bysshe Stein, "Emily Dickinson's Parodic Masks," *University of Kansas City Review* 36 (Autumn 1969): 54-55.

DICKINSON, EMILY

"Again--His Voice Is at the Door--"

Miller, *The Poetry of Emily Dickinson*, 200-204.

"All That I Do"

Diehl, *Emily Dickinson and the Romantic Imagination*, 77-78.

"All These My Banners Be"

Miller, *The Poetry of Emily Dickinson*, 150-52.

"Alone, I Cannot Be--"

Porter, *The Art of Emily Dickinson's Early Poetry*, 118-19.

"Although I Put Away His Life--"

Juhasz, *The Undiscovered Continent*, 125-27.

"Angels, in the Early Morning"

Barker, *Lunacy of Light*, 68-69.

"The Angle of a Landscape--"

Cameron, *Lyric Time*, 4-5.

Johnson, *Emily Dickinson: Perception and the Poet's Quest*, 115-16.

Barton Levi St. Armand, *Emily Dickinson and Her Culture: The Soul's Society* (Cambridge: Cambridge University Press, 1984), 222-24.

"Apparently with No Surprise"

Herbert R. Coursen, Jr., "Nature's Center," *CE* 24 (Mar. 1963): 468-69.

Perrine, *Sound and Sense*, 126-27.

"'Arcturus' Is His Other Name"

Budick, *Emily Dickinson and the Life of Language*, 126.

Wallace, *God Be with the Clown*, 85-87.

"As By the Dead We Love to Sit"

J. Burbick, "Emily Dickinson and the Economics of Desire," *AL* 58 (Oct. 1986): 372-73.

Edgar F. Daniels, *Expl* 35 (Winter 1976): 10-11.

Nat Henry, *Expl* 31 (Jan. 1973): 35.

Nat Henry, *Expl* 35 (Winter 1976): 26-27.

Johnson, *Emily Dickinson: Perception and the Poet's Quest*, 82-83.

Robert L. Lair, *Expl* 25 (Mar. 1967): 58.

Laurence Perrine, *Expl* 33 (Feb. 1975): 49.

Laurence Perrine, *Expl* 36 (Spring 1978): 32.

"As Far from Pity as Complaint"

Duncan, *Emily Dickinson*, 79-80.

"As Frost Is Best Conceived"

Barker, *Lunacy of Light*, 72-73.

"As Imperceptibly as Grief"

Blair, *The Literature of the United States*, 2:751.

Andrew Hook, *American Literature in Context, III: 1865-1900* (London: Metheun, 1983), 56-59.

Johnson, *Emily Dickinson*, 106-9.

Frank Rashid, "Emily Dickinson's Voice of Endings," *ESQ*, no. 118 (First Quarter, 1985): 30.

"As Summer into Autumn Slips"

Mossberg, *Emily Dickinson: When a Writer Is a Daughter*, 81-82.

"As the Starved Maelstrom Laps the Navies"

Cameron, *Lyric Time*, 16-18.

Weisbuch, *Emily Dickinson's Poetry*, 20-21.

"As Watchers Hang upon the East"

Brenda Ann Catto, *Expl* 33 (Mar. 1975): 55.

Cody, *After Great Pain*, 428-30.

Ford, *Heaven Beguiles the Tired*, 76-77.

Laurence Perrine, *Expl* 35 (Winter 1976): 4-5.

"At Half Past Three, a Single Bird"

Douglas Anderson, "Presence and Place in Emily Dickinson's Poetry," *NEQ* 57 (June 1984): 209-11.

Cameron, *Lyric Time*, 176-77.

Archibald MacLeish, "The Private World: Poems of Emily Dickinson," in Sewall, *Emily Dickinson: A Collection of Critical Essays*, 152-53.

Robert Russell, *Expl* 16 (Oct. 1957): 3. Reprinted in *The Explicator Cyclopedia* 1:55-56.

Weisbuch, *Emily Dickinson's Poetry*, 121-22.

"Aurora Is the Effort"

John Mann, "Emily Dickinson, Emerson, and the Poet as Namer," *NEQ* 51 (Dec. 1978): 481.

Kenneth B. Newell, *Expl* 20 (Sept. 1961): 5.

"Banish Air From Air--"

Nicholas Ruddick, *Expl* 40 (Summer 1982): 31.

"The Bat Is Dun, With Wrinkled Wings--"

Anderson, *Emily Dickinson's Poetry*, 108-11.

"Because I Could Not Stop for Death"

Abad, *A Formal Approach to Lyric Poetry*, 141-43.

Anderson, *Emily Dickinson's Poetry*, 241-46, 248-49.

Christopher Benfey, *Emily Dickinson: Lives of a Poet* (New York: George Braziller, 1986), 82-85.

Paula Bennet, *My Life a Loaded Gun: Female Creativity and Feminist Poetics* (Boston: Beacon Press, 1986), 46-49.

Blair, *The Literature of the United States*, 2:750.

Bloom, *A Map of Misreading*, 184-86.

H.A. Bouraoui, "'Leaning Against the Sun': Emily Dickinson, the Poet as Seer," *RS* 37 (Sept. 1969): 208-17.

Budick, *Emily Dickinson and the Life of Language*, 223-27.

E. Miller Budick, "Temporal Consciousness and the Perception of Eternity in Emily Dickinson," *ELWIU* 10 (Fall 1983): 235-37.

Frances Bzowski, "A Continuation of the Tradition of the Irony of Death," *DicS*, no. 54 (Bonus 1984): 33-37.

Cameron, *Lyric Time*, 121-28.

Chase, *Emily Dickinson*, 249-51. Abridged in Gwynn, Condee, and Lewis, *The Case for Poetry*, 105-6; in Davis, *14 by Emily Dickinson*, 109-11.

Daiches and Charvat, *Poems in English*, 727.

Bert Case Diltz, *Sense or Nonsense: Contemporary Education at the Crossroads* (Toronto: McClelland & Stewart, 1972), 83-89.

Denis Donoghue, *Emily Dickinson*, University of Minnesota Pamphlets on American Writers, no. 81 (Minneapolis: University of Minnesota Press, 1969), 37-39.

Eberwein, *Dickinson: Strategies*, 216-18.

Paul Ferlazzo, "The Deadly Beau in Two Poems by Emily Dickinson, *DicS*, no. 19 (Dec. 1971): 133-36.

Ford, *Heaven Beguiles the Tired*, 122-23.

Eunice Glenn, "Emily Dickinson's Poetry: A Revaluation, " *SR* 51 (Autumn 1943): 585-88.

Griffith, *The Long Shadow*, 126-34.

Theodore Hoepfner, "'Because I Could Not Stop for Death,'" *AL* 29 (Mar. 1957): 96.

Thomas Johnson, *Emily Dickinson: An Interpretive Biography* (Cambridge: Harvard University Press, 1955), 222-24.

Ankey Larrabeee, "Three Studies in Modern Poetry," in Davis, *14 by Emily Dickinson*, 105-7.

John F. Lynen, "Three Uses of the Present: The Historian's, the Critic's, and Emily Dickinson's," *CE* 28 (Nov. 1966): 134-35.

Jerome McGann, "The Text, the Poem, and the Problem of Historical Method," *NLH* 12 (Winter 1981): 278-85.

Martz, *The Poem of the Mind*, 94-95.

Miller, *The Poetry of Emily Dickinson*, 193-94.

Pollak, *Dickinson: The Anxiety of Gender*, 190-92.

B.N. Raina, *Expl* 43 (Spring 1985): 11.

James Reeves, "Introduction to Selected Poems of Emily Dickinson," in Sewall, *Emily Dickinson: A Collection of Critical Essays*, 125-26.

Robinson, *Emily Dickinson: Looking to Canaan*, 51-53.

William E. Rogers, *The Three Genres and the Interpretation of Lyric* (Princeton: Princeton University Press, 1983), 97-101.

Barton Levi St. Armand, *Emily Dickinson and Her Culture: The Soul's Society* (Cambridge: Cambridge University Press, 1984), 71-73.

Sanders, *The Discovery of Poetry*, 344-46.

Michael Staub, "A Dickinson Diagnosis," *DicS*, no. 54 (Bonus 1984): 43-46.

Tate, *Reactionary Essays on Poetry and Ideas*, 13-16, 22-25. Reprinted in Tate, *On the Limits of Poetry*, 205-8; in Locke, Gibson, and Arms, *Readings for Liberal Education*, 173-74; 3d ed., 158-59. Abridged in Gwynn, Condee, and Lewis, *The Case for Poetry*, 105. Reprinted in Feidelson and Brodtkorb, *Interpretations of American Literature*, 204-5; in Ferlazzo, *Critical Essays on Emily Dickinson*, 87-88; in Tate, *Reason in Madness*, 14-15.

Unger and O'Connor, *Poems for Study*, 547-48.

John E. Walsh, *The Hidden Life of Emily Dickinson* (New York: Simon & Schuster, 1971), 161-66.

Weisbuch, *Emily Dickinson's Poetry*, 113-17.

J.S. Wheatcroft, "Emily Dickinson's White Robes," *Criticism* 5 (Spring 1963): 144-45.

Wheeler, *The Design of Poetry*, 172-75.

Winters, *Maule's Curse*, 154-56. Reprinted in Winters, *In Defense of Reason*, 288-90. Abridged in Gwynn, Condee, and Lewis, *The Case for Poetry*, 105. Reprinted in Ferlazzo, *Critical Essays on Emily Dickinson*, 97-98.

"Bees Are Black, with Gilt Surcingles--"

Cameron, *Lyric Time*, 9-10.

"Before I Got My Eyes Put Out"

Douglas Anderson, "Presence and Place in Emily Dickinson's Poetry," *NEQ* 57 (June 1984): 220-21.

Barker, *Lunacy of Light*, 87-88.

Budick, *Emily Dickinson and the Life of Language*, 117-21.

E. Miller Budick, "When the Soul Selects: Emily Dickinson's Attack on New England Symbolism," *AL* 51 (Nov. 1979): 360-63.

Cody, *After Great Pain*, 422-24.

James Guthrie, "'Before I Got My Eyes Put Out': Dickinson's Illness and Its Effects on Her Poetry," *DicS*, no. 42 (First Half 1982): 16-21.

Johnson, *Emily Dickinson: Perception and the Poet's Quest*, 48-51.

B.J. Rogers, "The Truth Told Slant: Emily Dickinson's Poetic Mode," *TSLL* 14 (Summer 1972): 333.

"Before the Ice Is in the Pools"

J.S. Wheatcroft, "Emily Dickinson's White Robes," *Criticism* 5 (Spring 1963): 136.

"Behind Me--Dips Eternity--"

Anderson, *Emily Dickinson's Poetry*, 280-83.

Sharon Cameron, "'A Loaded Gun': Dickinson and the Dialectic of Rage," *PMLA* 93 (May 1978): 430-31. Reprinted in Cameron, *Lyric Time*, 74-76.

Diehl, *Emily Dickinson and The Romantic Imagination*, 151-53.

Henry Wells, *Introduction to Emily Dickinson* (Chicago: Packard & Co., 1947), 149-50.

"Best Things Dwell out of Sight"

Benfey, *Emily Dickinson and the Problem of Others*, 37-40.

"The Bible Is an Antique Volume"

Austin Warren, "Emily Dickinson," in Sewall, *Emily Dickinson: A Collection of Critical Essays*, 107-8.

"A Bird Came Down the Walk"

Douglas Anderson, "Presence and Place in Emily Dickinson's Poetry," *NEQ* 57 (June 1984): 221-22.

E. Miller Budick, "The Dangers of Living in the World: Aspects of Dickinson's Epistemology, Cosmology, and Symbolism," *ESQ* 29 (Fourth Quarter 1983): 217-22.

Budick, *Emily Dickinson and the Life of Language*, 62-65.

Cameron, *Lyric Time*, 6-7.

Frederick I. Carpenter, "Emily Dickinson and the Rhymes of Dream," *University of Kansas City Review* 20 (Winter 1953): 119-20.

J. Kirby, *Expl* 2 (June 1944): 61. Reprinted in *The Explicator Cyclopedia* 1:57.

Loving, *Emily Dickinson: The Poet on the Second Story*, 55-57.

Eleanor Wilner, "The Poetics of Emily Dickinson," *ELH* 38 (Mar. 1971): 147-54.

Edith Wylder, *The Last Face: Emily Dickinson's Manuscripts* (Albuquerque: University of New Mexico Press, 1971), 44-48.

"The Birds Begun at Four O'Clock--"

Douglas Anderson, "Presence and Place in Emily Dickinson's Poetry," *NEQ* 57 (June 1984): 211-13.

"Blazing in Gold--and"

Anderson, *Emily Dickinson's Poetry*, 136-38.

E. Miller Budick, "The Dangers of Living in the World: Aspects of Dickinson's Epistemology, Cosmology, and Symbolism," *ESQ* 29 (Fourth Quarter 1983): 208-10.

Budick, *Emily Dickinson and the Life of Language*, 1-6.

Lois A, Cuddy, "The Influence of Latin Poetics on Emily Dickinson's Style," *CLS* 13 (Sept. 1976): 221-24.

"Bloom--Is the Result--to Meet a Flower"

Martin, *An American Triptych*, 157-58.

"Bloom Upon the Mountain--Stated--"

Christanne Miller, "How 'Low Feet' Stagger: Disruptions of Language in Dickinson's Poetry," in Juhasz, *Feminist Critics Read Emily Dickinson*, 149-50.

"The Body Grows Without--"

Benfey, *Emily Dickinson and the Problem of Others*, 82-84.

Mudge, *Emily Dickinson and the Image of Home*, 207-9.

"The Brain--Is Wider than the Sky--"

Juhasz, *The Undiscovered Continent*, 26-27.

"Bring Me the Sunset in a Cup"

Mudge, *Emily Dickinson and the Image of Home*, 174-76.
Wallace, *God Be with the Clown*, 93-94.

"The Bustle in a House"

Ford, *Heaven Beguiles the Tired*, 152-54.
Raymond J. Jordan, *Expl* 21 (Feb. 1963): 49.

"The Butterfly Obtains"

Donald E. Houghton, *Expl* 27 (Sept. 1968): 5.

"By My Window Have I for Scenery--"

Budick, *Emily Dickinson and the Life of Language*, 182-85.

"Came a Wind Like a Bugle"

Mario L. D'Avanzo, "'Came a Wind Like a Bugle': Dickinson's Poetic Apocalypse," *Renascence* 17 (Fall 1964): 29-31.

"The Chariot"

Allen Tate, "Emily Dickinson," in Feidelson and Brodtkorb, *Interpretations of American Literature*, 204-5.

"A Clock Stopped--Not the Mantel's"

Anderson, *Emily Dickinson's Poetry*, 234-38.
Donald W. Bolin, *Expl* 22 (Dec. 1963): 27.

Cameron, *Lyric Time*, 103-6.

Ford, *Heaven Beguiles the Tired*, 109-10.

L.C. Knights, "Defining the Self: Poems of Emily Dickinson," *SR* 91 (Summer 1983): 363-65.

Lucas, *Emily Dickinson and Riddle*, 76-78.

Earl Roy Miner, *Expl* 13 (Oct. 1954): 18. Reprinted in *The Explicator Cyclopedia* 1:57-58.

Laurence Perrine, *Expl* 14 (Oct. 1955):4. Reprinted in *The Explicator Cyclopedia* 1:59.

Porter, *The Art of Emily Dickinson's Early Poetry*, 167-68.

Robinson, *Emily Dickinson: Looking to Canaan*, 121-23.

William Rossky, *Expl* 22 (Sept. 1963): 3.

B.A. Scheffler, "Emily Dickinson's 'A Clock Stopped,'" *MSE* 1 (Fall 1967): 52-54.

"A Coffin--Is a Small Domain"

Sharon Cameron, "Naming As History: Dickinson's Poems of Definition," *CritI* 5 (Winter 1978): 236-37. Reprinted in Cameron, *Lyric Time*, 38-39.

"Come Slowly--Eden"

Diehl, *Emily Dickinson and The Romantic Imagination*, 17-18.

Juhasz, *The Undiscovered Continent*, 103-4.

Porter, *The Art of Emily Dickinson's Early Poetry*, 35.

Weisbuch, *Emily Dickinson's Poetry*, 24-25.

"Conscious Am I in my Chamber--"

Douglas Anderson, "Presence and Place in Emily Dickinson's Poetry," *NEQ* 57 (June 1984): 213-14.

Juhasz, *The Undiscovered Continent*, 155-57.

"The Crickets Sang"

Simon Tugwell, *Expl* 23 (Feb. 1965): 46.

"Crisis Is a Hair"

Juhasz, *The Undiscovered Continent*, 60-62.

"Crumbling Is Not an Instant's Act"

Charles R. Anderson, "The Conscious Self in Emily Dickinson's Poetry," *AL* 31 (Nov. 1959): 297-98.

Sharon Cameron, "Naming As History: Dickinson's Poems of Definition," *CritI* 5 (Winter 1978): 240-41. Reprinted in Cameron, *Lyric Time*, 43-44.

"The Daisy Follows Soft the Sun"

Gilbert and Gubar, *The Madwoman in the Attic*, 600-603.

Margaret Homans, "'Oh, Vision of Language!'": Dickinson's Poems of Love and Death," in Juhasz, *Feminist Critics Read Emily Dickinson*, 118-20.

Kimpel, *Emily Dickinson as Philosopher*, 178-80.

Loving, *Emily Dickinson: The Poet on the Second Story*, 7-8.

"The Dandelion's Pallid Tube"

Marilyn D. De Eulis, "Whitman's 'The First Dandelion' and Emily Dickinson's 'The Dandelion's Pallid Tube," *WWR* 25 (Mar. 1979): 29-32.

"Dare You See a Soul at the White Heat?"

Cameron, *Lyric Time*, 198-200.

Gilbert and Gubar, *The Madwoman in the Attic*, 612-13.

Salska, *Walt Whitman and Emily Dickinson*, 88-90.

Whicher, *This Was a Poet*, 242-43.

Judith Wilt, "Emily Dickinson: Playing House," *Boundary 2* 12 (Winter 1984): 162-63.

"A Day! Help! Help! Another Day!"

Cody, *After Great Pain*, 334-35.

"Dear Sue, Your--Riches--Taught Me--Poverty!"

Rebecca Patterson, "Emily Dickinson's Jewel Imagery," *AL* 42 (Jan. 1974): 516-19.

"Death Is a Dialogue Between"

Virginia Adair, *Expl* 27 (Mar. 1969): 52.

Benfey, *Emily Dickinson and the Problem of Others*, 101-2.

Chase, *Emily Dickinson*, 175-76.

Perrine, *The Art of Total Relevance*, 120-21.

Lee Richmond, "Death is a Dialogue Between," *DicS*, no. 23 (First Half 1973): 171.

"Death Is a Supple Suitor"

Sharon Cameron, "Naming As History: Dickinson's Poems of Definition," *CritI* 5 (Winter 1978): 239.

Paul Ferlazzo, "The Deadly Beau in Two Poems by Emily Dickinson, *DicS*, no. 19 (Dec. 1971): 136-38.

"Delight Is as the Flight--"

Johnson, *Emily Dickinson: Perception and the Poet's Quest*, 84-85.

Juhasz, *The Undiscovered Continent*, 86-90.

"Delight's Despair at Setting"

Sherwood, *Circumference and Circumstance*, 160-61.

"Despair's Advantage Is Achieved"

Wolosky, *Emily Dickinson: A Voice of War*, 85-86.

"Did the Harebell Loose Her Girdle"

Weisbuch, *Emily Dickinson's Poetry*, 16-17.

"The Difference Between Despair"

Juhasz, *The Undiscovered Continent*, 36-37.

"Doom Is the House without the Door--"

Sharon Cameron, "Naming As History: Dickinson's Poems of Definition," *CritI* 5 (Winter 1978): 235-36.

Judith Wilt, "Emily Dickinson: Playing House," *Boundary 2* 12 (Winter 1984): 158-59.

"Drama's Vitallest Expression Is the Common Day"

Gilbert and Gubar, *The Madwoman in the Attic*, 585-86.

"Dust Is the Only Secret"

Ford, *Heaven Beguiles the Tired*, 89-92.

Archibald MacLeish, "The Private World: Poems of Emily Dickinson," in Sewall, *Emily Dickinson: A Collection of Critical Essays*, 157-58.

"Each Life Converges to Some Centre--"

Mudge, *Emily Dickinson and the Image of Home*, 110-11.

Wolosky, *Emily Dickinson: A Voice of War*, 21-23.

"Each Scar I'll Keep for Him"

Porter, *Dickinson: The Modern Idiom*, 110-11.

"Egypt, Thou Knew'st Too Well"

Patterson, *Emily Dickinson's Imagery*, 154-55.

"Elysium Is as Far as To"

R.P. Blackmur, "Emily Dickinson's Notation," in Sewall, *Emily Dickinson: A Collection of Critical Essays*, 82-83.

Roland Hagenbuchle, "Precision and Indeterminacy in the Poetry of Emily Dickinson," *ESQ*, no. 20 (First Quarter 1974): 48-49.

John F. Lynen, "Three Uses of the Present: The Historian's, the Critic's, and Emily Dickinson's," *CE* 28 (Nov. 1966): 135.

Stephen Whicher, *Expl* 19 (Apr. 1961): 45. Reprinted in *The Explicator Cyclopedia* 1:59.

"Endanger It, and the Demand"

Benfey, *Emily Dickinson and the Problem of Others*, 42.

"Escape Is Such a Thankful Word"

Kimpel, *Emily Dickinson as Philosopher*, 75-76.

"Essential Oils Are Wrung--"

Anderson, *Emily Dickinson's Poetry*, 64-68.

Murray Arndt, "Emily Dickinson and the Limits of Language," *DicS*, no. 57 (First Half 1986): 24-27.

Cameron, *Lyric Time*, 195-96.

Miller, *Emily Dickinson: A Poet's Grammar*, 2-6.

Sherwood, *Circumference and Circumstance*, 212-14.

"Except the Smaller Size"

Charles R. Anderson, "The Conscious Self in Emily Dickinson's Poetry," *AL* 31 (Nov. 1959): 295-96.

"Expectation--Is Contentment"

Juhasz, *The Undiscovered Continent*, 92-94.

"Experience Is the Angled Road"

Sharon Cameron, "Naming As History: Dickinson's Poems of Definition," *CritI* 5 (Winter 1978): 235-36. Reprinted in Cameron, *Lyric Time*, 37-38.

"Exultation Is the Going"

Budick, *Emily Dickinson and the Life of Language*, 52-53.

Duncan, *Emily Dickinson*, 43.

"'Faith' Is a Fine Invention"

Anderson, *Emily Dickinson's Poetry*, 34-36.

Paul Witherington, *Expl* 26 (Apr. 1968): 62.

"Farther in Summer than the Birds"

Anderson, *Emily Dickinson's Poetry*, 150-55.

Barker, *Lunacy of Light*, 129-32.

Cameron, *Lyric Time*, 182-85.

Frederick I. Carpenter, "Emily Dickinson and the Rhymes of Dream," *University of Kansas City Review* 20 (Winter 1953): 118.

Frederick I. Carpenter, *Expl* 8 (Mar. 1950): 33. Reprinted in *The Explicator Cyclopedia* 1:59-60.

Chase, *Emily Dickinson*, 171-72.

Diehl, *Emily Dickinson and The Romantic Imagination*, 97-98.

Eberwein, *Dickinson: Strategies*, 190-91.

Robert H. Elias and Helen L. Elias, *Expl* 11 (Oct. 1952): 5.

Greg Johnson, *Emily Dickinson: Perception and the Poet's Quest*, 104-6, 185-88.

Thomas Johnson, *Emily Dickinson: An Interpretive Biography* (Cambridge: Harvard University Press, 1955), 185-87.

Sidney E. Lind, "Emily Dickinson's 'Farther in Summer Than the Birds' and Nathaniel Hawthorne's 'The Old Manse,'" *AL* 39 (May 1967): 163-69.

Miller, *Emily Dickinson: A Poet's Grammar*, 88-90.

Linda Munk, "Recycling Language: Emily Dickinson's Religious Wordplay," *ESQ* 32 (Fourth Quarter 1986): 236-37.

Porter, *Dickinson: The Modern Idiom*, 21-23, 28-29.

Rene Rapin, *Expl* 12 (Feb. 1954): 24. Reprinted in *The Explicator Cyclopedia* 1:60-61.

Frank Rashid, "Emily Dickinson's Voice of Endings," *ESQ* 31, no. 118 (First Quarter, 1985): 24-26, 30-32.

Marshall Van Duesen, *Expl* 13 (Mar. 1955): 33. Reprinted in *The Explicator Cyclopedia* 1:61-64.

Charles Child Walcutt, "Introduction," *The Explicator Cyclopedia* 1:xvii-xviii.

Winters, *Maule's Curse*, 158-59. Reprinted in Winters, *In Defense of Reason*, 292-93; in Blair, Hornberger, and Stewart, *The Literature of the United States*, 2:752; in Ferlazzo, *Critical Essays on Emily Dickinson*, 100-101.

"The Farthest Thunder That I Heard"

Donald Thackrey, "Emily Dickinson's Approach to Poetry," *University of Nebraska Studies*, no. 13 (Nov. 1954), 39-40.

"The Feet of People Walking Home"

Ted-Larry Pebworth and Jay Jay Claude Summers, *Expl* 27 (May 1969): 76.

"The First Day's Night Had Come--"

Cody, *After Great Pain*, 315-19.

Griffith, *The Long Shadow*, 101-4.

Mossberg, *Emily Dickinson: When a Writer Is a Daughter*, 25-27.

Pollak, *Dickinson: The Anxiety of Gender*, 19-20.

Robinson, *Emily Dickinson: Looking to Canaan*, 128-30.

Constance Rooke, "'The First Day's Night Had Come': An Explication of J. 410," *DicS*, no. 24 (Second Half 1973): 221-23.

Wallace, *God Be with the Clown*, 103-4.

"Fitter to See Him, I May Be"

Wolosky, *Emily Dickinson: A Voice of War*, 80-82.

"Flowers--Well--If Anybody"

Sherwood, *Circumference and Circumstance*, 28-29.

"For Every Bird a Nest"

George Monteiro, *Expl* 37 (Fall 1978): 28.

Barton Levi St. Armand, "Dickinson's 'For Every Bird A Nest,'" *Expl* 35 (Spring 1977): 34-35.

"For This--Accepted Breath"

Wolosky, *Emily Dickinson: A Voice of War*, 158-60.

"Four Trees--upon a Solitary Acre--"

Douglas Anderson, "Presence and Place in Emily Dickinson's Poetry," *NEQ* 57 (June 1984): 222-23.

Christopher Benfey, *Emily Dickinson: Lives of a Poet* (New York: George Braziller, 1986), 44-45.

Benfey, *Emily Dickinson and the Problem of Others*, 113-17.

E. Miller Budick, "The Dangers of Living in the World: Aspects of Dickinson's Epistemology, Cosmology, and Symbolism," *ESQ* 29 (Fourth Quarter 1983): 212-13.

Budick, *Emily Dickinson and the Life of Language*, 17-18.

Joanne Diehl, "'Ransom in a Voice': Language as Defense in Dickinson's Poetry," in Juhasz, *Feminist Critics Read Emily Dickinson*, 164-65.

Johnson, *Emily Dickinson: Perception and the Poet's Quest*, 37-38.

L.C. Knights, "Defining the Self: Poems of Emily Dickinson," *SR* 91 (Summer 1983): 372-74.

Miller, *Emily Dickinson: A Poet's Grammar*, 70-71.

Porter, *Dickinson: The Modern Idiom*, 163-64.

Sherwood, *Circumference and Circumstance*, 198-99.

Carole Taylor, "Kierkegaard and the Ironic Voices of Emily Dickinson," *JEGP* 77 (Oct. 1978): 571-72.

Wolosky, *Emily Dickinson: A Voice of War*, 2-4.

"From Blank to Blank"

Barker, *Lunacy of Light*, 85-86.

J. Burbick, "Emily Dickinson and the Economics of Desire," *AL* 58 (Oct. 1986): 372-73.

"The Frost Was Never Seen--"

Diehl, *Emily Dickinson and The Romantic Imagination*, 51-54.

"The Gentian Weaves Her Fringes"

Kathryn Etter, *Expl* 40 (Spring 1982): 34.

"Given in Marriage unto Thee"

Porter, *Dickinson: The Modern Idiom*, 197-98.

"Glass Was the Street--in Tinsel Peril"

Porter, *Dickinson: The Modern Idiom*, 72-73.

"Glory Is That Bright Tragic Thing"

Chase, *Emily Dickinson*, 148-49.

"God Gave a Loaf to Every Bird"

Mossberg, *Emily Dickinson: When a Writer Is a Daughter*, 138-39.

"God Made the Little Gentian--"

Barker, *Lunacy of Light*, 81-82.

"Going to Heaven!"

Porter, *The Art of Emily Dickinson's Early Poetry*, 64-66.

"Go Not Too Near a House of Rose"

Warren Beck, "Poetry's Chronic Disease," *EJ* 33 (Sept. 1944): 362-63.

Macklin Thomas, "Analysis of the Experience in Lyric Poetry," *CE* 9 (Mar. 1948): 320-21.

David W. Thompson, "Interpretative Reading as Symbolic Action," *QJS* 42 (Dec. 1956): 395.

"The Grass So Little Has to Do"

Anderson, *Emily Dickinson's Poetry*, 100-102.

Ruth McNaughton, "The Imagery of Emily Dickinson," *University of Nebraska Studies*, no. 4 (Jan. 1949), 39-41.

"Great Streets of Silence Led Away"

Cameron, *Lyric Time*, 162-65.

Yvor Winters, "Emily Dickinson and the Limits of Judgment," in Ferlazzo, *Critical Essays on Emily Dickinson*, 96-97.

"Growth of Man--Like Growth of Nature--"

Budick, *Emily Dickinson and the Life of Language*, 160-61.

Mossberg, *Emily Dickinson: When a Writer Is a Daughter*, 160-62.

Sherwood, *Circumference and Circumstance*, 173-74.

Barbara J. Williams, "A Room of Her Own: Emily Dickinson as Woman Artist," in *Feminist Criticism: Essays on Theory, Poetry, and Prose*, ed. C.L. Brown and K. Olson (Metuchen: Scarecrow Press, 1983), 19-80.

"Had I Presumed to Hope--"

Johnson, *Emily Dickinson: Perception and the Poet's Quest*, 59-60.

"The Hallowing of Pain"

Juhasz, *The Undiscovered Continent*, 58-60.

"The Harm of Years Is on Him"

Charles R. Anderson, "The Conscious Self in Emily Dickinson's Poetry," *AL* 31 (Nov. 1959): 296-97.

"The Heart Asks Pleasure First"

Frederic I. Carpenter, "Emily Dickinson and the Rhymes of Dream," *University of Kansas City Review* 20 (Winter 1953): 115.

"'Heaven' Has Different Signs--To Me--"

Weisbuch, *Emily Dickinson's Poetry*, 70-71.

"'Heaven'--Is What I Cannot Reach!"

Linda Munk, "Recycling Language: Emily Dickinson's Religious Wordplay," *ESQ* 32 (Fourth Quarter 1986): 238-39.

Porter, *The Art of Emily Dickinson's Early Poetry*, 117-18.

Weisbuch, *Emily Dickinson's Poetry*, 64-65.

"The Heaven Vests for Each"

Wolosky, *Emily Dickinson: A Voice of War*, 122-24.

"He Forgot--and I--Remembered"

Dorothy Oberhaus, "'Tender Pioneer': Emily Dickinson's Poems on the Life of Christ," *AL* 59 (Oct. 1987): 350-51.

"He Fumbles at Your Soul"

Chase, *Emily Dickinson*, 204-5.

Joanne Dobson, "Oh, Susie, It Is Dangerous: Emily Dickinson and the Archetype," in Juhasz, *Feminist Critics Read Emily Dickinson*, 81-82.

Miller, *Emily Dickinson: A Poet's Grammar*, 113-18.

"He Gave Away His Life--"

Dorothy Oberhaus, "'Tender Pioneer': Emily Dickinson's Poems on the Life of Christ," *AL* 59 (Oct. 1987): 354-58.

"He Put the Belt Around My Life"

Eunice Glenn, "Emily Dickinson's Poetry: A Revaluation," *SR* 51 (Autumn 1943): 580-82.

Linda Munk, "Recycling Language: Emily Dickinson's Religious Wordplay," *ESQ* 32 (Fourth Quarter 1986): 241-42.

Sherwood, *Circumference and Circumstance*, 86-87.

George Tackes, *Expl* 42 (Fall 1983): 26.

"Her Breast Is Fit for Pearls"

Mudge, *Emily Dickinson and the Image of Home*, 15-16.

"Her Sweet Turn to Leave the Homestead"

Porter, *Dickinson: The Modern Idiom*, 68-70.

"He Strained My Faith--"

Lindberg-Seyersted, *The Voice of the Poet*, 175-77.

Mossberg, *Emily Dickinson: When a Writer Is a Daughter*, 130-31.

"He Touched Me, So I Live to Know"

Chester P. Sadowy, *Expl* 37 (Fall 1978): 4.

"He Was Weak, and I Was Strong--Then--"

Cody, *After Great Pain*, 145-47.

Rebecca Patterson, *The Riddle of Emily Dickinson* (Boston: Houghton Mifflin, 1951), 152-53.

"His Mansion in the Pool"

Kimpel, *Emily Dickinson as Philosopher*, 153-54.

"His Mind of Man, a Secret Makes"

Benfey, *Emily Dickinson and the Problem of Others*, 84-86.

"Hope Is a Strange Invention"

Charles R. Anderson, "The Conscious Self in Emily Dickinson's Poetry," *AL* 31 (Nov. 1959): 301-2.

"Hope Is a Subtle Glutton--"

Sharon Cameron, "Naming As History: Dickinson's Poems of Definition," *CritI* 5 (Winter 1978): 232-33.

"A House upon the Hight"

Mudge, *Emily Dickinson and the Image of Home*, 211-12.

Laurence Perrine, *Expl* 36 (Spring 1978): 14.

Salska, *Walt Whitman and Emily Dickinson*, 155-56.

Eleanor Wilner, "The Poetics of Emily Dickinson," *ELH* 38 (Mar. 1971): 140-41.

Judith Wilt, "Emily Dickinson: Playing House," *Boundary 2* 12 (Winter 1984): 156-57.

"How Brittle Are the Piers"

Dorothy Oberhaus, "'Tender Pioneer': Emily Dickinson's Poems on the Life of Christ," *AL* 59 (Oct. 1987): 345-46.

"How Human Nature Dotes"

Ford, *Heaven Beguiles the Tired*, 149-50.

"How Many Schemes May Die"

Weisbuch, *Emily Dickinson's Poetry*, 14-16.

"How Many Times These Low Feet Staggered"

Ford, *Heaven Beguiles the Tired*, 85-87.

"How the Old Mountains Drip with Sunset"

Porter, *Dickinson: The Modern Idiom*, 30-32.

Robinson, *Emily Dickinson: Looking to Canaan*, 165-67.

"I Asked No Other Thing"

Vivian R. Pollak, "'That Fine Prosperity': Economic Metaphors in Emily Dickinson's Poetry," *MLQ* 34 (June 1973): 169-70.

"I Cannot Dance upon My Toes"

Anderson, *Emily Dickinson's Poetry*, 21-23.

Gilbert and Gubar, *The Madwoman in the Attic*, 633-34.

Mossberg, *Emily Dickinson: When a Writer Is a Daughter*, 156-58.

Barbara A.C. Mossberg, "'Everyone Else Is Prose': Emily Dickinson's Lack of Community Spirit," in Ferlazzo, *Critical Essays on Emily Dickinson*, 226-28.

Pollak, *Dickinson: The Anxiety of Gender*, 238-40.

Porter, *The Art of Emily Dickinson's Early Poetry*, 11-12.

Norman Talbot, "The Child, The Actress, and Miss Emily Dickinson," *SoRA* 5 (June 1972): 108.

"I Cannot Live with You"

Sharon Cameron, "'A Loaded Gun': Dickinson and the Dialectic of Rage," *PMLA* 93 (May 1978): 431-33. Reprinted in Cameron, *Lyric Time*, 78-82.

Gail Donohue, "I Cannot Live with You," *DicS*, no. 46 (Bonus 1983): 3-9.

Duncan, *Emily Dickinson*, 65-67.

Eunice Glenn, "Emily Dickinson's Poetry: A Revaluation," *SR* 51 (Autumn 1943): 582-85.

Mudge, *Emily Dickinson and the Image of Home*, 180-82.

Pollak, *Dickinson: The Anxiety of Gender*, 181-83.

"I Can Wade Grief"

Chase, *Emily Dickinson*, 201-3.

John Cody, *Expl* 37 (Fall 1978): 15.

William Howard, *Expl* 14 (Dec. 1955): 17. Reprinted in *The Explicator Cyclopedia* 1:64.

Juhasz, *The Undiscovered Continent*, 96-99.

"I Cross Till I Am Weary"

Johnson, *Emily Dickinson: Perception and the Poet's Quest*, 181-83.

"I Died for Beauty"

Abad, *A Formal Approach to Lyric Poetry*, 139-41.

Budick, *Emily Dickinson and the Life of Language*, 113-15.

Cameron, *Lyric Time*, 209-10.

Frederic I. Carpenter, "Emily Dickinson and the Rhymes of Dream," *University of Kansas City Review* 20 (Winter 1953): 116-17.

Chase, *Emily Dickinson*, 196-98.

Diehl, *Emily Dickinson and The Romantic Imagination*, 120-21.

Edith Stamm, "Emily Dickinson: Poetry and Punctuation," in Davis, *14 by Emily Dickinson*, 59-64.

Francis Stoddard, "Technique in Emily Dickinson's Poems," in *The Recognition of Emily Dickinson*, ed. Caesar Blake and Carlton Wells (Ann Arbor: University of Michigan Press, 1964), 51-53.

"I Dreaded That First Robin So"

Anderson, *Emily Dickinson's Poetry*, 199-202.

Chase, *Emily Dickinson*, 170-71.

John Mann, "Emily Dickinson, Emerson, and the Poet as Namer," *NEQ* 51 (Dec. 1978): 485-88.

Russell St. C. Smith, *Expl* 5 (Feb. 1947): 31. Reprinted in *The Explicator Cyclopedia* 1:64-65.

"I Dwell in Possibility--"

Benfey, *Emily Dickinson and the Problem of Others*, 28, 33.

David Green, "Emily Dickinson: The Spatial Drama of Centering," *ELWIU* 7 (Fall 1980): 192-93.

Juhasz, *The Undiscovered Continent*, 19-20.

Weisbuch, *Emily Dickinson's Poetry*, 12-13.

"I Felt a Cleaving in My Mind--"

Budick, *Emily Dickinson and the Life of Language*, 210-11.

Cody, *After Great Pain*, 293-94.

Gilbert and Gubar, *The Madwoman in the Attic*, 627-28.

"I Felt a Funeral, in My Brain"

Anderson, *Emily Dickinson's Poetry*, 208-10.

Brooks, Lewis, and Warren, *American Literature*, 1245.

Budick, *Emily Dickinson and the Life of Language*, 205-9.

E. Miller Budick, "Temporal Consciousness and the Perception of Eternity in Emily Dickinson," *ELWIU* 10 (Fall 1983): 230-33.

Cameron, *Lyric Time*, 96-98.

Dickinson, *Suggestions for Teachers of "Introduction to Literature,"* 34.

Andrew Gibson, "Emily Dickinson and the Poetry of Hypothesis," *EIC* 33 (July 1983): 233-34.

Griffith, *The Long Shadow*, 245-50.

Philip, "Valley News: Emily Dickinson at Home and Beyond," in Lee, *Nineteenth-Century American Poetry*, 67-68.

Pollak, *Dickinson: The Anxiety of Gender*, 211-14.

Porter, *The Art of Emily Dickinson's Early Poetry*, 36-38, 146-47.

Porter, *Dickinson: The Modern Idiom*, 120-21.

Robinson, *Emily Dickinson: Looking to Canaan*, 111-14.

B.J. Rogers, "The Truth Told Slant: Emily Dickinson's Poetic Mode," *TSLL* 14 (Summer 1972): 332-33.

Barton Levi St. Armand, *Emily Dickinson and Her Culture: The Soul's Society* (Cambridge: Cambridge University Press, 1984), 107-9.

Sherwood, *Circumference and Circumstance*, 106-9.

William Bysshe Stein, "Emily Dickinson's Parodic Masks," *University of Kansas City Review* 36 (Autumn 1969): 52-54.

John E. Walsh, *The Hidden Life of Emily Dickinson* (New York: Simon & Schuster, 1971), 158-60.

Weisbuch, *Emily Dickinson's Poetry*, 103-7.

"If I Can Stop One Heart from Breaking"

Perrine, *The Art of Total Relevance*, 119-20.

"If I May Have It, When It's Dead"

J. Burbick, "Emily Dickinson and the Economics of Desire," *AL* 58 (Oct. 1986): 372-73.

Margaret Homans, "Oh, Vision of Language!": Dickinson's Poems of Love and Death," in Juhasz, *Feminist Critics Read Emily Dickinson*, 126.

Whicher, *This Was a Poet*, 281-83.

"If I Should Die"

Barker, *Lunacy of Light*, 64-65.

Vivian R. Pollak, "'That Fine Prosperity': Economic Metaphors in Emily Dickinson's Poetry," *MLQ* 34 (June 1973): 164-67.

"I Found the Words to Every Thought"

Donald Thackrey, "Emily Dickinson's Approach to Poetry," *University of Nebraska Studies*, no. 13 (Nov. 1954), 25-26.

"If Pain for Peace Prepares"

Barker, *Lunacy of Light*, 122-23.

Lois A. Cuddy, "The Influence of Latin Poetics on Emily Dickinson's Style," *CLS* 13 (Sept. 1976): 215-18.

"If Recollecting Were Forgetting"

Loving, *Emily Dickinson: The Poet on the Second Story*, 6-7.

"If She Had Been the Mistletoe"

Porter, *The Art of Emily Dickinson's Early Poetry*, 24-25.

"If Your Nerve, Deny You"

Cameron, *Lyric Time*, 155-57.

Porter, *The Art of Emily Dickinson's Early Poetry*, 165.

"If You Were Coming in the Fall"

Budick, *Emily Dickinson and the Life of Language*, 201-2.

E. Miller Budick, "Temporal Consciousness and the Perception of Eternity in Emily Dickinson," *ELWIU* 10 (Fall 1983): 227-28.

Frederick Keefer and Deborah Vlahos, *Expl* 29 (Nov. 1970): 23.

Lee J. Richmond, "Emily Dickinson's 'If You Were Coming in the Fall': An Explication," *EJ* 59 (Sept. 1970): 771-73.

Salska, *Walt Whitman and Emily Dickinson*, 143-45.

Genevieve Taggard, *The Life and Mind of Emily Dickinson* (New York: Knopf, 1930), 309-11.

"I Gained It So--"

Johnson, *Emily Dickinson: Perception and the Poet's Quest*, 114-15.

"I Gave Myself to Him--"

Wolosky, *Emily Dickinson: A Voice of War*, 107-8.

"I Got So I Could Hear His Name--"

Cameron, *Lyric Time*, 58-61.

Duncan, *Emily Dickinson*, 54-56.

Pollak, *Dickinson: The Anxiety of Gender*, 177-80.

Porter, *The Art of Emily Dickinson's Early Poetry*, 173-75.

Wolosky, *Emily Dickinson: A Voice of War*, 118-21.

"I Had Been Hungry, All the Years"

Cody, *After Great Pain*, 39-43, 129-32.

Mossberg, *Emily Dickinson: When a Writer Is a Daughter*, 139-40.

Mudge, *Emily Dickinson and the Image of Home*, 82-83.

Pollak, *Dickinson: The Anxiety of Gender*, 127-29.

"I Had No Time to Hate--"

Andrew Gibson, "Emily Dickinson and the Poetry of Hypothesis," *EIC* 33 (July 1983): 226-27.

"I Had Not Minded--Walls--"

Budick, *Emily Dickinson and the Life of Language*, 80-82, 101-12.

E. Miller Budick, "'I Had Not Minded--Walls--': The Method and Meaning of Emily Dickinson's Symbolism," *CP* 9 (Fall 1976): 5-12.

Kimpel, *Emily Dickinson as Philosopher*, 261-62.

Robert Merideth, *Expl* 23 (Nov. 1964): 25.

Rebecca Patterson, "Emily Dickinson's 'Double' Tim: Masculine Identification," *AI* 28 (Winter 1971): 340-42.

Patterson, *Emily Dickinson's Imagery*, 45-47.

Salska, *Walt Whitman and Emily Dickinson*, 84-85.

Sherwood, *Circumference and Circumstance*, 88-91.

Van Doren, *Introduction to Poetry*, 13-16.

"I Had Some Things That I Called Mine"

Jane Donahue Eberwein, *Expl* 42 (Spring 1984): 31.

"I Have a Bird in Spring"

Porter, *The Art of Emily Dickinson's Early Poetry*, 21-22.

"I Have a King, Who Does Not Speak"

Virginia Ogden Birdsall, "Emily Dickinson's Intruder in the Soul," *AL* 27 37 (Mar. 1965): 55.

Joanne Dobson, "Oh, Susie, It Is Dangerous: Emily Dickinson and the Archetype," in Juhasz, *Feminist Critics Read Emily Dickinson*, 86-87.

Theodora Ward, *The Capsule of the Mind: Chapters in the Life of Emily Dickinson* (Cambridge: Harvard University Press, 1961), 44-46.

"I Have Never Seen 'Volcanoes'--"

Robinson, *Emily Dickinson: Looking to Canaan*, 153-55.

"I Heard a Fly Buzz When I Died"

Anderson, *Emily Dickinson's Poetry*, 231-32.

Katrina Bachinger, *Expl* 43 (Spring 1985): 12.

Ronald Beck, *Expl* 26 (Dec. 1967): 31.

M. Boruch, "Dickinson Descending," *GaR* 40 (Winter 1986): 863-77.

Budick, *Emily Dickinson and the Life of Language*, 168-74.

Cameron, *Lyric Time*, 112-15.

Chase, *Emily Dickinson*, 246-48.

John Ciardi, *Expl* 14 (Jan. 1956): 22. Reprinted in *The Explicator Cyclopedia* 1:65-66.

James T. Connelly, *Expl* 25 (Dec. 1966): 34.

Eberwein, *Dickinson: Strategies*, 219.

Ford, *Heaven Beguiles the Tired*, 112-14.

Thomas W. Ford, "Thoreau's Cosmic Mosquito and Dickinson's Terrestrial Fly," *NEQ* 48 (Dec. 1975): 487-504.

Gerhard Friedrich, *Expl* 13 (Apr. 1955): 35. Reprinted in *The Explicator Cyclopedia* 1:65.

Griffith, *The Long Shadow*, 134-37.

Eugene Hollahan, *Expl* 25 (Sept. 1966): 6.

Caroline Hogue, *Expl* 20 (Nov. 1961): 26. Reprinted in *The Explicator Cyclopedia* 1:66.

Lucas, *Emily Dickinson and Riddle*, 63-65.

Ruth McNaughton, "The Imagery of Emily Dickinson," *University of Nebraska Studies*, no. 4 (Jan. 1949), 50-52.

George Monteiro, *Expl* 43 (Fall 1984): 43.

Pollak, *Dickinson: The Anxiety of Gender*, 192-94.

John Rachal, "Probing the Final Mystery in Dickinson's 'I Heard a Fly Buzz' and 'I've Seen a Dying Eye,'" *DicS*, no. 39 (First Half 1981): 44-47.

Robinson, *Emily Dickinson: Looking to Canaan*, 116-18.

B.J. Rogers, "The Truth Told Slant: Emily Dickinson's Poetic Mode," *TSLL* 14 (Summer 1972): 333-34.

Benjamin T. Spencer, "Criticism: Centrifugal and Centripetal," *Criticism* 8 (Spring 1966): 141-43.

Wallace, *God Be with the Clown*, 94-96.

Weisbuch, *Emily Dickinson's Poetry*, 99-102.

Wheeler, *The Design of Poetry*, 189-92.

"I Held a Jewel in My Fingers--"

Joseph Ditta, "The Jewel and the Amethyst: Poet and Persona in Emily Dickinson," *DicS*, no. 42 (First Half 1982): 30-37.

Mossberg, *Emily Dickinson: When a Writer Is a Daughter*, 171-72.

"I Knew That I Had Gained"

Porter, *Dickinson: The Modern Idiom*, 76-79.

"I Know Some Lonely Houses Off the Road"

Virginia Ogden Birdsall, "Emily Dickinson's Intruder in the Soul," *AL* 37 (Mar. 1965): 56-59.

Budick, *Emily Dickinson and the Life of Language*, 156-58.

Karl Keller, *The Only Kangaroo among the Beauty: Emily Dickinson and America* (Baltimore: Johns Hopkins University Press, 1979), 323-25.

Myron Ochshorn, *Expl* 11 (Nov. 1952): 12. Reprinted in *The Explicator Cyclopedia* 1:66-67.

Judith Wilt, "Emily Dickinson: Playing House," *Boundary 2* 12 (Winter 1984): 158.

"I Know That He Exists"

Griffith, *The Long Shadow*, 73-76.

Karl Keller, *The Only Kangaroo among the Beauty: Emily Dickinson and America* (Baltimore: Johns Hopkins University Press, 1979), 62-64.

James Machor, "Emily Dickinson and Feminine Rhetoric," *ArQ* 36 (Summer 1980): 137-38.

Laurence Perrine, "Emily Dickinson's 'I Know That He Exists,'" *CEA Forum* 8 (Oct. 1978): 8, 11-12.

"I Learned--at Least--What Home Could Be--"

Mudge, *Emily Dickinson and the Image of Home*, 215-17.

"I Like a Look of Agony"

Benfey, *Emily Dickinson and the Problem of Others*, 91-93.

Ford, *Heaven Beguiles the Tired*, 107-8.

"I Like to See It Lap the Miles"

Abad, *A Formal Approach to Lyric Poetry*, 342-44.

Anderson, *Emily Dickinson's Poetry*, 14-16.

George Arms, *Expl* 2 (May 1944): Q31.

Chase, *Emily Dickinson*, 226-28.

William Freedman, *Expl* 40 (Spring 1982): 30.

F.J. Hoffman, "The Technological Fallacy in Contemporary Poetry," *AL* 21 (Mar. 1949): 97. Reprinted in Stageberg and Anderson, *Poetry as Experience*, 460.

Andrew Hook, *American Literature in Context*. Vol. 3, *1865-1900* (London: Metheun, 1983), 62-64.

Robert E. Lowrey, "'Boanerges': An Encomium for Edward Dickinson," *ArQ* 26 (Spring 1970): 54-58.

P.F. O'Connell, "Emily Dickinson's Train: Iron Horse or 'Rough Beast'?" *AL* 52 (Nov. 1979): 469-75.

Jim Philip, "Valley News: Emily Dickinson at Home and Beyond," in Lee, *Nineteenth-Century American Poetry*, 74-75.

Walsh, *Doors into Poetry*, 15-18.

George Whicher, in Davis, *14 by Emily Dickinson*, 91-93.

Nathalia Wright, "Emily Dickinson's Boanerges and Thoreau's Atropos on the Same Line?" in Davis, *14 by Emily Dickinson*, 96-98.

"I Lived on Dread--"

Juhasz, *The Undiscovered Continent*, 55-57.

"I Live with Him--I See His Face--"

Cameron, *Lyric Time*, 82-83.

Pollak, *Dickinson: The Anxiety of Gender*, 179-81.

"I'll Tell You How the Sun Rose"

Budick, *Emily Dickinson and the Life of Language*, 7-8.

Jerome, *Poetry: Premeditated Art*, 144.

Kher, *The Landscape of Absence*, 219-21.

Wilbur Scott, *Expl* 7 (Nov. 1948): 14. Reprinted in *The Explicator Cyclopedia* 1:67-68.

Suzanne M. Wilson, "Structural Patterns in the Poetry of Emily Dickinson," *AL* 35 (Mar. 1963): 56-57.

"I'm Ceded--I've Stopped Being Theirs"

Paula Bennet, *My Life a Loaded Gun: Female Creativity and Feminist Poetics* (Boston: Beacon Press, 1986), 81-82.

Chase, *Emily Dickinson*, 156-57.

Mossberg, *Emily Dickinson: When a Writer Is a Daughter*, 158-60.

Pollak, *Dickinson: The Anxiety of Gender*, 118-20.

Adrienne Rich, "Vesuvius at Home: The Power of Emily Dickinson," in Ferlazzo, *Critical Essays on Emily Dickinson*, 186.

"I Meant to Find Her When I Came--"

Pollak, *Dickinson: The Anxiety of Gender*, 135-37.

"I Meant to Have But Modest Means"

Griffith, *The Long Shadow*, 31-35.

Dorothy Huff Oberhaus, "'Engine Against th' Almightie': Emily Dickinson and Prayer," *ESQ* 32 (Third Quarter 1986): 159-60.

Vivian R. Pollak, "'That Fine Prosperity': Economic Metaphors in Emily Dickinson's Poetry," *MLQ* 34 (June 1973): 170-71.

Wallace, *God Be with the Clown*, 87-88.

"I Measure Every Grief I Meet"

Benfey, *Emily Dickinson and the Problem of Others*, 88-91.

William Doreski, "'An Exchange of Territory': Dickinson's Fascicle 27," *ESQ* 32 (First Quarter 1986): 58-60.

Duncan, *Emily Dickinson*, 62-63.

Linda Munk, "Recycling Language: Emily Dickinson's Religious Wordplay," *ESQ* 32 (Fourth Quarter 1986): 242-45.

"Immured in Heaven"

Thomas H. Johnson, *Expl* 11 (Mar. 1953): 36.

"I'm Nobody! Who Are You?"

Eberwein, *Dickinson: Strategies*, 61-62.

Jane Eberwein, "I'm Nobody! Who Are You?" *DicS*, no. 46 (Bonus 1983): 9-15.

Adrienne Rich, "Vesuvius at Home: The Power of Emily Dickinson," in Ferlazzo, *Critical Essays on Emily Dickinson*, 181-82.

"I'm the Little 'Heart's Ease'!"

Kimpel, *Emily Dickinson as Philosopher*, 128-29.

"I'm Wife--I've Finished That--"

Gilbert and Gubar, *The Madwoman in the Attic*, 589-90.

Kimpel, *Emily Dickinson as Philosopher*, 158-59.

Mossberg, *Emily Dickinson: When a Writer Is a Daughter*, 46-47.

Pollak, *Dickinson: The Anxiety of Gender*, 172-73.

Porter, *The Art of Emily Dickinson's Early Poetry*, 68-70.

"I Never Felt at Home--Below--"

Barker, *Lunacy of Light*, 46-48.

Sandra Gilbert, "The Wayward Nun Beneath the Hill," in Juhasz, *Feminist Critics Read Emily Dickinson*, 48-49.

David Lloyd, "The Adult Voice in Dickinson's Child Poems," *DicS*, no. 49 (June 1984): 25-27.

Mossberg, *Emily Dickinson: When a Writer Is a Daughter*, 120-21.

"I Never Hear the One is Dead"

Myron Ochshorn, "In Search of Emily Dickinson," *New Mexico Quarterly Review* 23 (Spring 1953): 101-2, 104.

Robinson, *Emily Dickinson: Looking to Canaan*, 92-94.

Weisbuch, *Emily Dickinson's Poetry*, 147-48.

"I Never Lost As Much But Twice"

Nina Baym, "God, Father, and Lover in Emily Dickinson's Poetry," in *Puritan Influences in American Literature*, ed. Emory Elliot (Urbana: University of Illinois Press, 1979), 199-201.

Allen D. Lackey, *Expl* 34 (Nov. 1975): 18.

George Monteiro, *Expl* 30 (Sept. 1971): 7.

Vivian R. Pollak, "'That Fine Prosperity': Economic Metaphors in Emily Dickinson's Poetry," *MLQ* 34 (June 1973): 168-69.

Rene Rapin, *Expl* 31 (Mar. 1973): 52.

Sherwood, *Circumference and Circumstance*, 34-36.

Whicher, *This Was a Poet*, 108-9.

"I Never Saw a Moor"

Benfey, *Emily Dickinson and the Problem of Others*, 25.

W. Herget, *Expl* 30 (Oct. 1962): 13.

Johnson, *Emily Dickinson: Perception and the Poet's Quest*, 57-58.

Robert Meredith, "Emily Dickinson and the Acquisitive Society," *NEQ* 37 (Dec. 1964): 448-51.

Thomas Werge, "'Checks' in 'I Never Saw a Moor,'" *AN&Q* 12 (Mar. 1974): 101-2.

"I Never Told the Buried Gold"

Paula Bennet, *My Life a Loaded Gun: Female Creativity and Feminist Poetics* (Boston: Beacon Press, 1986), 51-52.

Thomas Johnson, *Emily Dickinson: An Interpretive Biography* (Cambridge: Harvard University Press, 1955), 87-89.

Miller, *The Poetry of Emily Dickinson*, 36-37.

"In Falling Timbers Buried--"

Judith Wilt, "Emily Dickinson: Playing House," *Boundary 2* 12 (Winter 1984): 160.

"In Snow Thou Comest"

Walter Hesford, "In Snow Thou Comest," *DicS*, no. 46 (Bonus 1983): 15-20.

"In Winter, in My Room"

Barker, *Lunacy of Light*, 93-95.

Cody, *After Great Pain*, 180-82.

Griffith, *The Long Shadow*, 177-83, 284-87.

Karl Keller, *The Only Kangaroo among the Beauty: Emily Dickinson and America* (Baltimore: Johns Hopkins University Press, 1979), 268-70.

Mudge, *Emily Dickinson and the Image of Home*, 104-6.

Whicher, *This Was a Poet*, 186-87.

"I Play at Riches to Appease"

Mossberg, *Emily Dickinson: When a Writer Is a Daughter*, 141-43.

Barbara Mossberg, "Emily Dickinson's Nursery Rhymes," in Juhasz, *Feminist Critics Read Emily Dickinson*, 61-62.

"I Prayed, at First, a Little Girl"

Lindberg-Seyersted, *The Voice of the Poet*, 40-42.

Mossberg, *Emily Dickinson: When a Writer Is a Daughter*, 122-24.

"I Put New Blossoms in the Glass"

Jim Philip, "Valley News: Emily Dickinson at Home and Beyond," in Lee, *Nineteenth-Century American Poetry*, 63-65.

"I Read My Sentence--Steadily--"

Anderson, *Emily Dickinson's Poetry*, 204-7.

Cameron, *Lyric Time*, 108-9.

"I Reason, Earth Is Short"

Ford, *Heaven Beguiles the Tired*, 100-101.

George Monteiro, *Expl* 38 (Summer 1980): 23.

"I Reckon--When I Count at All--"

Anderson, *Emily Dickinson's Poetry*, 93-94.

Barker, *Lunacy of Light*, 105-6.

Diehl, *Emily Dickinson and The Romantic Imagination*, 90-91.

Kimpel, *Emily Dickinson as Philosopher*, 34-36.

Miller, *The Poetry of Emily Dickinson*, 107-8.

Weisbuch, *Emily Dickinson's Poetry*, 174-76.

Wolosky, *Emily Dickinson: A Voice of War*, 153-54.

"I Rose--Because He Sank--"

Diehl, *Emily Dickinson and The Romantic Imagination*, 81-83.

Rebecca Patterson, *The Riddle of Emily Dickinson* (Boston: Houghton Mifflin, 1951), 155.

"I Saw No Way--the Heavens Were Stitched--"

Cameron, *Lyric Time*, 8-9.

Eberwein, *Dickinson: Strategies*, 193-94.

Salska, *Walt Whitman and Emily Dickinson*, 129-30.

"I Shall Know Why--When Time Is Over"

Diehl, *Emily Dickinson and The Romantic Imagination*, 102-3.

"I Should Have Been Too Glad, I See"

Anderson, *Emily Dickinson's Poetry*, 194-96.

Sharon Cameron, "'A Loaded Gun': Dickinson and the Dialectic of Rage," *PMLA* 93 (May 1978): 424-25. Reprinted in Cameron, *Lyric Time*, 62-65.

Myron Ochshorn, "In Search of Emily Dickinson," *New Mexico Quarterly Review* 23 (Spring 1953): 103-6.

Wolosky, *Emily Dickinson: A Voice of War*, 95-97.

"I Should Not Dare to Leave My Friend"

Kimpel, *Emily Dickinson as Philosopher*, 102-4.

"I Started Early--Took My Dog"

Virginia Ogden Birdsall, "Emily Dickinson's Intruder in the Soul," *AL* 37 (Mar. 1965): 61-64.

Eric W. Carlson, *Expl* 20 (May 1962): 72. Reprinted in *The Explicator Cyclopedia* 1:69-70.

Cody, *After Great Pain*, 305-7.

Kate Flores, *Expl* 9 (May 1951): 47. Reprinted in *The Explicator Cyclopedia* 1:68-69.

Griffith, *The Long Shadow*, 18-24.

George S. Lensing, *Expl* 31 (Dec. 1972): 30.

Miller, *Emily Dickinson: A Poet's Grammar*, 73-75.

Laurence Perrine, *Expl* 10 (Feb. 1952): 28. Reprinted in *The Explicator Cyclopedia* 1:69.

Pollak, *Dickinson: The Anxiety of Gender*, 114-16.

Salska, *Walt Whitman and Emily Dickinson*, 81-82.

John E. Walsh, *The Hidden Life of Emily Dickinson* (New York: Simon & Schuster, 1971), 106-9.

Weisbuch, *Emily Dickinson's Poetry*, 53-56.

Yvor Winters, "Emily Dickinson and the Limits of Judgment," in Ferlazzo, *Critical Essays on Emily Dickinson*, 94-95.

Winters, *Forms of Discovery*, 267-68.

Wallace, *God Be with the Clown*, 80-81.

"It Always Felt To Me--a Wrong"

Robinson, *Emily Dickinson: Looking to Canaan*, 82-83.

Marilyn Teichert, "The Divine Adversary: The Image of God in 3 Poems," *DicS*, no. 46 (Bonus 1983): 21-29.

"I Taste a Liquor Never Brewed"

Thomas Baily Aldrich, "In Re Emily Dickinson," in Davis, *14 by Emily Dickinson*, 11-13.

Anderson, *Emily Dickinson's Poetry*, 73-76.

Barker, *Lunacy of Light*, 128-29.

Chase, *Emily Dickinson*, 228-29.

John Cody, *Expl* 36 (Spring 1978): 7.

Hennig Cohen, *Expl* 33 (Jan. 1975): 41.

Lloyd M. Davis, *Expl* 23 (Mar. 1965): 53.

Wallace W. Douglas, *English "A" Analyst*, no. 4, 1-3.

Cecil D. Eby, "'I Taste a Liquor Never Brewed': A Variant Reading," *AL* 36 (Jan. 1965): 516-18.

A. Scott Garrow, "A Note on Manzanilla," *AL* 35 (Nov. 1963): 366.

Charles J. Hauser, *Expl* 31 (Sept. 1972): 2.

William Dean Howells, "Editor's Study," in Davis, *14 by Emily Dickinson*, 9-11.

Thomas Johnson, in Davis, *14 by Emily Dickinson*, 14-15.

Juhasz, *The Undiscovered Continent*, 106-8.

Raymond G. Malbone, *Expl* 26 (Oct. 1967): 14.

Frank Rashid, "Emily Dickinson's Voice of Endings," *ESQ*, no. 118 (First Quarter, 1985): 26-27.

Salska, *Walt Whitman and Emily Dickinson*, 48-49.

William Bysshe Stein, "Emily Dickinson's Parodic Masks," *University of Kansas City Review* 36 (Autumn 1969): 49-52.

Genevieve Taggard, *The Life and Mind of Emily Dickinson* (New York: Knopf, 1930), 267-70.

"It Ceased to Hurt Me, Though So Slow"

Juhasz, *The Undiscovered Continent*, 74-76.

"It Dropped So Low--in My Regard"

Archibald A. Hill, "Figurative Structure and Meaning: Two Poems by Emily Dickinson," *TSLL* 16 (Spring 1974): 206-8. Reprinted in *Constituent and Pattern in Poetry* (Austin: University of Texas Press, 1976), 133-35.

Ted-Larry Pebsorth, "The Lusterward of Dickinson's Silver Shelf," *AN&Q* 12 (Oct. 1973): 18.

James Reeves, "Introduction to Selected Poems of Emily Dickinson," in Sewall, *Emily Dickinson: A Collection of Critical Essays*, 121-22.

"I Tend My Flowers for Thee--"

Budick, *Emily Dickinson and the Life of Language*, 67-68.

"I Think I Was Enchanted"

Barker, *Lunacy of Light*, 99-101.

Gilbert and Gubar, *The Madwoman in the Attic*, 647-49.

Porter, *Dickinson: The Modern Idiom*, 204-6.

Donald Thackrey, "Emily Dickinson's Approach to Poetry," *University of Nebraska Studies*, no. 13 (Nov. 1954), 61-62.

"I Think Just How My Shape Will Rise"

Weisbuch, *Emily Dickinson's Poetry*, 128-29.

"I Thought that Nature Was Enough"

Benfey, *Emily Dickinson and the Problem of Others*, 17-18.

"I Tie My Hat--I Crease My Shawl--"

Barker, *Lunacy of Light*, 49-50.

Sharon Cameron, "'A Loaded Gun': Dickinson and the Dialectic of Rage," *PMLA* 93 (May 1978): 431-33. Reprinted in Cameron, *Lyric Time*, 76-78.

Mossberg, *Emily Dickinson: When a Writer Is a Daughter*, 196-98.

Pollak, *Dickinson: The Anxiety of Gender*, 202-6.

Robinson, *Emily Dickinson: Looking to Canaan*, 96-98.

"It Might Be Lonelier"

Patterson, *Emily Dickinson's Imagery*, 175-76.

"I Took My Powers in My Hands"

Nora M. Fitzgerald, *Expl* 43 (Winter 1985): 20.

Henry Wells, *Introduction to Emily Dickinson* (Chicago: Packard & Co., 1947), 193-94.

"It's Easy to Invent a Life"

Ford, *Heaven Beguiles the Tired*, 103-5.

Vivian R. Pollak, "'That Fine Prosperity': Economic Metaphors in Emily Dickinson's Poetry," *MLQ* 34 (June 1973): 167-68.

"It Sifts from Leaden Sieves--"

Barker, *Lunacy of Light*, 83-84.

Cameron, *Lyric Time*, 174-76.

"It's Like the Light,--"

Henry Wells, *Introduction to Emily Dickinson* (Chicago: Packard & Co., 1947), 162-63.

"It Sounded As If the Streets Were Running"

Anderson, *Emily Dickinson's Poetry*, 140-43.

"It Struck Me--Every Day--"

Sherwood, *Circumference and Circumstance*, 107-9.

"It Was a Quiet Way--"

Joanne Dobson, "Oh, Susie, It Is Dangerous: Emily Dickinson and the Archetype," in Juhasz, *Feminist Critics Read Emily Dickinson*, 90-91.

"It Was Not Death, for I Stood Up"

Anderson, *Emily Dickinson's Poetry*, 212-15.

Sharon Cameron, "Naming As History: Dickinson's Poems of Definition," *CritI* 5 (Winter 1978): 245-48. Reprinted in Cameron, *Lyric Time*, 48-52.

Cody, *After Great Pain*, 326-28.

John Crabbe, "A Thing Without Feathers," *DicS*, no. 34 (Second Half 1978): 3-6.

Diehl, *Emily Dickinson and The Romantic Imagination*, 117-18.

Griffith, *The Long Shadow*, 187-92.

Juhasz, *The Undiscovered Continent*, 65-70.

L.C. Knights, "Defining the Self: Poems of Emily Dickinson," *SR* 91 (Summer 1983): 361-62.

Miller, *Emily Dickinson: A Poet's Grammar*, 78-80.

Laurence Perrine, "Structure and Pronominal Reference in 'It Was Not Death,'" *DicS*, no. 38 (Second Half 1980): 34-36.

Pollak, *Dickinson: The Anxiety of Gender*, 214-17.

Robinson, *Emily Dickinson: Looking to Canaan*, 118-21.

B.J. Rogers, "The Truth Told Slant: Emily Dickinson's Poetic Mode," *TSLL* 14 (Summer 1972): 334-35.

Edith Wylder, *The Last Face: Emily Dickinson's Manuscripts* (Albuquerque: University of New Mexico Press, 1971), 22-26.

"It Was Too Late for Man--"

Benfey, *Emily Dickinson and the Problem of Others*, 69.

Dorothy Huff Oberhaus, "'Engine Against th' Almightie': Emily Dickinson and Prayer," *ESQ* 32 (Third Quarter 1986): 157-58.

"It Would Have Starved a Gnat--"

Mossberg, *Emily Dickinson: When a Writer Is a Daughter*, 136-38.

Barbara Mossberg, "Emily Dickinson's Nursery Rhymes," in Juhasz, *Feminist Critics Read Emily Dickinson*, 58-59.

Pollak, *Dickinson: The Anxiety of Gender*, 131-32.

Theodora Ward, *The Capsule of the Mind: Chapters in the Life of Emily Dickinson* (Cambridge: Harvard University Press, 1961), 11-12.

"It Would Never Be Common--More--I Said--"

Joanne Diehl, "'Ransom in a Voice': Language as Defense in Dickinson's Poetry," in Juhasz, *Feminist Critics Read Emily Dickinson*, 170-72.

Christanne Miller, "How 'Low Feet' Stagger: Disruptions of Language in Dickinson's Poetry," in Juhasz, *Feminist Critics Read Emily Dickinson*, 147-48.

"I've Dropped My Brain--My Soul Is Numb"

Charles R. Anderson, "The Conscious Self in Emily Dickinson's Poetry," *AL* 31 (Nov. 1959): 299-301.

Cody, *After Great Pain*, 324-26.

Diehl, *Emily Dickinson and the Romantic Imagination*, 45-46.

"I've Known a Heaven, Like a Tent--"

Patterson, *Emily Dickinson's Imagery*, 150-51.

"I've None to Tell Me to But Thee"

Porter, *Dickinson: The Modern Idiom*, 132-33.

"I've Seen a Dying Eye"

Ford, *Heaven Beguiles the Tired*, 115-17.

Griffith, *The Long Shadow*, 233-38.

John Rachal, "Probing the Final Mystery in Dickinson's 'I Heard a Fly Buzz' and 'I've Seen a Dying Eye,'" *DicS*, no. 39 (First Half 1981): 44-47.

"I Was the Slightest in the House"

Barbara J. Williams, "A Room of Her Own: Emily Dickinson as Woman Artist," in *Feminist Criticism: Essays on Theory, Poetry, and Prose*, ed. C.L. Brown and K. Olson (Metuchen: Scarecrow Press, 1983), 86-87.

"I Watched the Moon Around the House"

L.C. Knights, "Defining the Self: Poems of Emily Dickinson," *SR* 91 (Summer 1983): 370-71.

"I Would Not Paint--a Picture--"

Diehl, *Emily Dickinson and The Romantic Imagination*, 19-20.

"I Years Had Been from Home"

Steven Axelrod, "Terror in the Everyday: Emily Dickinson's 'I Years Had Been From Home,'" *CP* 6 (Spring 1973): 53-56.

Cody, *After Great Pain*, 129-38.

James E. Miller, Jr., "Emily Dickinson: The Thunder's Tongue," *MinnR* 2 (Spring 1962): 299-303.

Mudge, *Emily Dickinson and the Image of Home*, 78-81.

"Just Lost, When I Was Saved!"

Johnson, *Emily Dickinson: Perception and the Poet's Quest*, 19-21.

Loving, *Emily Dickinson: The Poet on the Second Story*, 15-16.

Porter, *The Art of Emily Dickinson's Early Poetry*, 32-33.

Sherwood, *Circumference and Circumstance*, 45-46.

"Lain in Nature--So Suffice Us--"

Ford, *Heaven Beguiles the Tired*, 145-47.

"The Lamp Burns Sure Within"

Stuart Lewis, *Expl* 28 (Sept. 1969): 4.

"The Last Night That She Lived"

Abad, *A Formal Approach to Lyric Poetry*, 160-64.

Harry Modean Campbell, *Expl* 8 (May 1950): 54. Reprinted in *The Explicator Cyclopedia* 1:70-71.

Ford, *Heaven Beguiles the Tired*, 154-56.

Griffith, *The Long Shadow*, 113-21.

Johnson, *Emily Dickinson: Perception and the Poet's Quest*, 170-72.

James Reeves, "Introduction to Selected Poems of Emily Dickinson," in Sewall, *Emily Dickinson: A Collection of Critical Essays*, 124-25.

Yvor Winters, "Emily Dickinson and the Limits of Judgment," in Ferlazzo, *Critical Essays on Emily Dickinson*, 99-100.

"Let Us Play Yesterday"

Mossberg, *Emily Dickinson: When a Writer Is a Daughter*, 147-52.

"Life--Is What We Make It--"

Kimpel, *Emily Dickinson as Philosopher*, 221-22.

Dorothy Oberhaus, "'Tender Pioneer': Emily Dickinson's Poems on the Life of Christ," *AL* 59 (Oct. 1987): 342-45.

"A Light Exists in Spring"

Cameron, *Lyric Time*, 178-81.

Griffith, *The Long Shadow*, 85-93, 97-100.

Kher, *The Landscape of Absence*, 60-62.

"The Lightning Playeth--All the While--"

Sherwood, *Circumference and Circumstance*, 191-93.

"Like Eyes That Looked on Wastes--"

Cameron, *Lyric Time*, 141-42.

Margaret Homans, "'Oh, Vision of Language!': Dickinson's Poems of Love and Death," in Juhasz, *Feminist Critics Read Emily Dickinson*, 121-23.

Mossberg, *Emily Dickinson: When a Writer Is a Daughter*, 178-81.

Pollak, *Dickinson: The Anxiety of Gender*, 144-45.

Porter, *Dickinson: The Modern Idiom*, 169-70.

"A Little Bread--a Crust--A Crumb"

Porter, *The Art of Emily Dickinson's Early Poetry*, 144-45.

"A Little East of Jordan"

Duncan, *Emily Dickinson*, 50-51.

"A Little Madness in the Spring"

Sherwood, *Circumference and Circumstance*, 197-98.

"The Loneliness One Dare Not Sound--"

Andrew Gibson, "Emily Dickinson and the Poetry of Hypothesis," *EIC* 33 (July 1983): 225-26.

David Green, "Emily Dickinson: The Spatial Drama of Centering," *ELWIU* 7 (Fall 1980): 197-98.

Kimpel, *Emily Dickinson as Philosopher*, 55-56.

John Mann, "Emily Dickinson, Emerson, and the Poet as Namer," *NEQ* 51 (Dec. 1978): 482-83.

Mudge, *Emily Dickinson and the Image of Home*, 108-9.

"The Lonesome for They Know Not What--"

Eberwein, *Dickinson: Strategies*, 172-73.

Lindberg-Seyersted, *The Voice of the Poet*, 82-83.

"Longing Is Like the Seed"

Cameron, *Lyric Time*, 34-35.

Sharon Cameron, "Naming As History: Dickinson's Poems of Definition," *CritI* 5 (Winter 1978): 233-34.

"A Loss of Something Ever Felt I--"

Cody, *After Great Pain*, 40-42.

Barbara J. Williams, "A Room of Her Own: Emily Dickinson as Woman Artist," in *Feminist Criticism: Essays on Theory, Poetry, and Prose*, ed. C.L. Brown and K. Olson (Metuchen: Scarecrow Press, 1983), 78.

"The Love a Life Can Show Below"

Weisbuch, *Emily Dickinson's Poetry*, 68-69.

"Make Me a Picture of the Sun"

Porter, *The Art of Emily Dickinson's Early Poetry*, 82-83.

"The Malay--Took the Pearl--"

Paula Bennet, *My Life a Loaded Gun: Female Creativity and Feminist Poetics* (Boston: Beacon Press, 1986), 52-53.

Patterson, *Emily Dickinson's Imagery*, 89-91.

Rebecca Patterson, *The Riddle of Emily Dickinson* (Boston: Houghton Mifflin, 1951), 258-60.

Pollak, *Dickinson: The Anxiety of Gender*, 154-56.

Theodora Ward, *The Capsule of the Mind: Chapters in the Life of Emily Dickinson* (Cambridge: Harvard University Press, 1961), 62-64.

Weisbuch, *Emily Dickinson's Poetry*, 56-58.

Eleanor Wilner, "The Poetics of Emily Dickinson," *ELH* 38 (Mar. 1971): 143-44.

"Manzanilla"

George Monteiro, *Expl* 43 (Spring 1985): 16.

"Me from Myself--to Banish--"

Cody, *After Great Pain*, 331-32.

Juhasz, *The Undiscovered Continent*, 17-18.

"A Mien to Move a Queen"

F. DeWolfe Miller, "Emily Dickinson: Self-Portrait in the Third Person," *NEQ* 46 (Mar. 1973): 119-24.

"Mine--by the Right of the White Election"

Juhasz, *The Undiscovered Continent*, 100-103.

"A Mine There Is No Man Would Own"

Vivian R. Pollak, "'That Fine Prosperity': Economic Metaphors in Emily Dickinson's Poetry," *MLQ* 34 (June 1973): 177-78.

"The Moon upon Her Fluent Route"

Winters, *Forms of Discovery*, 270-71.

Wolosky, *Emily Dickinson: A Voice of War*, 28-30.

"More Life Went Out, When He Went"

R. Blackmur, "Emily Dickinson: Notes on Prejudice and Fact," *SoR* 3 (Autumn 1937): 337-41.

Blackmur, *Expense of Greatness*, 126-30. Reprinted in Blackmur, *Language as Gesture*, 40-43.

Cameron, *Lyric Time*, 149-51.

Chase, *Emily Dickinson*, 47-48.

Robinson, *Emily Dickinson: Looking to Canaan*, 155-57.

Sherwood, *Circumference and Circumstance*, 100-102.

"The Morns Are Meeker Than They Were--"

Margaret Homans, *Women Writers and Poetic Identity* (Princeton: Princeton University Press, 1980), 197-98.

"Much Madness Is Divinest Sense"

Abad, *A Formal Approach to Lyric Poetry*, 133-34.

R.P. Blackmur, "Emily Dickinson's Notation," in Sewall, *Emily Dickinson: A Collection of Critical Essays*, 86-87.

Cynthia Griffin Wolff, *Expl* 36 (Summer 1978): 3.

"Must Be a Wo--"

Diehl, *Emily Dickinson and the Romantic Imagination*, 57-58.

Kimpel, *Emily Dickinson as Philosopher*, 26-27.

"My Cocoon Tightens--Colors Tease--"

Barker, *Lunacy of Light*, 123-24.

Diehl, *Emily Dickinson and The Romantic Imagination*, 106-7.

"My Faith Is Larger Than the Hills--"

Wolosky, *Emily Dickinson: A Voice of War*, 14-17.

"My Life Closed Twice"

Perry D. Luckett, *Expl* 40 (Spring 1982): 32.

"My Life Had Stood--a Loaded Gun--"

Anderson, *Emily Dickinson's Poetry*, 172-76.

Christopher Benfey, *Emily Dickinson: Lives of a Poet* (New York: George Braziller, 1986), 86-89.

Paula Bennet, *My Life a Loaded Gun: Female Creativity and Feminist Poetics* (Boston: Beacon Press, 1986), 5-8.

Louise Bogan, "A Mystical Poet," in Sewall, *Emily Dickinson: A Collection of Critical Essays*, 142-43.

Sharon Cameron, "'A Loaded Gun': Dickinson and the Dialectic of Rage," *PMLA* 93 (May 1978): 425-30. Reprinted in Cameron, *Lyric Time*, 65-68.

Amy Cherry, "'A Prison Gets to Be a Friend," *DicS*, no. 49 (June 1984): 12-14.

Cody, *After Great Pain*, 399-415.

Albert Gelpi, "Emily Dickinson and the Deerslayer: The Dilemma of the Woman Poet in America," *SJS* 2 (May 1977): 81-90.

Gilbert and Gubar, *The Madwoman in the Attic*, 608-10.

Thomas Johnson, *Emily Dickinson: An Interpretive Biography* (Cambridge: Harvard University Press, 1955), 138-40.

Loving, *Emily Dickinson: The Poet on the Second Story*, 45-46.

Miller, *Emily Dickinson: A Poet's Grammar*, 34-36, 71-72, 122-26.

Mossberg, *Emily Dickinson: When a Writer Is a Daughter*, 19-23.

Laurence Perrine, *Expl* 21 (Nov. 1962): 21.

The Poetry Workshop, Columbus, Georgia, *Expl* 15 (May 1957): 51. Reprinted in *The Explicator Cyclopedia* 1:71-72.

Pollak, *Dickinson: The Anxiety of Gender*, 150-54.

Porter, *Dickinson: The Modern Idiom*, 215-17.

Adrienne Rich, "Vesuvius at Home: The Power of Emily Dickinson," in Ferlazzo, *Critical Essays on Emily Dickinson*, 186-88.

Robinson, *Emily Dickinson: Looking to Cannan*, 158-61.

Edgar Stocker, "Essay, no. Two: We Roam in Sovereign Woods," *DicS*, no. 42 (First Half 1982): 43-50.

Weisbuch, *Emily Dickinson's Poetry*, 25-30.

Whicher, *This Was a Poet*, 278-80.

Wolosky, *Emily Dickinson: A Voice of War*, 92-95.

"My Period Had Come for Prayer--"

Dorothy Huff Oberhaus, "'Engine Against th' Almightie': Emily Dickinson and Prayer," *ESQ* 32 (Third Quarter 1986): 166-69.

"My Portion Is Defeat--Today--"

Wolosky, *Emily Dickinson: A Voice of War*, 56-57.

"Myself Was Formed--a Carpenter--"

Judith Wilt, "Emily Dickinson: Playing House," *Boundary 2* 12 (Winter 1984): 160-61.

"My Triumph Lasted Till the Drums"

Wolosky, *Emily Dickinson: A Voice of War*, 51-52.

"My Wheel Is in the Dark"

Mabel Howard, William Howard, and Emily Harvey, *Expl* 17 (Nov. 1958): 12. Reprinted in *The Explicator Cyclopedia* 1:72-73.

"A Narrow Fellow in the Grass"

Johnson, *Emily Dickinson: Perception and the Poet's Quest*, 35-37.

Karl Keller, *The Only Kangaroo among the Beauty: Emily Dickinson and America* (Baltimore: Johns Hopkins University Press, 1979), 268-70.

L.C. Knights, "Defining the Self: Poems of Emily Dickinson," *SR* 91 (Summer 1983): 367-69.

"Nature and God--I Neither Knew"

Benfey, *Emily Dickinson and the Problem of Others*, 60-62.

Chase, *Emily Dickinson*, 164-65.

"'Nature' Is What We See--"

Margaret Homans, *Women Writers and Poetic Identity* (Princeton: Princeton University Press, 1980), 190-91.

Juhasz, *The Undiscovered Continent*, 38-41.

Kimpel, *Emily Dickinson as Philosopher*, 187-88.

"Nature, the Gentlest Mother, Is"

Margaret Homans, *Women Writers and Poetic Identity* (Princeton: Princeton University Press, 1980), 199-200.

Ruth McNaughton, "The Imagery of Emily Dickinson," *University of Nebraska Studies*, no. 4 (Jan. 1949), 34-36.

"The Nearest Dream Recedes--Unrealized--"

Benfey, *Emily Dickinson and the Problem of Others*, 69-71.

Loving, *Emily Dickinson: The Poet on the Second Story*, 20-21.

Miller, *The Poetry of Emily Dickinson*, 53-56.

Norman Talbot, "The Child, The Actress, and Miss Emily Dickinson," *SoRA* 5 (June 1972): 107-8.

"The Night Was Wide and Furnished Scant"

Whicher, *This Was a Poet*, 274-75.

"Nobody Knows This Little Rose"

Karen Durdurand, "Another Dickinson Poem Published in Her Lifetime,"*AL* 54 (Oct. 1983): 434-37.

"No Brigadier Throughout the Year"

Sr. Victoria Marie Forde, S.C., *Expl* 27 (Feb. 1969): 41

"No Crowd That Has Occurred"

Lindberg-Seyersted, *The Voice of the Poet*, 248-49.

Robinson, *Emily Dickinson: Looking to Canaan*, 46-49.

Sherwood, *Circumference and Circumstance*, 171-72.

"No Man Can Compass a Despair--"

Juhasz, *The Undiscovered Continent*, 41-42.

Wolosky, *Emily Dickinson: A Voice of War*, 24-26.

"No Man Saw Awe, Nor to His House"

B.J. Smith, "ED: 'Vicinity to Laws,'" *DicS*, no. 56 (Second Half 1985): 47-49.

Judith Wilt, "Emily Dickinson: Playing House," *Boundary 2* 12 (Winter 1984): 163-64.

"No Rack Can Torture Me"

Eunice Glenn, "Emily Dickinson's Poetry: A Revaluation," *SR* 51 (Autumn 1943): 577-78.

B.J. Rogers, "The Truth Told Slant: Emily Dickinson's Poetic Mode," *TSLL* 14 (Summer 1972): 332.

"Not in This World to See His Face"

Kimpel, *Emily Dickinson as Philosopher*, 137-38.

Loving, *Emily Dickinson: The Poet on the Second Story*, 87-88.

"Not with a Club the Heart Is Broken"

Mordecai Marcus, *Expl* 20 (Mar. 1962): 54.

"Of All the Souls That Stand Create"

Abad, *A Formal Approach to Poetry*, 137-39.

E. Miller Budick, "When the Soul Selects: Emily Dickinson's Attack on New England Symbolism," *AL* 51 (Nov. 1979): 358-59.

Chase, *Emily Dickinson*, 158-59.

Christanne Miller, "How 'Low Feet' Stagger: Disruptions of Language in Dickinson's Poetry," in Juhasz, *Feminist Critics Read Emily Dickinson*, 139-41.

Richard Wilbur, "Sumptuous Destitution," in Sewall, *Emily Dickinson: A Collection of Critical Essays*, 134-35.

"Of All the Sounds Despatched Abroad"

Thomas Johnson, *Emily Dickinson: An Interpretive Biography* (Cambridge: Harvard University Press, 1955), 114-16.

Miller, *The Poetry of Emily Dickinson*, 72-74.

"Of Bronze--and Blaze--"

Anderson, *Emily Dickinson's Poetry*, 47-57.

Robert Gillespie, "A Circumference of Emily Dickinson," *NEQ* 46 (June 1973): 258-60.

David Hiatt, *Expl* 21 (Sept. 1962): 6.

Jo. C. Searles, "The Art of Dickinson's 'Household Thought,'" *CP* 6 (Spring 1973): 46-51.

Sherwood, *Circumference and Circumstance*, 98-99, 206-7.

"Of Chambers as the Cedars--"

Benfey, *Emily Dickinson and the Problem of Others*, 33-34.

"Of Course--I Prayed--"

Marilyn C. Teichert, "The Divine Adversary: The Image of God in 3 Poems," *DicS*, no. 46 (Bonus 1983): 21-29.

"Of Death I Try to Think Like This"

Nancy McClaran, *Expl* 35 (Winter 1976): 18-19.

Patterson, *Emily Dickinson's Imagery*, 55-56.

"Of God We Ask One Favor"

Mildred K. Travis, *Expl* 40 (Fall 1981): 31.

"Oh Could We Climb Where Moses Stood"

Porter, *The Art of Emily Dickinson's Early Poetry*, 60-61.

"One Blessing Had I Than the Rest"

Johnson, *Emily Dickinson: Perception and the Poet's Quest*, 136-40.

Juhasz, *The Undiscovered Continent*, 63-65.

Vivian R. Pollak, "'That Fine Prosperity': Economic Metaphors in Emily Dickinson's Poetry," *MLQ* 34 (June 1973): 178-79.

"One Crown That No One Seeks"

Dorothy Oberhaus, "'Tender Pioneer': Emily Dickinson's Poems on the Life of Christ," *AL* 59 (Oct. 1987): 349-50.

"One Crucifixion Is Recorded--Only--"

Dorothy Oberhaus, "'Tender Pioneer': Emily Dickinson's Poems on the Life of Christ," *AL* 59 (Oct. 1987): 351-54.

Robinson, *Emily Dickinson: Looking to Canaan*, 130-31.

Weisbuch, *Emily Dickinson's Poetry*, 80-81.

"One Day Is There of the Series"

Paul O. Williams, *Expl* 23 (Dec. 1964): 28.

"One Dignity Delays for All--"

Duncan, *Emily Dickinson*, 82-84.

Erhardt H. Essig, *Expl* 23 (Oct. 1964): 16.

Pierre Michel, "The Last Stanza of Emily Dickinson's 'One Dignity Delays for All--," *ES* 50 (Feb. 1969): 98-100

"One Life of So Much Consequence"

Rebecca Patterson, "Emily Dickinson's Jewel Imagery," *AL* 42 (Jan. 1971): 514-15.

"One Need Not Be a Chamber--to Be Haunted"

Charles R. Anderson, "The Conscious Self in Emily Dickinson's Poetry," *AL* 31 (Nov. 1959): 304-5.

David Green, "Emily Dickinson: The Spatial Drama of Centering," *ELWIU* 7 (Fall 1980): 198-99.

"One Sister Have I in Our House"

Pollak, *Dickinson: The Anxiety of Gender*, 137-40.

"One Year Ago--Jots What?"

David Luisi, "Some Aspects of Emily Dickinson's Food and Liquor Poems," *ES* 52 (Feb. 1971): 38.

Miller, *The Poetry of Emily Dickinson*, 131-33.

"The Only News I Know"

Ralph Marcellino, "Emily Dickinson," *CE* 7 (Nov. 1945): 102-3.

"On This Wondrous Sea"

George Monteiro, *Expl* 33 (May 1975): 74

"Our Journey Had Advanced"

Harold Bloom, "Poetic Crossing II: American Stances," *GaR* 30 (Winter 1976): 787-90.

Cameron, *Lyric Time*, 109-11.

Chase, *Emily Dickinson*, 165-66.

Robert Gillespie, "A Circumference of Emily Dickinson," *NEQ* 46 (June 1973): 266-71.

Johnson, *Emily Dickinson: Perception and the Poet's Quest*, 184-5.

Douglas Novich Leonard, *Expl* 41 (Summer 1983): 29.

Weisbuch, *Emily Dickinson's Poetry*, 50-52.

Yvor Winters, "Emily Dickinson and the Limits of Judgment," in Ferlazzo, *Critical Essays on Emily Dickinson*, 98-99.

"Our Little Kinsmen--After Rain"

Sherwood, *Circumference and Circumstance*, 195-97.

"Ourselves Were Wed One Summer--Dear--"

Rebecca Patterson, *The Riddle of Emily Dickinson* (Boston: Houghton Mifflin, 1951), 124-26.

Pollak, *Dickinson: The Anxiety of Gender*, 141-42.

Barbara J. Williams, "A Room of Her Own: Emily Dickinson as Woman Artist," in *Feminist Criticism: Essays on Theory, Poetry, and Prose*, ed. C.L. Brown and K. Olson (Metuchen: Scarecrow Press, 1983), 85.

"Our Share of Night To Bear--"

Archibald MacLeish, "The Private World: Poems of Emily Dickinson," in Sewall, *Emily Dickinson: A Collection of Critical Essays*, 151.

"Over the Fence--"

Barker, *Lunacy of Light*, 45.

"Pain--Has an Element of Blank--"

Douglas Anderson, "Presence and Place in Emily Dickinson's Poetry," *NEQ* 57 (June 1984): 216-17.

Cameron, *Lyric Time*, 161-62.

"Pass to Thy Rendezvous of Light"

Norman Talbot, "The Child, The Actress, and Miss Emily Dickinson," *SoRA* 5 (June 1972): 120-23.

"Perception of an Object Costs"

Juhasz, *The Undiscovered Continent*, 46-48.

"Pink--Small--and Punctual"

Travis Du Priest, "Pink--Small--and Punctual," *DicS*, no. 46 (Bonus 1983): 20-21.

"A Pit--But Heaven Over It--"

Wolosky, *Emily Dickinson: A Voice of War*, 5-9.

"The Poets Light But Lamps"

Helene Knox, *Expl* 41 (Fall 1982): 31.

Stuart Lewis, *Expl* 28 (Sept. 1969): 4.

Mudge, *Emily Dickinson and the Image of Home*, 111-12.

Barton Levi St. Armand, "Emily Dickinson and the Occult: The Rosicrucian Connection," *PrS* 51 (Winter 1977-1978): 351-56.

"Poor Little Heart"

Kimpel, *Emily Dickinson as Philosopher*, 175-76.

J.S. Wheatcroft, "Emily Dickinson's White Robes," *Criticism* 5 (Spring 1963): 137.

"Portraits Are to Daily Faces"

Simon Tugwell, "Notes on Two Poems by Emily Dickinson," *N&Q* 13 (Sept. 1966): 342.

"Praise It--'Tis Dead"

James S. Mullican, *Expl* 27 (Apr. 1969): 62.

"Presentiment--Is That Long Shadow--on the Lawn"

Abad, *A Formal Approach to Lyric Poetry*, 39-40.

Mario L. D'Avanza, "Emily Dickinson's and Emerson's 'Presentiment,'" *ESQ*, no. 58 (Part 4 1970): 157-59.

David H. Hirsch, "Emily Dickinson's 'Presentiment,'" *AN&Q* 1 (Nov. 1962): 36-37.

Laurence Perrine, "Emily Dickinson's 'Presentiment' Again," *AN&Q* 3 (Apr. 1965): 119.

"A Prison Gets to Be a Friend"

Amy Cherry, "'A Prison Gets to Be a Friend," *DicS*, no. 49 (June 1984): 9-12.

Mudge, *Emily Dickinson and the Image of Home*, 224-26.

Pollak, *Dickinson: The Anxiety of Gender*, 129-31.

"The Province of the Saved"

Miller, *Emily Dickinson: A Poet's Grammar*, 94-96.

Weisbuch, *Emily Dickinson's Poetry*, 86-87.

"Publication--Is the Auction"

Anderson, *Emily Dickinson's Poetry*, 59-60.

Benfey, *Emily Dickinson and the Problem of Others*, 35-36.

Mario L. D'Avanza, "'Unto the White Creator': The Snow of Dickinson and Emerson," *NEQ* 45 (June 1972): 278-80.

Eberwein, *Dickinson: Strategies*, 43.

Pollak, *Dickinson: The Anxiety of Gender*, 229-30.

Vivian R. Pollak, "'That Fine Prosperity': Economic Metaphors in Emily Dickinson's Poetry," *MLQ* 34 (June 1973): 176-77.

"The Rat Is the Concisest Tenant"

Barker, *Lunacy of Light*, 96-97.

"Rearrange a Wife's Affection!"

Paula Bennet, *My Life a Loaded Gun: Female Creativity and Feminist Poetics* (Boston: Beacon Press, 1986), 80-81.

R.P. Blackmur, "Emily Dickinson's Notation," in Sewall, *Emily Dickinson: A Collection of Critical Essays*, 84-85.

Eberwein, *Dickinson: Strategies*, 107-8.

Sandra Gilbert, "The Wayward Nun Beneath the Hill," in Juhasz, *Feminist Critics Read Emily Dickinson*, 33-35.

Mossberg, *Emily Dickinson: When a Writer Is a Daughter*, 173-74.

Pollak, *Dickinson: The Anxiety of Gender*, 169-71.

"Red Sea"

Barton Levi St. Armand, *Expl* 43 (Spring 1985): 17.

"Remembrance Has a Rear and Front--"

Mudge, *Emily Dickinson and the Image of Home*, 2-4.

"Remorse--Is Memory--Awake--"

Sharon Cameron, "Naming As History: Dickinson's Poems of Definition," *CritI* 5 (Winter 1978): 234-36. Reprinted in Cameron, *Lyric Time*, 35-36.

Griffith, *The Long Shadow*, 201-4.

Mudge, *Emily Dickinson and the Image of Home*, 190-91.

Wolosky, *Emily Dickinson: A Voice of War*, 77-79.

"Renunciation--Is a Piercing Virtue--"

R.P. Blackmur, "Emily Dickinson: Notes on Prejudice and Fact," *SoR* 3 (Autumn 1937): 333-36.

Blackmur, *Expense of Greatness*, 119-23.

Sharon Cameron, "Naming As History: Dickinson's Poems of Definition," *CritI* 5 (Winter 1978): 237-39. Reprinted in Cameron, *Lyric Time*, 39-41.

Johnson, *Emily Dickinson: Perception and the Poet's Quest*, 52-53.

Juhasz, *The Undiscovered Continent*, 129-32.

Kher, *The Landscape of Absence*, 240-41.

Mudge, *Emily Dickinson and the Image of Home*, 113-14.

Porter, *Dickinson: The Modern Idiom*, 45-46.

Weisbuch, *Emily Dickinson's Poetry*, 173-74.

"Rests at Night"

Barker, *Lunacy of Light*, 77-78.

"Reverse Cannot Befall"

Charles R. Anderson, *Expl* 18 (May 1960): 46. Reprinted in *The Explicator Cyclopedia* 1:74-75; in Locke, Gibson, and Arms, *Readings for Liberal Education*, 4th ed., 154-55; 5th ed., 133-34.

"Revolution Is the Pod"

Celia Anderson, "Deep Dyed Politics in ED's 'Revolution Is the Pod,'" *DicS*, no. 49 (June 1984): 3-8.

"The Robin Is the One"

Laurence Perrine, *Expl* 33 (Dec. 1974): 33.

"The Robin's My Criterion for Tune--"

Porter, *The Art of Emily Dickinson's Early Poetry*, 86-87.

"A Route of Evanescence"

Anderson, *Emily Dickinson's Poetry*, 114-17.

Frank Davidson, "A Note on Emily Dickinson's Use of Shakespeare," *NEQ* 18 (Sept. 1945): 407-8.

Roland Hagenbuchle, "Precision and Indeterminacy in the Poetry of Emily Dickinson," *ESQ*, no. 20 (First Quarter 1974): 33-40.

Thomas Johnson, "Emily Dickinson," in Davis, *14 by Emily Dickinson*, 139-40.

Lucas, *Emily Dickinson and Riddle*, 122-24.

John Lynen, "Three Uses of the Present: The Historian's, the Critic's and Emily Dickinson's," *CE* 28 (Nov. 1966): 131-32.

Archibald MacLeish, "The Private World: Poems of Emily Dickinson," in Sewall, *Emily Dickinson: A Collection of Critical Essays*, 153.

Rebecca Patterson, "Emily Dickinson's Hummingbird," in Davis, *14 by Emily Dickinson*, 140-48.

Porter, *The Art of Emily Dickinson's Early Poetry*, 76-77.

Grover Smith, *Expl* 7 (May 1949): 54. Reprinted in *The Explicator Cyclopedia* 1:75-76.

Linda J. Taylor, "Shakespeare and Circumference: Dickinson's Hummingbird and *The Tempest*," *ESQ*, no. 23 (Fourth Quarter 1977): 252-61.

Whicher, *This Was a Poet*, 261-63.

"Safe in Their Alabaster Chambers"

Anderson, *Emily Dickinson's Poetry*, 269-75.

Mother Angela Carson, O.S.U., *Expl* 17 (June 1959): 62. Reprinted in *The Explicator Cyclopedia* 1:77.

William Howard, *Expl* 17 (June 1969): 62. Reprinted in *The Explicator Cyclopedia* 1:76-77.

Karl Keller, *The Only Kangaroo among the Beauty: Emily Dickinson and America* (Baltimore: Johns Hopkins University Press, 1979), 190-93.

Lucas, *Emily Dickinson and Riddle*, 98-101.

Miller, *The Poetry of Emily Dickinson*, 52-53.

Porter, *The Art of Emily Dickinson's Early Poetry*, 168-70.

Porter, *Dickinson: The Modern Idiom*, 25-27.

David Porter, "Emily Dickinson: The Poetics of Doubt," *ESQ*, no. 60 Supplement (Summer 1970): 92-93.

Robinson, *Emily Dickinson: Looking to Canaan*, 53-55.

Norman Talbot, "The Child, The Actress, and Miss Emily Dickinson," *SoRA* 5 (June 1972): 106.

Weisbuch, *Emily Dickinson's Poetry*, 109-13.

"Sang From the Heart, Sire"

Diehl, *Emily Dickinson and The Romantic Imagination*, 155-58.

Pollak, *Dickinson: The Anxiety of Gender*, 107-9.

"Satisfaction--Is the Agent"

Juhasz, *The Undiscovered Continent*, 91-92.

"The Saucer Holds a Cup"

Kimpel, *Emily Dickinson as Philosopher*, 168-69.

"Savior! I've No One Else To Tell"

Kimpel, *Emily Dickinson as Philosopher*, 240-41.
Jenijoy LaBelle, *Expl* 38 (Summer 1980): 34.

"The Savior Must Have Been"

Dorothy Oberhaus, "'Tender Pioneer': Emily Dickinson's Poems on the Life of Christ," *AL* 59 (Oct. 1987): 346-47.

"'Secrets' Is a Daily Word"

Kimpel, *Emily Dickinson as Philosopher*, 92-94.

"The Service without Hope"

Miller, *Emily Dickinson: A Poet's Grammar*, 83-84.

"Severer Service of Myself"

Miller, *The Poetry of Emily Dickinson*, 207-9.
Pollak, *Dickinson: The Anxiety of Gender*, 199-202.

"'Shall I Take Thee?' the Poet Said"

B.J. Smith, "ED: 'Vicinity to Laws,'" *DicS*, no. 56. (Second Half 1985): 45-47.
Donald Thackrey, "Emily Dickinson's Approach to Poetry," *University of Nebraska Studies*, no. 13 (Nov. 1954), 11-12.

"She Bore It Till the Simple Veins"

Archibald MacLeish, "The Private World: Poems of Emily Dickinson," in Sewall, *Emily Dickinson: A Collection of Critical Essays*, 156-57.

Porter, *The Art of Emily Dickinson's Early Poetry*, 63-64.

Sherwood, *Circumference and Circumstance*, 39-41.

"She Laid Her Docile Crescent Down"

Diehl, *Emily Dickinson and The Romantic Imagination*, 63-64.

"She Rose to His Requirement -- Dropt"

Gilbert and Gubar, *The Madwoman in the Attic*, 588-91.

Johnson, *Emily Dickinson: Perception and the Poet's Quest*, 133-35.

Juhasz, *The Undiscovered Continent*, 114-16.

"She Sweeps with Many-colored Brooms"

Laurence Perrine, "Dickinson Distorted," *CE* 36 (Oct. 1974): 212-13.

"The Sky Is Low, The Clouds Are Mean"

Susan Miles, "The Irregularities of Emily Dickinson," in Ferlazzo, *Critical Essays on Emily Dickinson*, 69-70.

"Sleep Is Supposed to Be"

Barker, *Lunacy of Light*, 127-28.

Mossberg, *Emily Dickinson: When a Writer Is a Daughter*, 80-81.

Weisbuch, *Emily Dickinson's Poetry*, 6-8.

"The Snow That Never Drifts"

Ralph Marcellino, *Expl* 13 (Apr. 1955): 36. Reprinted in *The Explicator Cyclopedia* 1:77.

"Softened by Time's Consumate Plush"

Chatman, *An Introduction to the Language of Poetry*, 63-64.

"So Glad We Are"

Owen P. Thomas, Jr., *Expl* 18 (Nov. 1959): 10. Reprinted in *The Explicator Cyclopedia* 1:77-78.

"So Has a Daisy Vanished"

Weisbuch, *Emily Dickinson's Poetry*, 18-19.

"A Solemn Thing--It Was--I Said--"

Sandra Gilbert, "The Wayward Nun Beneath the Hill," in Juhasz, *Feminist Critics Read Emily Dickinson*, 31-32.

Miller, *The Poetry of Emily Dickinson*, 14-15.

"A Solemn Thing within the Soul"

Barker, *Lunacy of Light*, 48.

Robinson, *Emily Dickinson: Looking to Canaan*, 41-42.

Kher, *The Landscape of Absence*, 251-53.

David Luisi, "Some Aspects of Emily Dickinson's Food and Liquor Poems," *ES* 52 (Feb. 1971): 38-39.

"Some Arrows Slay but Whom They Strike"

J.S. Wheatcroft, "Emily Dickinson's White Robes," *Criticism* 5 (Spring 1963): 139-40.

"Some One Prepared This Mighty Show"

Benfey, *Emily Dickinson and the Problem of Others*, 43-45.

"Some Things That Fly There Be"

Porter, *The Art of Emily Dickinson's Early Poetry*, 31-32, 80.

"Some--Work For Immortality--"

Laurence Perrine, *Expl* 40 (Fall 1981): 32.

"So Much Of Heaven Has Gone from Earth"

Richard J. Ripley, *Expl* 42 (Fall 1983): 27.

"So Much Summer"

Porter, *Dickinson: The Modern Idiom*, 103-4.

"Son Of None"

Peggy Anderson, *Expl* 41 (Fall 1982): 32.

"The Soul Has Bandaged Moments"

Cameron, *Lyric Time*, 7-8.

John Cody, "The Soul Has Bandaged Moments," in *Critics on Emily Dickinson*, ed. Richard Rupp (Coral Gables: University of Miami Press, 1972), 90-92.

David Green, "Emily Dickinson: The Spatial Drama of Centering," *ELWIU* 7 (Fall 1980): 196-97.

Griffith, *The Long Shadow*, 215-21.

Peckham and Chatman, *Word, Meaning, Poem*, 303-11.

Adrienne Rich, "Vesuvius at Home: The Power of Emily Dickinson," in Ferlazzo, *Critical Essays on Emily Dickinson*, 190.

Weisbuch, *Emily Dickinson's Poetry*, 122-24.

"The Soul Selects Her Own Society--"

Abad, *A Formal Approach to Lyric Poetry*, 135-38.

Elizabeth Bowman, *Expl* 29 (Oct. 1970): 13.

Budick, *Emily Dickinson and the Life of Language*, 138-43.

E. Miller Budick, "When the Soul Selects: Emily Dickinson's Attack on New England Symbolism," *AL* 51 (Nov. 1979): 353-56.

Paul Faris, *Expl* 25 (Apr. 1967): 65.

Griffith, *The Long Shadow*, 209-12.

Archibald A. Hill, "Figurative Structure and Meaning: Two Poems by Emily Dickinson," *TSLL* 16 (Spring 1974): 196-206. Reprinted in Archibald A. Hill, *Constituent and Pattern in Poetry* (Austin: University of Texas Press, 1976), 123-33.

Juhasz, *The Undiscovered Continent*, 14-16.

Will C. Jumper, *Expl* 29 (Sept. 1970): 5.

Kher, *The Landscape of Absence*, 256-57.

James Machor, "Emily Dickinson and Feminine Rhetoric," *ArQ* 36 (Summer 1980): 145-46.

Henry F. Pommer, *Expl* 3 (Feb. 1945): 32. Reprinted in *The Explicator Cyclopedia* 1:78.

Larry Rubin, *Expl* 30 (Apr. 1972): 67.

Simon Tugwell, *Expl* 27 (Jan. 1969): 37.

Van Doren, *Introduction to Poetry*, 39-42.

Paul Witherington, "The Neighborhood Humor of Dickinson's 'The Soul Selects Her Own Society,'" *CP* 2 (Fall 1969): 5-8.

Wolosky, *Emily Dickinson: A Voice of War*, 128-29.

"The Soul's Distinct Connection"

Sharon Cameron, "Naming As History: Dickinson's Poems of Definition," *CritI* 5 (Winter 1978): 244-45. Reprinted in Cameron, *Lyric Time*, 47-48.

"The Soul Should Always Stand Ajar"

Virginia Ogden Birdsall, "Emily Dickinson's Intruder in the Soul," *AL* 37 (Mar. 1965): 59-60.

Chase, *Emily Dickinson*, 129-30.

"The Soul's Superior Instants"

Suzanne M. Wilson, "Emily Dickinson and the Twentieth-Century Poetry of Sensibility," *AL* 36 (Nov. 1964): 351-52.

"The Spider Holds a Silver Ball"

Johnson, *Emily Dickinson: Perception and the Poet's Quest*, 44-45.

Martin, *An American Triptych*, 133-34.

"A Spider Sewed at Night"

Anderson, *Emily Dickinson's Poetry*, 125-27.

Cameron, *Lyric Time*, 5-6.

Gilbert and Gubar, *The Madwoman in the Attic*, 635-37.

Johnson, *Emily Dickinson: Perception and the Poet's Quest*, 43-44.

Salska, *Walt Whitman and Emily Dickinson*, 78-79.

"A Still--Volcano--Life--"

Barker, *Lunacy of Light*, 117-19.

"Struck, Was I, Nor Yet by Lightning--"

Cody, *After Great Pain*, 440-42.

"Success Is Counted Sweetest"

Abad, *A Formal Approach to Lyric Poetry*, 134-35.

Andrew Gibson, "Emily Dickinson and the Poetry of Hypothesis," *EIC* 33 (July 1983): 229-30.

Pollak, *Dickinson: The Anxiety of Gender*, 125.

Whicher, *This Was a Poet*, 202-3.

Richard Wilbur, "Sumptuous Destitution," in Sewall, *Emily Dickinson: A Collection of Critical Essays*, 131-32.

"Summer Begins to Have the Look"

Johnson, *Emily Dickinson*, 109-10.

"Summer Has Two Beginnings"

Lawrence A. Walz, *Expl* 33 (Oct. 1974): 16.

"The Sun Is The One"

Ralph Marcellino, *Expl* 40 (Spring 1982): 29.

"The Sun--Just Touched the Morning--"

Cody, *After Great Pain*, 430-31.

"The Sun Kept Stooping--Stooping--Low!"

Barker, *Lunacy of Light*, 109-10.

"Superfluous Were the Sun"

Brita Lindberg, "Further Notes on a Poem by Emily Dickinson," *N&Q* 15 (May 1968): 179-80.

"Sweet Mountains--Ye Tell Me No Lie--"

Barker, *Lunacy of Light*, 110-11.

Joanne Diehl, "'Ransom in a Voice': Language as Defense in Dickinson's Poetry," in Juhasz, *Feminist Critics Read Emily Dickinson*, 166-68.

"Sweet--Safe--Houses"

Lindberg-Seyersted, *The Voice of the Poet*, 87-88.

"Taken From Men This Morning"

Henry Wells, *Introduction to Emily Dickinson* (Chicago: Packard & Co., 1947), 260-61.

"Tell All the Truth But Tell It Slant--"

Wallace, *God Be with the Clown*, 78-79.

"Tell Me!"

Wallace, *God Be with the Clown*, 82-83.

"The Test of Love--Is Death"

Dorothy Oberhaus, "'Tender Pioneer': Emily Dickinson's Poems on the Life of Christ," *AL* 59 (Oct. 1987): 347-49.

"That After Horror--That 'Twas Us"

Willis J. Buckingham, *Expl* 40 (Summer 1982): 34.
Cameron, *Lyric Time*, 106-8.

"Their Height in Heaven Comforts Not--"

Mudge, *Emily Dickinson and the Image of Home*, 209-10.
Wolosky, *Emily Dickinson: A Voice of War*, 104-5.

"There Are Two Ripenings"

Laurence Perrine, *Expl* 31 (Apr. 1973): 65.

"There Came a Day at Summer's Full,"

Mother Mary Anthony, "Emily Dickinson's Scriptural Echoes," *MR* 2 (Spring 1961): 557-61.

Budick, *Emily Dickinson and the Life of Language*, 213-23.

Griffith, *The Long Shadow*, 158-62.

Caroline Hogue, *Expl* 11 (Dec. 1952): 17. Reprinted in *The Explicator Cyclopedia* 1:78-79.

William Howard, *Expl* 12 (Apr. 1954): 41. Reprinted in *The Explicator Cyclopedia* 1:80-81.

Loving, *Emily Dickinson: The Poet on the Second Story*, 39-40.

Miller, *The Poetry of Emily Dickinson*, 75-76.

Pollak, *Dickinson: The Anxiety of Gender*, 167-68.

"There Came a Wind Like a Bugle"

Lindberg-Seyersted, *The Voice of the Poet*, 152-53.

"There Is a June When Corn Is Cut"

Wolosky, *Emily Dickinson: A Voice of War*, 113-15.

"There Is a Morn by Men Unseen--"

Joanne Diehl, "'Ransom in a Voice': Language as Defense in Dickinson's Poetry," in Juhasz, *Feminist Critics Read Emily Dickinson*, 159-60.

"There Is Another Sky"

Douglas Anderson, "Presence and Place in Emily Dickinson's Poetry," *NEQ* 57 (June 1984): 206-7.

Barker, *Lunacy of Light*, 104-5.

Diehl, *Emily Dickinson and The Romantic Imagination*, 89-90.

"There Is a Pain--So Utter--"

Juhasz, *The Undiscovered Continent*, 44-46.

"There Is No Frigate Like a Book"

Perrine, *Sound and Sense*, 32; 2d ed., 38.

"There's a Certain Slant of Light"

Anderson, *Emily Dickinson's Poetry*, 215-18.

Cameron, *Lyric Time*, 100-103.

Curtis Dahl, *Expl* 45 (Spring 1987): 37-38.

Diehl, *Emily Dickinson and The Romantic Imagination*, 54-56.

Denis Donoghue, *Emily Dickinson*, University of Minnesota Pamphlets on American Writers, no. 81 (Minneapolis: University of Minnesota Press, 1969), 31-33.

Duncan, *Emily Dickinson*, 76-77.

Griffith, *The Long Shadow*, 26-28.

Kher, *The Landscape of Absence*, 80-81.

Lindberg-Seyersted, *The Voice of the Poet*, 147-48, 194-95.

George Monteiro, *Expl* 31 (Oct. 1972): 13.

Elizabeth F. Perlmutter, "Hide and Seek: Emily Dickinson's Use of the Existential Sentence," *Lang&S* 10 (Spring 1977): 110-14.

Laurence Perrine, *Expl* 11 (May 1953): 50. Reprinted in *The Explicator Cyclopedia* 1:80.

Pollak, *Dickinson: The Anxiety of Gender*, 217-21.

Barton Levi St. Armand, *Emily Dickinson and Her Culture: The Soul's Society* (Cambridge: Cambridge University Press, 1984), 239-40.

Sherwood, *Circumference and Circumstance*, 96-97.

Donald Thackrey, "Emily Dickinson's Approach to Poetry," *University of Nebraska Studies*, no. 13 (Nov. 1954), 76-80.

Winters, *In Defense of Reason*, 283-99.

"There's Been a Death, in the Opposite House"

M. Boruch, "Dickinson Descending," *GaR* 40 (Winter 1986): 863-77.

William Doreski, "'An Exchange of Territory': Dickinson's Fascicle 27," *ESQ* 32 (First Quarter 1986): 57-58.

"There's Something Quieter Than Sleep"

Ford, *Heaven Beguiles the Tired*, 79-81.

Porter, *The Art of Emily Dickinson's Early Poetry*, 26-28.

"These Are the Days When Birds Come Back--"

Anderson, *Emily Dickinson's Poetry*, 145-49.

George Arms, *Expl* 2 (Feb. 1944): 29. Reprinted in *The Explicator Cyclopedia* 1:80-81.

Robert L. Berner, *Expl* 30 (May 1972): 78.

Budick, *Emily Dickinson and the Life of Language*, 54-60.

Lindberg-Seyersted, *The Voice of the Poet*, 143-44.

Ruth McNaughton, "The Imagery of Emily Dickinson," *University of Nebraska Studies*, no. 4 (Jan. 1949), 13-14.

Sherwood, *Circumference and Circumstance*, 30-31.

Marshall Van Deusen, *Expl* 12 (Apr. 1954): 40. Reprinted in *The Explicator Cyclopedia* 1:80-81.

"These Are the Signs to Nature's Inns--"

Mudge, *Emily Dickinson and the Image of Home*, 162-63.

"These--Saw Visions--"

Miller, *The Poetry of Emily Dickinson*, 205-7.

"They Leave Us with the Infinite."

Carole Taylor, "Kierkegaard and the Ironic Voices of Emily Dickinson," *JEGP* 77 (Oct. 1978): 579-80.

"They Shut Me Up in Prose--"

Mossberg, *Emily Dickinson: When a Writer Is a Daughter*, 107-9.

"This Chasm, Sweet, Upon My Life"

Gilbert and Gubar, *The Madwoman in the Attic*, 628-30.

"This Consciousness That Is Aware"

Charles R. Anderson, "The Conscious Self in Emily Dickinson's Poetry," *AL* 31 (Nov. 1959): 304-5.

Martin, *An American Triptych*, 117-18.

Sherwood, *Circumference and Circumstance*, 224-25.

"This Is a Blossom of the Brain"

Martin, *An American Triptych*, 158-59.

Porter, *Dickinson: The Modern Idiom*, 65-66.

Weisbuch, *Emily Dickinson's Poetry*, 60-62.

"This Is My Letter to the World"

Miller, *Emily Dickinson: A Poet's Grammar*, 8-9.

"This Was a Poet"

Budick, *Emily Dickinson and the Life of Language*, 127-29.

Cameron, *Lyric Time*, 197-89.

Diehl, *Emily Dickinson and The Romantic Imagination*, 64-66.

Jane Donahue Eberwein, "Doing Without: Dickinson as Yankee Woman Poet," in Ferlazzo, *Critical Essays on Emily Dickinson*, 207-8.

George E. Fortenberry, *Expl* 35 (Spring 1977): 26-27.

Miller, *Emily Dickinson: A Poet's Grammar*, 76-78, 118-22.

Pollak, *Dickinson: The Anxiety of Gender*, 232-34.

Sherwood, *Circumference and Circumstance*, 210-12.

"This World Is Not Conclusion"

Anderson, *Emily Dickinson's Poetry*, 267-68.

Thomas Johnson, "Emily Dickinson," in Davis, *14 by Emily Dickinson*, 81-82.

Kimpel, *Emily Dickinson as Philosopher*, 228-30.

Sr. Mary Humiliata, "Emily Dickinson--Mystic Poet?" in Davis, *14 by Emily Dickinson*, 75-81.

Henry Wells, in Davis, *14 by Emily Dickinson*, 72-75.

"Tho' I Get Home How Late--How Late--"

Weisbuch, *Emily Dickinson's Poetry*, 43-45.

"Those--Dying Then,"

Carole Taylor, "Kierkegaard and the Ironic Voices of Emily Dickinson," *JEGP* 77 (Oct. 1978): 573-74.

"Those Not Live Yet"

Kimpel, *Emily Dickinson as Philosopher*, 290-91.

Dorothy Waugh, *Expl* 15 (Jan. 1957): 22. Reprinted in *The Explicator Cyclopedia* 1:82-83.

"The Thought Beneath So Slight a Film"

James E. White, "Emily Dickinson: Metaphysician and Miniaturist," *CEA* 29 (Mar. 1967): 17-18.

"Three Times--We Parted--Breath--And I--"

Johnson, *Emily Dickinson: Perception and the Poet's Quest*, 158-59.

"Through the Strait Pass of Suffering--"

Sharon Cameron, "'A Loaded Gun': Dickinson and the Dialectic of Rage," *PMLA* 93 (May 1978): 433-34.

Pollak, *Dickinson: The Anxiety of Gender*, 89-90.

"Till Death--Is Narrow Loving--"

Diehl, *Emily Dickinson and The Romantic Imagination*, 141-43.

"The Tint I Cannot Take Is Best"

Diehl, *Emily Dickinson and The Romantic Imagination*, 166-67.

Sr. Ellen Fitzgerald, *Expl* 28 (Nov. 1969): 29.

"'Tis Opposites--Entice--"

Joseph Ditta, "The Jewel and the Amethyst: Poet and Persona in Emily Dickinson," *DicS*, no. 42 (First Half 1982): 30-37.

Margaret Homans, *Women Writers and Poetic Identity* (Princeton: Princeton University Press, 1980), 180-81.

"'Tis So Appalling--It Exhilarates"

Carole Taylor, "Kierkegaard and the Ironic Voices of Emily Dickinson," *JEGP* 77 (Oct. 1978): 577-78.

"'Tis So Much Joy! 'Tis So Much Joy!"

Mossberg, *Emily Dickinson: When a Writer Is a Daughter*, 167-68.

"'Tis Sunrise--Little Maid--Hast Thou"

Gilbert and Gubar, *The Madwoman in the Attic*, 623.

"Title Divine--Is Mine"

Sharon Cameron, "'A Loaded Gun': Dickinson and the Dialectic of Rage," *PMLA* 93 (May 1978): 434-35. Reprinted in Cameron, *Lyric Time*, 85-87.

Eunice Glenn, "Emily Dickinson's Poetry: A Revaluation," *SR* 51 (Autumn 1943): 578-80.

Juhasz, *The Undiscovered Continent*, 109-14.

Kher, *The Landscape of Absence*, 162-64.

Martin, *An American Triptych*, 103-4.

Mudge, *Emily Dickinson and the Image of Home*, 96-98.

Laurence Perrine, "Dickinson Distorted," *CE* 36 (Oct. 1974): 213.

Porter, *Dickinson: The Modern Idiom*, 206-8.

"To Fight Aloud Is Very Brave"

Curtis Dahl, "'To Fight Aloud' and 'The Charge of the Light Brigade': Dickinson on Tennyson," *NEQ* (Mar. 1979): 94-99.

Ford, *Heaven Beguiles the Tired*, 77-78.

"To Hear an Oriole Sing"

Benfey, *Emily Dickinson and the Problem of Others*, 20-22.

B.J. Rogers, "The Truth Told Slant: Emily Dickinson's Poetic Mode," *TSLL* 14 (Summer 1972): 331-32.

Donald Thackrey, "Emily Dickinson's Approach to Poetry," *University of Nebraska Studies*, no. 13 (Nov. 1954), 78-80.

"To Know Just How He Suffered--Would Be Dear--"

Juhasz, *The Undiscovered Continent*, 141-43.

"To Learn the Transport By the Pain--"

Diehl, *Emily Dickinson and The Romantic Imagination*, 101-2.

Porter, *The Art of Emily Dickinson's Early Poetry*, 131-34.

"To Lose One's Faith"

Friedman and McLaughlin, *Poetry: An Introduction to Its Form and Art*, 47-48, 75-76, 120-21.

"To Make a Prairie It Takes a Clover and a Bee"

Budick, *Emily Dickinson and the Life of Language*, 178-81.

"To My Small Hearth His Fire Came"

Mudge, *Emily Dickinson and the Image of Home*, 122-23.

"To Pile Like Thunder to It's Close"

Diehl, *Emily Dickinson and The Romantic Imagination*, 78-79.

Miller, *Emily Dickinson: A Poet's Grammar*, 126-30.

"To Scan a Ghost, Is Faint"

Salska, *Walt Whitman and Emily Dickinson*, 53-54.

"To the Bright East She Flies"

Ford, *Heaven Beguiles the Tired*, 172-74.

"To Undertake Is to Achieve"

Richard B. Sewall, *Expl* 6 (June 1948): 51. Reprinted in *The Explicator Cyclopedia* 1:83-84.

"A Transport One Cannot Contain"

Sherwood, *Circumference and Circumstance*, 43-44.

"Triumph--May Be of Several Kinds--"

Sherwood, *Circumference and Circumstance*, 172-73.

"'Twas Crisis--All the Length Had Passed--

Ford, *Heaven Beguiles the Tired*, 117-19.

"'Twas Like a Maelstrom, With a Notch,"

Budick, *Emily Dickinson and the Life of Language*, 153-56.

Cameron, *Lyric Time*, 93-95.

Dickinson, *Suggestions for Teachers of "Introduction to Literature,"* 34.

Martha Fodaski, *Expl* 19 (Jan. 1961): 24. Reprinted in *The Explicator Cyclopedia* 1:84-86.

Griffith, *The Long Shadow*, 51-56.

Juhasz, *The Undiscovered Continent*, 70-74.

Myron Ochshorn, "In Search of Emily Dickinson," *New Mexico Quarterly Review* 23 (Spring 1953): 103-6.

Sherwood, *Circumference and Circumstance*, 124-26.

"'Twas Such a Little--Little Boat"

Johnson, *Emily Dickinson: Perception and the Poet's Quest*, 18-19.

"'Twas the Old--Road--through Pain"

Austin Warren, "Emily Dickinson," in Sewall, *Emily Dickinson: A Collection of Critical Essays*, 102-3.

"'Twas Warm--at First--Like Us--"

Sharon Cameron, "Naming As History: Dickinson's Poems of Definition," *CritI* 5 (Winter 1978): 240. Reprinted in Cameron, *Lyric Time*, 42-43.

Ford, *Heaven Beguiles the Tired*, 114-15.

Griffith, *The Long Shadow*, 122-24.

Porter, *Dickinson: The Modern Idiom*, 193-94.

Winters, *Forms of Discovery*, 268-69.

"Two Butterflies Went Out at Noon"

Frederick Asals, "Dickinson's 'Two Butterflies Went Out at Noon,'" *ESQ*, no. 63 (Spring 1971): 29-31.

Laurence Perrine, "The Importance of Tone in the Interpretation of Literature," *CE* 24 (Feb. 1963): 390. Reprinted in Perrine, *The Art of Total Relevance*, 20-21.

"Two Swimmers Wrestled on a Spar--"

Diehl, *Emily Dickinson and The Romantic Imagination*, 178-80.

Porter, *The Art of Emily Dickinson's Early Poetry*, 47-48.

"Victory Comes Late"

Kher, *The Landscape of Absence*, 168-69.

Katherine A. Monteiro, *Expl* 44 (Winter 1986): 30.

Mossberg, *Emily Dickinson: When a Writer Is a Daughter*, 115-17.

Wolosky, *Emily Dickinson: A Voice of War*, 60-62.

"Water, Is Taught By Thirst"

Margaret Homans, *Women Writers and Poetic Identity* (Princeton: Princeton University Press, 1980), 178-79.

"Water Makes Many Beds"

James S. Mullican, *Expl* 27 (Nov. 1968): 23.

"The Way I Read a Letter's--This--"

Benfey, *Emily Dickinson and the Problem of Others*, 48-49.

Loving, *Emily Dickinson: The Poet on the Second Story*, 85-86.

"We Don't Cry--Tim and I"

Cody, *After Great Pain*, 122-24.

Kimpel, *Emily Dickinson as Philosopher*, 138-40.

"We Dream--It Is Good We Are Dreaming"

Budick, *Emily Dickinson and the Life of Language*, 151-53.

Diehl, *Emily Dickinson and The Romantic Imagination*, 79-81.

Johnson, *Emily Dickinson: Perception and the Poet's Quest*, 150-52.

Miller, *Emily Dickinson: A Poet's Grammar*, 80-83.

"We Grow Accustomed to the Dark--"

Juhasz, *The Undiscovered Continent*, 22-24.

Sherwood, *Circumference and Circumstance*, 119-20.

"We Learned the Whole of Love"

Henry Wells, *Introduction to Emily Dickinson* (Chicago: Packard & Co., 1947), 61-62.

"We Miss Her, Not Because We See--"

Porter, *Dickinson: The Modern Idiom*, 47-48.

"We Never Know How High We Are"

Weisbuch, *Emily Dickinson's Poetry*, 144-45.

"Went Up a Year This Evening!"

Lucas, *Emily Dickinson and Riddle*, 58-61.
Porter, *The Art of Emily Dickinson's Early Poetry*, 101-3.

"We Play at Paste--"

Norman Talbot, "The Child, The Actress, and Miss Emily Dickinson," *SoRA* 5 (June 1972): 107.
Weisbuch, *Emily Dickinson's Poetry*, 56.

"We Should Not Mind So Small a Flower"

Kenneth B. Newell, *Expl* 19 (June 1961): 65.

"We Talked As Girls Do--"

Pollak, *Dickinson: The Anxiety of Gender*, 146-47.

"What Care the Dead, for Canticleer"

Rebecca Patterson, "The Cardinal Points of Symbolism of Emily Dickinson," *MQ* 14 (Summer 1973): 308.

"What I See Not, I Better See"

Jane F. Crosthwaite, *Expl* 36 (Spring 1978): 10.

"What Is --'Paradise'--"

Weisbuch, *Emily Dickinson's Poetry*, 65-67.

"What Mystery Pervades a Well!"

Anderson, *Emily Dickinson's Poetry*, 86-88.

Benfey, *Emily Dickinson and the Problem of Others*, 77-79.

Kher, *The Landscape of Absence*, 38-40.

Patterson, *Emily Dickinson's Imagery*, 55.

"What Soft--Cherubic Creatures--"

Anderson, *Emily Dickinson's Poetry*, 12-14.

Brooks, Lewis, and Warren, *American Literature*, 1241.

Robert Franicevich, *Expl* 35 (Fall 1976): 5-6.

Nancy Lenz Harvey, *Expl* 28 (Oct. 1969): 17.

Ruth McNaughton, "The Imagery of Emily Dickinson," *University of Nebraska Studies*, no. 4 (Jan. 1949), 11-12.

Dwight H. Purdy, *Expl* 33 (Apr. 1975): 67.

"What Would I Give to See His Face"

Lindberg-Seyersted, *The Voice of the Poet*, 145-47.

"When I Count the Seeds"

Porter, *The Art of Emily Dickinson's Early Poetry*, 25-26, 81-82.

"When I Have Seen the Sun Emerge"

Barker, *Lunacy of Light*, 71-72.

"When I Hoped I Feared"

Wilson O. Clough, *Expl* 10 (Nov. 1951): 10. Reprinted in *The Explicator Cyclopedia* 1:86-87.

Caroline Hogue, *Expl* 10 (May 1952): 49. Reprinted in *The Explicator Cyclopedia* 1:87-88.

"When I Hoped, I Recollect"

Lindberg-Seyersted, *The Voice of the Poet*, 257-58.

Mudge, *Emily Dickinson and the Image of Home*, xiv-xvi.

"When We Stand on Top of Things--"

Robinson, *Emily Dickinson: Looking to Canaan*, 43-45.

"Where Ships of Purple Gently Toss"

Laurence Perrine, "The Nature of Proof in the Interpretation of Poetry," *EJ* 51 (Sept. 1962): 394-96. Reprinted in Perrine, *The Art of Total Relevance*, 12-14, 18.

"Where Thou Art--That--Is Home--"

Lindberg-Seyersted, *The Voice of the Poet*, 107-8.

"Whether My Bark Went Down at Sea --"

Johnson, *Emily Dickinson: Perception and the Poet's Quest*, 14-16.

"Who Never Lost, Are Unprepared"

Weisbuch, *Emily Dickinson's Poetry*, 22-23.

"Who Goes to Dine Must Take His Feast"

Benfey, *Emily Dickinson and the Problem of Others*, 18-19.

"The Whole of It Came Not at Once--"

Kimpel, *Emily Dickinson as Philosopher*, 42-43.

"Who Occupies This House?"

Myrth Jimmie Killingsworth, *Expl* 40 (Fall 1981): 33.

Loving, *Emily Dickinson: The Poet on the Second Story*, 71-72.

"'Why Do I Love' You, Sir?"

Porter, *Dickinson: The Modern Idiom*, 48-50.

Edith Wylder, *The Last Face: Emily Dickinson's Manuscripts* (Albuquerque: University of New Mexico Press, 1971), 56-64.

"Why--Do They Shut Me Out of Heaven?"

Mossberg, *Emily Dickinson: When a Writer Is a Daughter*, 110-11.

"Why Make It Doubt--It Hurts So--"

Gilbert and Gubar, *The Madwoman in the Attic*, 603-4.

"A Wife--at Daybreak I Shall Be"

Eberwein, *Dickinson: Strategies*, 174-75.

Juhasz, *The Undiscovered Continent*, 116-20.

Norman Talbot, "The Child, The Actress, and Miss Emily Dickinson," *SoRA* 5 (June 1972): 111.

"Wild Nights--Wild Nights"

Christ of Wegelin, *Expl* 26 (Nov. 1967): 25.

Cody, *After Great Pain*, 386-88.

James T. Connelly, *Expl* 25 (Jan. 1967): 44.

Duncan, *Emily Dickinson*, 71-73.

Porter, *The Art of Emily Dickinson's Early Poetry*, 70-72.

Suzanne M. Wilson, "Emily Dickinson and the Twentieth-Century Poetry of Sensibility," *AL* 36 (Nov. 1964): 353-54.

"The Wind Begun to Rock the Grass"

E. Miller Budick, "The Dangers of Living in the World: Aspects of Dickinson's Epistemology, Cosmology, and Symbolism," *ESQ* 29 (Fourth Quarter 1983): 210-11.

Budick, *Emily Dickinson and the Life of Language*, 15-16.

"The Wind Drew Off"

Connie M. Doyle, "Emily Dickinson's 'The Wind Drew Off,'" *ELN* 12 (Mar. 1975): 182-84.

"The Wind--Tapped Like a Tired Man"

Virginia Ogden Birdsall, "Emily Dickinson's Intruder in the Soul," *AL* 37 (Mar. 1965): 60-61.

Edward Bodie, Jr., *Expl* 46 (Fall 1987): 25-26.

"Winter is Good, His Hoar Delights Italic Flavor Yields"

Henry Wells, *Introduction to Emily Dickinson* (Chicago: Packard & Co., 1947), 110-11.

"Within My Garden, Rides a Bird"

Wallace, *God Be with the Clown*, 90-92.

"Wonder Is Not Precisely Knowing"

Friar and Brinnin, *Modern Poetry*, 456-57.

"A Word Made Flesh Is Seldom"

Anderson, *Emily Dickinson's Poetry*, 42-44.

Benfey, *Emily Dickinson and the Problem of Others*, 95-97.

Joanne Diehl, "'Ransom in a Voice': Language as Defense in Dickinson's Poetry," in Juhasz, *Feminist Critics Read Emily Dickinson*, 157-58.

Margaret Homans, *Women Writers and Poetic Identity* (Princeton: Princeton University Press, 1980), 212-13.

Wolosky, *Emily Dickinson: A Voice of War*, 145-47.

"The World Is Not Conclusion"

Eberwein, *Dickinson: Strategies*, 227-28.

"The World--Stands--Solemner--to Me--"

Pollak, *Dickinson: The Anxiety of Gender*, 163-65.

"A Wounded Deer--Leaps Highest--"

Salska, *Walt Whitman and Emily Dickinson*, 133-134.

Wallace, *God Be with the Clown*, 99-100.

"You Cannot Put a Fire Out--"

Barker, *Lunacy of Light*, 116-17.

"You're Right--'The Way Is Narrow'"

Ford, *Heaven Beguiles the Tired*, 97-99.

Vivian R. Pollak, "'That Fine Prosperity': Economic Metaphors in Emily Dickinson's Poetry," *MLQ* 34 (June 1973): 167.

"Your Riches--Taught Me--Poverty"

Paula Bennet, *My Life a Loaded Gun: Female Creativity and Feminist Poetics* (Boston: Beacon Press, 1986), 53-55.

Vivian R. Pollak, "'That Fine Prosperity': Economic Metaphors in Emily Dickinson's Poetry," *MLQ* 34 (June 1973): 174-75.

"You See I Cannot See--Your Lifetime--"

Joseph Ditta, "The Jewel and the Amethyst: Poet and Persona in Emily Dickinson," *DicS*, no. 42 (First Half 1982): 30-37.

"You've Seen Balloons Set--Haven't You?"

David Green, "'You've Seen Balloons Set--Haven't You?'" *DicS*, no. 37 (First Half 1980): 11-18.

Weisbuch, *Emily Dickinson's Poetry*, 40-42.

DU BOIS, W.E.B.

"The Burden of Black Women"

Arnold Rampersad, *The Art and Imagination of W.E.B. Du Bois* (Cambridge and London: Harvard University Press, 1976), 106.

"Children of the Moon"

Wilson J. Moses, "The Poetics of Ethiopianism: W.E.B. Du Bois and Literary Black Nationalism," *AL* 47 (Nov. 1975): 418-20.

"A Day in Africa"

Arnold Rampersad, *The Art and Imagination of W.E.B. Du Bois* (Cambridge and London: Harvard University Press, 1976), 107.

Arnold Rampersad, "W.E.B. Du Bois as a Man of Literature," *AL* 51 (Mar. 1979): 61-62.

"A Hymn to the Peoples"

Arnold Rampersad, *The Art and Imagination of W.E.B. Du Bois* (Cambridge and London: Harvard University Press, 1976), 108.

"A Litany of Atlanta"

Arnold Rampersad, *The Art and Imagination of W.E.B. Du Bois* (Cambridge and London: Harvard University Press, 1976), 104-5.

Arnold Rampersad, "W.E.B. Du Bois as a Man of Literature," *AL* 51 (Mar. 1979): 60-61.

DUNBAR, PAUL LAURENCE

"Accountability"

Dickson Bruce, "On Dunbar's 'Jingles in a Broken Tongue': Dunbar's Dialect Poetry and the Afro-American Folk Tradition," in Martin, *A Singer in the Dawn*, 106-9.

"An Ante-Bellum Sermon"

Dickson Bruce, "On Dunbar's 'Jingles in a Broken Tongue': Dunbar's Dialect Poetry and the Afro-American Folk Tradition," in Martin, *A Singer in the Dawn*, 102-6.

James Emanuel, "Radical Fire in the Poetry of Paul Laurence Dunbar," in Martin, *A Singer in the Dawn*, 87-88.

Peter Revell, *Paul Laurence Dunbar*, 86-87.

"The Colored Soldiers"

James Emanuel, "Radical Fire in the Poetry of Paul Laurence Dunbar," in Martin, *A Singer in the Dawn*, 86-87.

"Joggin' Erlong"

James Emanuel, "Radical Fire in the Poetry of Paul Laurence Dunbar," in Martin, *A Singer in the Dawn*, 80.

"Ode to Ethiopia"

Peter Revell, *Paul Laurence Dunbar*, 64-65.

"We Wear the Mask"

Peter Revell, *Paul Laurence Dunbar*, 71-72.

DWIGHT, TIMOTHY

"The Conquest of Canaan"

Leon Howard, *The Connecticut Wits* (Chicago: University of Chicago Press, 1943), 89-93.

Kenneth Silverman, *Timothy Dwight* (New York: Twayne, 1969), 24-45.

"Greenfield Hill"

Elliot, *Revolutionary Writers*, 70-88.

Leon Howard, *The Connecticut Wits* (Chicago: University of Chicago Press, 1943), 220-29.

Kenneth Silverman, *Timothy Dwight* (New York: Twayne, 1969), 52-79.

"The Triumph of Infidelity"

Kenneth Silverman, *Timothy Dwight* (New York: Twayne, 1969), 81-94.

EMERSON, RALPH WALDO

"The Adirondacs"

Joseph Jones, "Thought's New-Found Path and the Wilderness: 'The Adirondacs,'" in *Emerson: Prospect and Retrospect* (Cambridge: Harvard University Press, 1982), 105-19.

Carl F. Stauch, "The Mind's Voice: Emerson's Poetic Styles," *ESQ*, no. 60 Supplement (Summer 1970): 55-57.

Ronald Sudol, "'The Adirondacs' and Technology," in *Emerson Centenary Essays*, ed. Joel Myerson (Carbondale: Southern Illinois University, 1982), 173-79.

Philip G. Terrie, "Romantic Travelers in the Adirondac Wilderness," *AmerS* 24 (Fall 1983): 70-74.

"The Amulet"

Malloy, *A Study of Emerson's Major Poems*, 57-59.

"The Apology"

Malloy, *A Study of Emerson's Major Poems*, 55-57.

"Bacchus"

Michael Cowan, "The Loving Proteus: Metamorphosis in Emerson's Poetry," in *Characteristics of Emerson, Transcendental Poet, A Symposium*, ed. Carl Strauch (Hartford: Transcendental Books, 1975), 16-17.

Brian Harding, "'Frolic Architecture': Music and Metamorphosis in Emerson's Poetry," in Lee, *Nineteenth-Century American Poetry*, 107-8.

Malloy, *A Study of Emerson's Major Poems*, 39-43.

Bernard Paris, "Emerson's 'Bacchus,'" *MLQ* 23 (June 1962): 150-59.

Waggoner, *Emerson as Poet*, 142-46.

Yoder, *Emerson and the Orphic Poet in America*, 99-102.

"Beauty"

Vivian Hopkins, *Spires of Form: A Study of Emerson's Aesthetic Theory* (Cambridge: Harvard University Press, 1951), 122-23.

"Blight"

Stuart Levine, "Emerson and Modern Social Concepts," in *Emerson: Prospect and Retrospect* (Cambridge: Harvard University Press, 1982), 175-76.

"The Bohemian Hymn"

Richard E. Amacher, *Expl* 5 (June 1947): 55. Reprinted in *The Explicator Cyclopedia* 2:133-34.

Eric W. Carlson, "Emerson's 'The Bohemian Hymn,'" *ESQ* 6 (First Quarter 1957): 6-7.

"Bramha"

Abad, *A Formal Approach to Lyric Poetry*, 131.

Marilyn Baldwin, *Expl* 20 (Dec. 1961): 29. Reprinted in *The Explicator Cyclopedia* 2:135.

Dickinson, *Suggestions for Teachers of "Introduction to Literature,"* 26-27.

Robert Frost, "A Poet, Too, Must Learn the Magic Way of Poetry," *New York Times*, 21 Mar. 1954, 1.

Richard Greenleaf, "Emerson and Wordsworth," *Science and Society* 22 (Summer 1958): 229.

Gaylord C. LeRoy, *Expl* 20 (Dec. 1961): 29. Reprinted in *The Explicator Cyclopedia* 2:135-36.

Andrew M. McLean, "Emerson's Brahma as an Expression of Brahman," *NEQ* 42 (Mar. 1969): 115-22.

Malloy, *A Study of Emerson's Major Poems*, 60-69, 119-21.

John Russell, *Expl* 20 (Dec. 1961): 29. Reprinted in *The Explicator Cyclopedia* 2:134.

William Bysshe Stein, *Expl* 20 (Dec. 1961): 29. Reprinted in *The Explicator Cyclopedia* 2:134.

Van Doren, *Introduction to Poetry*, 90-93.

Waggoner, *Emerson as Poet*, 155-60.

Robert L. White, *Expl* 21 (Apr. 1963): 63.

"Celestial Love"

Malloy, *A Study of Emerson's Major Poems*, 72-79

"Compensation"

Richard VanDerBeets, "Compensatory Imagery in Emerson's Poem 'Compensation,'" *ESQ*, no. 63 (Spring 1971): 12-13.

"Concord Hymn"

George Arms, *Expl* 1 (Dec. 1942): 23. Reprinted in *The Explicator Cyclopedia* 2:136.

"Days"

George Arms, *Expl* 4 (Nov. 1945): 8. Reprinted in *The Explicator Cyclopedia* 2:136-37.

John Clendenning, "Emerson's 'Days': A Psychoanalytical Study," in *Characteristics of Emerson, Transcendental Poet, A Symposium*, ed. Carl Strauch (Hartford: Transcendental Books, 1975), 6-11.

Dickinson, *Suggestions for Teachers of "Introduction to Literature,"* 25-26.

Edward G. Fletcher, *Expl* 5 (Apr. 1947): 41. Reprinted in *The Explicator Cyclopedia* 2:138.

Linda S. Grimes, *Expl* 45 (Fall 1986): 22

Seymour L. Gross, "Emerson and Poetry," *SAQ* 54 (Jan. 1955): 93-94. Reprinted in *Critics on Emerson*, ed. Thomas Rountree (Coral Gables: University of Miami Press, 1973), 110-11.

Frances Hernandez, *Expl* 33 (Feb. 1975): 44.

Tyrus Hillway, *Expl* 34 (May 1976): 69.

Joseph Jones, *Expl* 4 (Apr. 1946): 47. Reprinted in *The Explicator Cyclopedia* 2:138-39.

Kirk and McCutcheon, *An Introduction to the Study of Poetry*, 35-36.

Malloy, *A Study of Emerson's Major Poems*, 25-29.

Porter, *Emerson and Literary Change*, 128-30.

Richard Tuerk, "Emerson's Darker Vision: 'Hamatreya' and 'Days,'" in *Characteristics of Emerson, Transcendental Poet, A Symposium*, ed. Carl Strauch (Hartford: Transcendental Books, 1975), 28-33.

Waggoner, *Emerson as Poet*, 172-78.

"Destiny"

Waggoner, *Emerson as Poet*, 127-29.

"Each and All"

George Arms, "The Dramatic Movement in Emerson's 'Each and All,'" *ELN* 1 (Mar. 1964): 207-11.

Walter Blair and Clarence Faust, "Emerson's Literary Method," *MP* 42 (Nov. 1944): 89-91.

Mario L. D'Avanzo, "Seeing and Hearing in 'Each and All,'" *ESQ*, no. 19 (Fourth Quarter 1973): 231-35.

S.L. Gross, "Emerson and Poetry," *SAQ* 54 (Jan. 1955): 89-91. Reprinted in *Critics on Emerson*, ed. Thomas Rountree (Coral Gables: University of Miami Press, 1973), 108-10.

Carl F. Strauch, "Emerson and the Doctrine of Sympathy," *SIR* 6 (Spring 1967): 157. Reprinted in *Critical Essays on Ralph Waldo Emerson*, ed. Robert Burkholder and Joel Myerson (Boston: G.K. Hall, 1983), 326-45.

R.A. Yoder, "The Development of Emerson's Poetic Style," *PMLA* 87 (Mar. 1972): 261.

"Etienne de La Boece"

Malloy, *A Study of Emerson's Major Poems*, 69-72.

"Ever the Rock of Ages Melts"

Karl Keller, "From Christianity to Transcendentalism: A Note on Emerson's Use of the Conceit," *AL* 39 (Mar. 1967): 94-98.

"Forbearance"

Carl F. Strauch, "Emerson and the Doctrine of Sympathy," *SIR* 6 (Spring 1967): 158-61. Reprinted in *Critical Essays on Ralph Waldo Emerson*, ed. Robert Burkholder and Joel Myerson (Boston: G.K. Hall, 1983), 326-45.

"Give All to Love"

Michael H. Cowan, *Expl* 18 (May 1960): 49. Reprinted in *The Explicator Cyclopedia* 2:138-39.

"Guy"

Carl F. Strauch, "Emerson and the Doctrine of Sympathy," *SIR* 6 (Spring 1967): 168-70. Reprinted in *Critical Essays on Ralph Waldo Emerson*, ed. Robert Burkholder and Joel Myerson (Boston: G.K. Hall, 1983), 326-45.

"Hamatreya"

Alice Petry, "The Meeting of the Twain: Emerson's 'Hamatreya,'" *ELN* 23 (Mar. 1986): 47-51.

Mohan Lal Sharma, *Expl* 26 (Apr. 1967): 63.

Warren Staebler, *Ralph Waldo Emerson* (New York: Twayne, 1973), 177-79.

Carl F. Strauch, "Emerson and the Doctrine of Sympathy," *SIR* 6 (Spring 1967): 172-74. Reprinted in *Critical Essays on Ralph Waldo Emerson*, ed. Robert Burkholder and Joel Myerson (Boston: G.K. Hall, 1983), 326-45.

Richard Tuerk, "Emerson's Darker Vision: 'Hamatreya' and 'Days,'" in *Characteristics of Emerson, Transcendental Poet, A Symposium*, ed. Carl Strauch (Hartford: Transcendental Books, 1975), 28-33.

Waggoner, *Emerson as Poet*, 147-55.

"Hermione"

Malloy, *A Study of Emerson's Major Poems*, 44-52.

"The House"

Brian Harding, "'Frolic Architecture': Music and Metamorphosis in Emerson's Poetry," in Lee, *Nineteenth-Century American Poetry*, 103-4.

"The Initial Love"

Carl Strauch, "Emerson's Adaption of Myth in 'The Initial Love,'" in *Characteristics of Emerson, Transcendental Poet, A Symposium*, ed. Carl Strauch (Hartford: Transcendental Books, 1975), 51-65.

"May-Day"

Porter, *Emerson and Literary Change*, 130-33.

"Merlin"

John Anderson, *The Liberating Gods: Emerson on Poets and Poetry* (Coral Gables: University of Miami Press, 1971), 38-40.

Mutlu Blasing, "Essaying the Poet: Emerson's Poetic Theory and Practice," *MLS* 15 (Spring 1985): 17-23. Revised in Blasing, *American Poetry*, 76-80.

Albert Gelpi, "Emerson: The Paradox of Organic Form," in *Emerson: Prophecy, Metamorphosis, and Influence*, ed. David Levin (New York: Columbia University Press, 1975), 166-69.

Brian Harding, "'Frolic Architecture': Music and Metamorphosis in Emerson's Poetry," in Lee, *Nineteenth-Century American Poetry*, 111-12.

Malloy, *A Study of Emerson's Major Poems*, 96-103.

Porter, *Emerson and Literary Change*, 88-91.

Waggoner, *Emerson as Poet*, 138-42.

Yoder, *Emerson and the Orphic Poet in America*, 145-50.

"Monadnoc"

Carl Dennis, "Emerson's Poetry of Mind and Nature," *ESQ*, no. 58 (Part 4 1970): 151-52.

Richard A. Grusin, "Emerson's Quotidian Apocalypse," *ESQ* 31, no. 120 (Third Quarter 1985): 149-63.

Brian Harding, "'Frolic Architecture': Music and Metamorphosis in Emerson's Poetry," in Lee, *Nineteenth-Century American Poetry*, 110-111.

Malloy, *A Study of Emerson's Major Poems*, 80-96.

R.A. Yoder, "The Development of Emerson's Poetic Style," *PMLA* 87 (Mar. 1972): 264-66.

Yoder, *Emerson and the Orphic Poet in America*, 124-27.

"Musketaquid"

Peach, *British Influence*, 74-75.

"My Garden"

Waggoner, *Emerson as Poet*, 164-66.

"Ode Inscribed to W.H. Channing"

George Arms, "Emerson's 'Ode Inscribed to W.H. Channing,'" *CE* 22 (Mar. 1961): 407-9.

Carl F. Strauch, "Emerson and the Doctrine of Sympathy," *SIR* 6 (Spring 1967): 170-74. Reprinted in *Critical Essays on Ralph Waldo Emerson*, ed. Robert Burkholder and Joel Myerson (Boston: G.K. Hall, 1983), 326-45.

Carl F. Strauch, "Emerson's 'Unwilling Senator': The Background and Meaning of the 'Ode Inscribed to W.H. Channing,'" *ESQ*, no. 42 Supplement (First Quarter 1966): 4-14.

Yoder, *Emerson and the Orphic Poet in America*, 129-32.

"The Poet"

John Anderson, *The Liberating Gods: Emerson on Poets and Poetry* (Coral Gables: University of Miami Press, 1971), 20-24, 44-46.

Vivian Hopkins, *Spires of Form: A Study of Emerson's Aesthetic Theory* (Cambridge: Harvard University Press, 1951), 47-49.

Seventeenth Century Poetry Group, University of Nebraska, *Expl* 33 (Mar. 1975): 54.

Yoder, *Emerson and the Orphic Poet in America*, 97-99, 116-17.

"Power"

William K. Bootorff, *Expl* 31 (Feb. 1973): 45.

"The Problem"

Malloy, *A Study of Emerson's Major Poems*, 29-36.

Warren Staebler, *Ralph Waldo Emerson* (New York: Twayne, 1973), 174-76.

R.A. Yoder, "The Development of Emerson's Poetic Style," *PMLA* 7 (Mar. 1972): 261-62.

Yoder, *Emerson and the Orphic Poet in America*, 109-12.

"The Rhodora"

Steven G. Axelrod, "Teaching Emerson's 'The Rhodora,'" *CEA* 36 (May 1974): 34-35.

S.L. Gross, "Emerson and Poetry," *SAQ* 54 (Jan. 1955): 91-93.

Matthiessen, *American Renaissance*, 49-50.

R.A. Yoder, "The Development of Emerson's Poetic Style," *PMLA* 7 (Mar. 1972): 267.

Yoder, *Emerson and the Orphic Poet in America*, 81-85.

"Rubies"

Malloy, *A Study of Emerson's Major Poems*, 59-60.

"Saadi"

John Anderson, *The Liberating Gods: Emerson on Poets and Poetry* (Coral Gables: University of Miami Press, 1971), 32-38.

Malloy, *A Study of Emerson's Major Poems*, 103-10.

"Seashore"

Michael Cowan, "The Loving Proteus: Metamorphosis in Emerson's Poetry," in *Characteristics of Emerson, Transcendental Poet, A Symposium*, ed. Carl Strauch (Hartford: Transcendental Books, 1975), 19-20.

"The Snow Storm"

Brian Harding, "'Frolic Architecture': Music and Metamorphosis in Emerson's Poetry," in Lee, *Nineteenth-Century American Poetry*, 100-103.

Matthiessen, *American Renaissance*, 138-39. Reprinted in Stageberg and Anderson, *Poetry as Experience*, 485-86.

Peach, *British Influence*, 73-74.

Porter, *Emerson and Literary Change*, 35-37.

Sr. Paula Reiten, O.S.B., *Expl* 22 (Jan. 1964): 39.

Yoder, *Emerson and the Orphic Poet in America*, 85-88.

"The Solution"

Porter, *Emerson and Literary Change*, 24-26.

"The Sphinx"

Carl Dennis, "Emerson's Poetry of Mind and Nature," *ESQ*, no. 58 (Part 4 1970): 150-51.

Malloy, *A Study of Emerson's Major Poems*, 5-25.

Leonard Neufeldt, *The House of Emerson* (Lincoln and London: University of Nebraska Press, 1982), 152-61.

Porter, *Emerson and Literary Change*, 80-81, 119-23.

E.J. Rose, "Melville, Emerson, and the Sphinx," *NEQ* 36 (June 1963): 249-58.

Melvin Storm, Jr., "The Riddle of 'The Sphinx': Another Approach," *ESQ*, no. 62 (Winter 1971): 44-48.

Carl F. Strauch, "Emerson and the Doctrine of Sympathy," *SIR* 6 (Spring 1967): 154-56. Reprinted in *Critical Essays on Ralph Waldo Emerson*, ed. Robert Burkholder and Joel Myerson (Boston: G.K. Hall, 1983), 326-45.

Waggoner, *Emerson as Poet*, 118-20.

Charles Child Walcutt, *Expl* 31 (Nov. 1972): 20.

Thomas R. Whitaker, "The Riddle of Emerson's 'Sphinx,'" *AL* 27 (May 1955): 179-95.

R.A. Yoder, "The Development of Emerson's Poetic Style," *PMLA* 87 (Mar. 1972): 264.

Yoder, *Emerson and the Orphic Poet in America*, 118-20.

"Terminus"

John Coakley, *Expl* 45 (Spring 1987): 25.

August H. Mason, *Expl* 4 (Mar. 1946): 37. Reprinted in *The Explicator Cyclopedia* 2:139.

"Threnody"

Walter Blair and Clarence Faust, "Emerson's Literary Method," *MP* 42 (Nov. 1944): 91-95.

N.A. Brittin, "Emerson and the Metaphysical Poets," *AL* 8 (Mar. 1936): 15.

Michael Cowan, "The Loving Proteus: Metamorphosis in Emerson's Poetry," in *Characteristics of Emerson, Transcendental Poet, A Symposium*, ed. Carl Strauch (Hartford: Transcendental Books, 1975), 14-16.

Brian Harding, "'Frolic Architecture': Music and Metamorphosis in Emerson's Poetry," in Lee, *Nineteenth-Century American Poetry*, 113-14.

Joel Porte, *Representative Man: Ralph Waldo Emerson in His Time* (New York: Oxford University Press, 1979), 186-93.

David Porter, "'Threnody' and Emerson's Poetic Failure," *ESQ*, no. 22 (First Quarter 1976): 1-13.

Porter, *Emerson and Literary Change*, 30-35.

"The Titmouse"

Carl Dennis, "Emerson's Poetry of Mind and Nature," *ESQ*, no. 58 (Part 4 1970): 148-49.

John K. McKee, "The Identity of Emerson's 'Titmouse,'" *AN&Q* 13 (June 1975): 151-52.

Carl F. Strauch, "The Mind's Voice: Emerson's Poetic Styles," *ESQ*, no. 60 Supplement (Summer 1970): 53-55.

Yoder, *Emerson and the Orphic Poet in America*, 157-59.

"Uriel"

Malloy, *A Study of Emerson's Major Poems*, 36-39.

Waggoner, *Emerson as Poet*, 136-38.

"Woodnotes"

John Anderson, *The Liberating Gods: Emerson on Poets and Poetry* (Coral Gables: University of Miami Press, 1971), 51-52.

Carl Dennis, "Emerson's Poetry of Mind and Nature," *ESQ*, no. 58 (Part 4 1970): 148-49.

Peach, *British Influence*, 51-56.

Carl F. Strauch, "Emerson and the Doctrine of Sympathy," *SIR* 6 (Spring 1967): 161-67. Reprinted in *Critical Essays on Ralph Waldo Emerson*, ed. Robert Burkholder and Joel Myerson (Boston: G.K. Hall, 1983), 326-45.

"Woodnotes II"

Brian Harding, "'Frolic Architecture': Music and Metamorphosis in Emerson's Poetry," in Lee, *Nineteenth-Century American Poetry*, 108-10.

Daniel Shea, "Emerson and the American Metamorphosis," in *Emerson: Prophecy, Metamorphosis, and Influence*, ed. David Levin (New York: Columbia University Press, 1975), 41-43.

Yoder, *Emerson and the Orphic Poet in America*, 121-23.

"The World-Soul"

Waggoner, *Emerson as Poet*, 123-26.

FIELD, EUGENE

"Little Boy Blue"

Laurence Perrine, "Are Tears Made of Sugar or Salt?" *IEY*, no. 8 (Fall 1963): 19-21.

Perrine, *The Art of Total Relevance*, 125-29.

FIELDS, JAMES T.

"The Captain's Daughter"

Daniels, *The Art of Reading Poetry*, 85-88.

FISKE, JOHN

"Upon the Much-To-Be Lamented Desease
of Reverend Mr. John Cotton . . ."

Astrid Schmitt-v. Muhlenfels, "John Fiske's Funeral Elegy on John Cotton," *EAL* 12 (Spring 1977): 49-62.

FRENEAU, PHILIP

"American Independence"

Jacob Axelrad, *Philip Freneau: Champion of Democracy* (Austin: University of Texas Press, 1967), 95-96.

"American Liberty"

Jacob Axelrad, *Philip Freneau: Champion of Democracy* (Austin: University of Texas Press, 1967), 62-64.

"The American Village"

William L. Andrews, "Goldsmith and Freneau in 'The American Village,'" *EAL* 5 (Fall 1970): 14-23.

Lewis Leary, *That Rascal Freneau: A Study in Literary Failure* (New Jersey: Rutgers University Press, 1941), 40-43.

Vitzthum, *Land and Sea*, 27-31.

"The Beauties of Santa Cruz"

Mary Bowden, *Philip Freneau* (Boston: Twayne, 1976), 48-51.

Jane Donahue Eberwein, "Freneau's 'The Beauties of Santa Cruz,'" *EAL* 12 (Winter 1977/1978): 271-76.

Vitzthum, *Land and Sea*, 35-38.

"The British Prison Ship"

Mary Bowden, *Philip Freneau* (Boston: Twayne, 1976), 61-63.

"Captain Jones's Invitation"

Vitzthum, *Land and Sea*, 82-86.

"The Departure"

Vitzthum, *Land and Sea*, 90-95.

"The Dying Elm, An Irregular Ode"

Vitzthum, *Land and Sea*, 39-44.

"The Dying Indian"

Vitzthum, *Land and Sea*, 53-55.

"Epistle"

Elliot, *Revolutionary Writers*, 166-67.

"A Farmer's Winter Evening, A Poem:
To the Nymph I Never Saw"

Vitzthum, *Land and Sea*, 31-35.

"Hermit of Saba"

Elliot, *Revolutionary Writers*, 168-69.

"The House of Night"

Mary Bowden, *Philip Freneau* (Boston: Twayne, 1976), 129-33.

"The Hurricane"

Vitzthum, *Land and Sea*, 59-63.

"The Indian Burying Ground"

George Arms, *Expl* 2 (May 1944): 55. Reprinted in *The Explicator Cyclopedia* 2:144.

Vitzthum, *Land and Sea*, 103-7.

George R. Wasserman, *Expl* 20 (Jan. 1962): 43. Reprinted in *The Explicator Cyclopedia* 2:141-42.

"The Indian Student"

Mary Bowden, *Philip Freneau* (Boston: Twayne, 1976), 161-63.

"A Journey from Philadelphia to New York"

Mary Bowden, *Philip Freneau* (Boston: Twayne, 1976), 82-84.

"The Lost Adventurer"

Vitzthum, *Land and Sea*, 66-71.

"Neversink"

Vitzthum, *Land and Sea*, 151-56.

"Picture of the Times"

Elliot, *Revolutionary Writers*, 164-66.

"The Pictures of Columbus"

Stephen Fender, *American Literature in Context*. Vol. 1, *1620-1830* (London: Metheun, 1983), 158-61.

"The Pilot of Hatteras"

Vitzthum, *Land and Sea*, 131-36.

"The Power of Fancy"

Mary Bowden, *Philip Freneau* (Boston: Twayne, 1976), 133-34.
Elliot, *Revolutionary Writers*, 137-39.

"The Rising Glory of America"

Mary Bowden, *Philip Freneau* (Boston: Twayne, 1976), 25-27.
Cecelia Tichi, *New World, New Earth: Environmental Reform in American Literature from the Puritans through Whitman* (New Haven: Yale University Press, 1979), 96-97.

"The Terrific Torpedoes"

Mary Bowden, *Philip Freneau* (Boston: Twayne, 1976), 73-74.

"To Cynthia"

Vitzthum, *Land and Sea*, 126-30.

"The Wild Honey Suckle"

Robert D. Arner, "Neoclassicism and Romanticism: A Reading of Freneau's 'The Wild Honey Suckle,'" *EAL* 9 (Spring 1974): 53-61.

Mary Bowden, *Philip Freneau* (Boston: Twayne, 1976), 147-48.

Brooks, Lewis, and Warren, *American Literature*, 207-8.

HAY, JOHN

"Golyer"

Kelly Thurman, *John Hay as a Man of Letters* (Reseda: Mojave Books, 1974), 20-21.

"Jim Bludso"

Daniels, *The Art of Reading Poetry*, 88-92.

"Little Breeches"

Robert Gale, *John Hay* (Boston: Twayne, 1978), 56-57.

HOLMES, OLIVER WENDELL

"An After-Dinner Poem"

Miriam Small, *Oliver Wendell Holmes* (New York: Twayne), 56-57.

"The Chambered Nautilus"

George Arms, *Expl* 4 (June 1946): 51. Reprinted in *The Explicator Cyclopedia* 2:161-62.

Arms, *The Fields Were Green*, 108-10.

Miriam Small, *Oliver Wendell Holmes* (New York: Twayne), 95-97.

"The Deacon's Masterpiece"

Arms, *The Fields Were Green*, 112-13.

Howard Webb, *Expl* 24 (Oct. 1965): 17.

"The Heart's Own Secret"

Miriam Small, *Oliver Wendell Holmes* (New York: Twayne), 68-69.

"The Living Temple"

George Arms, *Expl* 2 (Nov. 1943): 15. Reprinted in *The Explicator Cyclopedia* 2:162-63.

Arms, *The Fields Were Green*, 104-5.

"The Peau de Chagrin of State Street"

Arms, *The Fields Were Green*, 102.

"Two Sonnets: Harvard"

Arms, *The Fields Were Green*, 113-14.

"The Two Streams"

Arms, *The Fields Were Green*, 97-99.

George Arms, "'To Fix the Image All Unveiled and Warm,'" *NEQ* 19 (Dec. 1946): 534-37.

"The Voiceless"

Miriam Small, *Oliver Wendell Holmes* (New York: Twayne), 97-98.

HUMPHREYS, DAVID

"A Poem on Industry"

Leon Howard, *The Connecticut Wits* (Chicago: University of Chicago Press, 1943), 250-52.

"A Poem, on the Happiness of America"

Leon Howard, *The Connecticut Wits* (Chicago: University of Chicago Press, 1943), 125-31.

"A Poem on the Love of the Country"

Leon Howard, *The Connecticut Wits* (Chicago: University of Chicago Press, 1943), 253-54.

JOHNSON, JAMES WELDON

"The Crucifixion"

Fleming, *James Weldon Johnson*, 57-59.

"De Little Pickaninny's Gone to Sleep"

Fleming, *James Weldon Johnson*, 50-51.

"Fifty Years"

Fleming, *James Weldon Johnson*, 43-44.

"Let My People Go"

Fleming, *James Weldon Johnson*, 59-60.

"The White Witch"

Fleming, *James Weldon Johnson*, 46-47.

LANIER, SIDNEY

"The Centennial Meditation"

Jack De Bellis, *Sidney Lanier* (New York: Twayne, 1972), 97-99.

"Civil Rights"

Aubrey Starke, *Sidney Lanier: A Biographical and Critical Study* (Chapel Hill: University of North Carolina Press, 1933), 185-88.

"Corn"

Jack De Bellis, *Sidney Lanier* (New York: Twayne, 1972), 59-67.

Lincoln Lorenz, *The Life Of Sidney Lanier* (New York: Coward-McCann, 1935), 114-16.

Edd Winfield Parks, "Lanier as Poet," in Gohdes, *Essays on American Literature*, 189-90.

Aubrey Starke, *Sidney Lanier: A Biographical and Critical Study* (Chapel Hill: University of North Carolina Press, 1933), 188-94.

"A Florida Sunday"

Aubrey Starke, *Sidney Lanier: A Biographical and Critical Study* (Chapel Hill: University of North Carolina Press, 1933), 274-76.

"Hard Times in Elfland"

Aubrey Starke, *Sidney Lanier: A Biographical and Critical Study* (Chapel Hill: University of North Carolina Press, 1933), 289-90.

"Individuality"

Richard Webb and Edwin Coulson, *Sidney Lanier: Poet and Prosodist* (Athens: University of Georgia Press, 1941), 51-53.

"The Jacquerie"

Jack De Bellis, *Sidney Lanier* (New York: Twayne, 1972), 39-45.

"The Marshes of Glynn"

Jack De Bellis, *Sidney Lanier* (New York: Twayne, 1972), 109-25.

Philip Graham, "Sidney Lanier and the Pattern of Contrast," *AQ* 11 (Winter 1959): 506-7.

Lincoln Lorenz, *The Life of Sidney Lanier* (New York: Coward-McCann, 1935), 209-14.

Edd Winfield Parks, "Lanier as Poet," in Gohdes, *Essays on American Literature*, 196-98.

Edd Winfield Parks, *Sidney Lanier: The Man, The Poet, The Critic* (Athens: University of Georgia Press, 1968), 61-63.

Owen J. Reaner, "Lanier's 'The Marshes of Glynn' Revisited," *MissQ* 23 (Winter 1969-1970): 57-63.

Robert H. Ross, "'The Marshes of Glynn': A Study of Symbolic Obscurity," *AL* 32 (Jan. 1961): 403-16.

Aubrey Starke, *Sidney Lanier: A Biographical and Critical Study* (Chapel Hill: University of North Carolina Press, 1933), 312-15.

Allen Tate, *New Republic* 76 (30 Aug. 1933): 67-70.

R.P. Warren, "The Blind Poet: Sidney Lanier," *American Review* 2 (Nov. 1933): 42-45.

"My Springs"

Brooks and Warren, *Understanding Poetry*, 442-45.

Richard Webb and Edwin Coulson, *Sidney Lanier: Poet and Prosodist* (Athens: University of Georgia Press, 1941), 46-48.

"Night and Day"

Edd W. Parks, "Lanier's 'Night and Day,'" *AL* 30 (Mar. 1958): 117-18.

"The Psalm of the West"

Jack De Bellis, *Sidney Lanier* (New York: Twayne, 1972), 99-103.

Lincoln Lorenz, *The Life of Sidney Lanier* (New York: Coward-McCann, 1935), 164-66.

Aubrey Starke, *Sidney Lanier: A Biographical and Critical Study* (Chapel Hill: University of North Carolina Press, 1933), 248-52.

"Raven Days"

Jack De Bellis, *Sidney Lanier* (New York: Twayne, 1972), 51-53.

"The Revenge of Hamish"

Aubrey Starke, *Sidney Lanier: A Biographical and Critical Study* (Chapel Hill: University of North Carolina Press, 1933), 310-11.

"The Song of the Chattahooche"

Jack De Bellis, *Sidney Lanier* (New York: Twayne, 1972), 105-9.

"Sunrise"

Jack De Bellis, *Sidney Lanier* (New York: Twayne, 1972), 140-45.

Philip Graham, "Sidney Lanier and the Pattern of Contrast," *AQ* 11 (Winter 1959): 506.

Lincoln Lorenz, *The Life of Sidney Lanier* (New York: Coward-McCann, 1935), 280-86.

Edd Winfield Parks, "Lanier as Poet," in Gohdes, *Essays on American Literature*, 199-200.

Aubrey Starke, *Sidney Lanier: A Biographical and Critical Study* (Chapel Hill: University of North Carolina Press, 1933), 408-11.

"The Symphony"

Jack De Bellis, *Sidney Lanier* (New York: Twayne, 1972), 68-96.

C.H. Edwards, Jr., *Expl* 31 (Dec. 1972): 27.

Elisabeth J. Hogenes, *Expl* 16 (Oct. 1957): 4. Reprinted in *The Explicator Cyclopedia* 2:195-96.

Edd Winfield Parks, "Lanier as Poet," in Gohdes, *Essays on American Literature*, 190-93.

Edd Winfield Parks, *Sidney Lanier: The Man, The Poet, The Critic* (Athens: University of Georgia Press, 1968), 53-57.

Aubrey Starke, *Sidney Lanier: A Biographical and Critical Study* (Chapel Hill: University of North Carolina Press, 1933), 205-10.

LONGFELLOW, HENRY WADSWORTH

"Aftermath"

Arms, *The Fields Were Green*, 213-14.

"The Arsenal at Springfield"

Arvin, *Longfellow*, 75-76.

"Autumn Within"

Edward Hirsh, *Henry Wadsworth Longfellow* (Minneapolis: University of Minnesota Press, 1964), 29-30.

"The Building of the Ship"

Wagenknecht, *Henry Wadsworth Longfellow*, 79-81.

"Chaucer"

Nancy L. Tenfelde, *Expl* 22 (Mar. 1964): 55.

"The Courtship of Miles Standish"

Arvin, *Longfellow*, 173-80.

Brian Harding, *American Literature in Context*. Vol. 2, *1830-1865* (London: Mentheun, 1982), 164-72.

Edward Hirsh, *Henry Wadsworth Longfellow* (Minneapolis: University of Minnesota Press, 1964), 35-37.

Wagenknecht, *Henry Wadsworth Longfellow*, 104-13.

Cecil Williams, *Henry Wadsworth Longfellow* (New Haven: College and University Press, 1964), 164-68.

"The Cross of Snow"

Robert A. Durr, *Expl* 13 (Mar. 1955): 32. Reprinted in *The Explicator Cyclopedia* 2:196-97.

"The Day Is Done"

Edward Wagenknecht, *Henry Wadsworth Longfellow: Portrait of an American Humanist* (New York: Oxford University Press, 1966), 102-4.

"Divina Commedia, Sonnet I"

George Arms, *Expl* 2 (Oct. 1943): 7. Reprinted in *The Explicator Cyclopedia* 2:197.

Arms, *The Fields Were Green*, 211.

"Evangeline"

Arvin, *Longfellow*, 100-114.

Edward Hirsh, *Henry Wadsworth Longfellow* (Minneapolis: University of Minnesota Press, 1964), 34-35.

Wagenknecht, *Henry Wadsworth Longfellow*, 85-94.

Cecil Williams, *Henry Wadsworth Longfellow* (New Haven: College and University Press, 1964), 148-56.

"The Falcon of Ser Federigo"

Arms, *The Fields Were Green*, 218-19.

"The Fire of Drift-Wood"

Arms, *The Fields Were Green*, 212.

"Fire Worship"

Arvin, *Longfellow*, 189-90.

"The Golden Legend"

Arvin, *Longfellow*, 86-99.

Wagenknecht, *Henry Wadsworth Longfellow*, 175-80.

"Helen of Tyre"

Richard P. Benton, *Expl* 16 (June 1958): 54. Reprinted in *The Explicator Cyclopedia* 2:197-98.

"Hermes Trismegistus"

Arvin, *Longfellow*, 314-15.

"Hymn to the Night"

George Arms, *Expl* 1 (Oct. 1942): 7. Reprinted in *The Explicator Cyclopedia* 2:198.

"In the Churchyard at Cambridge"

Arms, *The Fields Were Green*, 208-9.

"John Endicott"

Edward Tucker, *The Shaping of Longfellow's "John Endicott"* (University of Virginia Press, 1985), 143-90.

Wagenknecht, *Henry Wadsworth Longfellow*, 180-84.

"Jugurtha"

Richard E. Amacher, *Expl* 6 (Feb. 1948): 29. Reprinted in *The Explicator Cyclopedia* 2:198-99.

Arms, *The Fields Were Green*, 215.

"Keramos"

Arvin, *Longfellow*, 300-302.

"Killed at the Ford"

Arms, *The Fields Were Green*, 221-22.

"King Robert of Sicily"

Arvin, *Longfellow*, 224-25.

"The Legend Beautiful"

Arvin, *Longfellow*, 223-24.

"The Masque of Pandora"

Arvin, *Longfellow*, 297-300.

"Michael Angelo"

Arvin, *Longfellow*, 279-287.

Wagenknecht, *Henry Wadsworth Longfellow*, 192-95.

"Morituri Salutamus"

Arvin, *Longfellow*, 302-4.

"My Lost Youth"

George Arms, "The Revision of 'My Lost Youth,'" *MLN* 61 (June 1946): 389-92.

"The Occultation of Orion"

Arvin, *Longfellow*, 76-77.

M. Zimmerman, "War and Peace: Longfellow's 'The Occultation of Orion,'" *AL* 38 (Jan. 1967): 540-46.

"Palingenesis"

Arvin, *Longfellow*, 197.

"Paul Revere's Ride"

N.H. Pearson, "Both Longfellows," *University of Kansas City Review* 16 (Summer 1950): 247.

"The Rainy Day"

Cecil Williams, *Henry Wadsworth Longfellow* (New Haven: College and University Press, 1964), 133-34.

"The Saga of King Olaf"

Arvin, *Longfellow*, 227-36.

"Seaweed"

Arms, *The Fields Were Green*, 209-11.

"Serenade"

Arms, *The Fields Were Green*, 220-21.

G. Thomas Tanselle, *Expl* 23 (Feb. 1965): 48.

"The Skeleton in Armor"

Wagenknecht, *Henry Wadsworth Longfellow*, 69-71.

"Snow-flakes"

Arms, *The Fields Were Green*, 207-8.

N.H. Pearson, "Both Longfellows," *University of Kansas City Review* 16 (Summer 1950): 252-53.

"The Song of Hiawatha"

Arvin, *Longfellow*, 162-73.

Brian Harding, *American Literature in Context*. Vol. 2, *1830-1865* (London: Mentheun, 1982), 176-80.

Edward Hirsh, *Henry Wadsworth Longfellow* (Minneapolis: University of Minnesota Press, 1964), 37-39.

Wagenknecht, *Henry Wadsworth Longfellow*, 95-103.

Cecil Williams, *Henry Wadsworth Longfellow* (New Haven: College and University Press, 1964), 156-64.

"The Spanish Student"

Arvin, *Longfellow*, 82-85.

Cecil Williams, *Henry Wadsworth Longfellow* (New Haven: College and University Press, 1964), 173-76.

"The Tide Rises, The Tide Falls"

Dickinson, *Suggestions for Teachers of "Introduction to Literature,"* 28.

LOWELL, JAMES RUSSELL

"Agassiz"

Arms, *The Fields Were Green*, 124-26.

"Auspex"

Richard E. Amacher, *Expl* 9 (Mar. 1951): 37. Reprinted in *The Explicator Cyclopedia* 2:200.

Arms, *The Fields Were Green*, 133-34.

"The Cathedral"

Arms, *The Fields Were Green*, 135-38.

"The Courtin'"

Milledge B. Seigler, *Expl* 8 (Nov. 1949): 14. Reprinted in *The Explicator Cyclopedia* 2:200-201.

"Fitz Adam's Story"

Arms, *The Fields Were Green*, 130-32.

"Ode Recited at the Harvard Commemoration"

Arms, *The Fields Were Green*, 138-40.

"To the Dandelion"

Arms, *The Fields Were Green*, 132-33.

"Woe for Religion"

Leon Howard, *Victorian Knight-Errant: A Study of the Early Literary Career of James Russell Lowell* (Berkeley: University of California Press, 1952), 66-69.

MARKHAM, EDWIN

"The Ballad of the Gallows-Bird"

Louis Filler, *The Unknown Edwin Markham: His Mystery and Its Significance* (Yellow Springs: Antioch Press, 1966), 176-83.

"The Man with the Hoe"

Lynn H. Harris, *Expl* 3 (Mar. 1945): 41. Reprinted in *The Explicator Cyclopedia* 1:215.

MELVILLE, HERMAN

"The Aeolian Harp"

Stein, *The Poetry of Melville's Late Years*, 53-54.

"After the Pleasure Party"

Richard Chase, *Herman Melville: A Critical Study* (New York: Macmillian, 1949), 220-24.

William Shurr, "Melville's Poems: The Late Agenda," in *A Companion to Melville Studies*, ed. John Bryant (New York: Greenwood Press, 1986), 362-63.

Shurr, *The Mystery of Iniquity*, 155-58.

William B. Stein, "Melville and the Creative Ethos," *Lock Haven Bulletin* 1 (Number Two 1960): 13-26. Reprinted in Stein, *The Poetry of Melville's Late Years,* 97-108.

Lawrance Thompson, *Melville's Quarrel with God* (Princeton: Princeton University Press, 1952), 341-46.

"Always with Us"

Stein, *The Poetry of Melville's Late Years*, 172-73.

"The Ambuscade"

Faye M. Lenarcic, *Expl* 43 (Fall 1984): 38.

Stein, *The Poetry of Melville's Late Years*, 206-8.

"America, I"

Adler, *War in Melville's Imagination*, 156-58.

Richard Chase, *Herman Melville: A Critical Study* (New York: Macmillian, 1949), 236-38.

George Monteiro, *Expl* 32 (May 1974): 72.

Michael Rogin, *Subversive Genealogy: The Politics and Art of Herman Melville* (New York: Knopf, 1983), 276-78.

"An American Aloe on Exhibition"

Stein, *The Poetry of Melville's Late Years*, 184-85.

"Amoroso"

Shurr, *The Mystery of Iniquity*, 195-96.

Stein, *The Poetry of Melville's Late Years*, 201-3.

"Apathy and Enthusiasm"

Adler, *War in Melville's Imagination*, 141.

"The Apparition: A Retrospect"

Adler, *War in Melville's Imagination*, 154-56.

Robert Penn Warren, "Melville the Poet," *KR* 8 (Spring 1946): 216-18.

Shurr, *The Mystery of Iniquity*, 42-43.

Stein, *The Poetry of Melville's Late Years*, 124-25.

"The Archipelago"

Stein, *The Poetry of Melville's Late Years*, 126-29.

"Armies in the Wilderness"

Adler, *War in Melville's Imagination*, 148-53.

"Art"

Leo Hamalian, *Expl* 8 (Mar. 1950): 40. Reprinted in *The Explicator Cyclopedia* 2:209-10.

Stein, *The Poetry of Melville's Late Years*, 110-11.

"At the Hostelry"

Shurr, *The Mystery of Iniquity*, 210-14.

Stein, *The Poetry of Melville's Late Years*, 228-46.

"The Attic Landscape"

Stein, *The Poetry of Melville's Late Years*, 120-21.

"The Avatar"

Stein, *The Poetry of Melville's Late Years*, 182-83.

"Ball's Bluff"

Adler, *War in Melville's Imagination*, 143-44.

"The Berg"

Lawrence Martin, Jr., "Melville and Christianity: The Late Poems," *MSE* 2 (Spring 1969): 14-15.

Ronald Mason, *The Spirit Above the Dust: A Study of Herman Melville* (Mamaroneck: Paul P. Appell, 1972), 220-22.

Stein, *The Poetry of Melville's Late Years*, 56-57.

"Billy in the Darbies"

Brooks, Lewis, and Warren, *American Literature*, 929-30.

"Bridegroom Dick"

Aaron Kramer, *Melville's Poetry: Toward the Enlarged Heart* (Rutherford: Fairleigh Dickinson University Press, 1972), 12-20.

Shurr, *The Mystery of Iniquity*, 129-30.

Stein, *The Poetry of Melville's Late Years*, 25-33.

"Butterfly Ditty"

Stein, *The Poetry of Melville's Late Years*, 162-63.

"C-----'s Lament"

Stein, *The Poetry of Melville's Late Years*, 91-93.

"Camoens"

Lawrance Thompson, *Melville's Quarrel with God* (Princeton: Princeton University Press, 1952), 346-350.

"The Chipmunk"

Stein, *The Poetry of Melville's Late Years*, 173-74.

"Clarel"

Newton Arvin, *Herman Melville* (New York: William Sloane, 1950), 206-9.

Merlin Bowen, *The Long Encounter: Self and Experience in the Writings of Herman Melville* (Chicago and London: University of Chicago Press, 1960), 79-118, 252-80.

Richard Chase, *Herman Melville: A Critical Study* (New York: Macmillian, 1949), 242-57.

Shirley Dettlaff, "Ionian Form and Esau's Waste: Melville's View of Art in *Clarel*," *AL* 54 (May 1982): 212-28.

Tyrus Hillway, *Herman Melville* (Boston: Twayne, 1963), 128-38.

Andrew Hook, "Melville's Poetry," in *Herman Melville: Reassessments*, ed. A. Robert Lee (London and Totowa: Vision Press; Barnes & Noble, 1984), 192-94.

Vincent Kenny, "Clarel," in *A Companion to Melville Studies*, ed. John Bryant (New York: Greenwood Press, 1986), 375-406.

A. Robert Lee, "'Eminently Adapted for Unpopularity'? Melville's Poetry," in Lee, *Nineteenth-Century American Poetry*, 134-40.

Ronald Mason, *The Spirit above the Dust: A Study of Herman Melville* (Mamaroneck: Paul P. Appell, 1972), 224-44.

Edwin Haviland Miller, *Melville* (New York: George Braziller, 1975), 326-41.

James Miller, Jr., *A Reader's Guide to Herman Melville* (New York: Octagon Books, 1973), 193-217.

Martin Pops, *The Melville Archetype* (Kent: Kent State University Press, 1970), 196-212.

Bernard Rosenthal, "Melville's Wandering Jews," in *Puritan Influences in American Literature*, ed. Emory Elliot (Urbana: University of Illinois Press, 1979), 167-92.

William Sedgewick, *Herman Melville: The Tragedy of Mind* (New York: Russell, 1962), 198-230.

Bryan Short, "Form as Vision in Herman Melville's *Clarel*," *AL* 50 (Jan. 1979): 553-69. Reprinted in *Herman Melville: Modern Critical Views*, ed. Harold Bloom (New York: Chelsea House, 1986), 183-96.

Shurr, *The Mystery of Iniquity*, 47-123.

Stein, *The Poetry of Melville's Late Years*, 10-13.

"Commemorative of a Naval Victory"

Brooks, Purser, and Warren, *An Approach to Literature*, 3d ed., 344-45; 4th ed., 342-43.

Shurr, *The Mystery of Iniquity*, 33-35.

"The Conflict of Convictions"

Adler, *War in Melville's Imagination*, 139-41.

Michael Rogin, *Subversive Genealogy: The Politics and Art of Herman Melville* (New York: Knopf, 1983), 269-71.

Shurr, *The Mystery of Iniquity*, 27-31.

Robert Penn Warren, "Melville the Poet," *KR* 8 (Spring 1946): 213-14, et passim.

"The Cuban Pirate"

Stein, *The Poetry of Melville's Late Years*, 185-86.

"The Devotion of the Flowers to Their Lady"

Stein, *The Poetry of Melville's Late Years*, 213-16.

"Donelson"

Adler, *War in Melville's Imagination*, 144-47.

"A Dutch Christmas up the Hudson in the Time of the Patroons"

Stein, *The Poetry of Melville's Late Years*, 176-77.

"The Enthusiast"

Stein, *The Poetry of Melville's Late Years*, 84-86.

"The Enviable Isles"

Stein, *The Poetry of Melville's Late Years*, 64-65.

"L'Envoi"

Stein, *The Poetry of Melville's Late Years*, 144-46.

"Far Off-Shore"

Stein, *The Poetry of Melville's Late Years*, 21-22.

"The Figure-Head"

Stein, *The Poetry of Melville's Late Years*, 61-62.

"Fragments of a Lost Gnostic Poem of the 12th Century"

Shurr, *The Mystery of Iniquity*, 164-66.

"From Beads for a Rosary"

Stein, *The Poetry of Melville's Late Years*, 212-13.

"Gettysburg: The Check"

Shurr, *The Mystery of Iniquity*, 20-23.

"The Good Craft 'Snow-Bird'"

Stein, *The Poetry of Melville's Late Years*, 59-61.

"The Great Pyramid"

Stein, *The Poetry of Melville's Late Years*, 133-36.

"A Ground Vine"

Stein, *The Poetry of Melville's Late Years*, 190-92.

"The Haglets"

Richard Harter Fogle, "The Themes of Melville's Later Poetry," *TSE* 11 (1961): 72-73.

Lawrence H. Martin, Jr., "Melville and Christianity: The Late Poems," *MSE* 2 (Spring 1969): 13-14.

Shurr, *The Mystery of Iniquity*, 132-33.

William B. Stein, "The Old Man and the Triple Goddess: Melville's 'The Haglets,'" *ELH* 25 (Mar. 1958): 43-59. Reprinted in Stein, *The Poetry of Melville's Late Years*, 36-51.

"Hearth Roses"

Stein, *The Poetry of Melville's Late Years*, 203-4.

"Hearts-of-Gold"

Stein, *The Poetry of Melville's Late Years*, 186-87.

"Herba Santa"

Stein, *The Poetry of Melville's Late Years*, 82-84.

"In a Bye-Canal"

Stein, *The Poetry of Melville's Late Years*, 113-17.

Robert Penn Warren, "Melville the Poet," *KR* 8 (Spring 1946): 209-11. Reprinted in *Herman Melville: Modern Critical Views*, ed. Harold Bloom (New York: Chelsea House, 1986), 106-7.

"In a Church of Padua"

Stein, *The Poetry of Melville's Late Years*, 118-19.

"In the Desert"

Stein, *The Poetry of Melville's Late Years*, 136-37.

"In the Hall of Marbles"

Stein, *The Poetry of Melville's Late Years*, 132-33.

"In the Turret"

Shurr, *The Mystery of Iniquity*, 35-37.

"Iris"

Stein, *The Poetry of Melville's Late Years*, 187-90.

"Jack Roy"

Stein, *The Poetry of Melville's Late Years*, 34-35.

"John Marr"

Stein, *The Poetry of Melville's Late Years*, 22-25.

"Lamia's Song"

Stein, *The Poetry of Melville's Late Years*, 96-97.

"Lee at the Capitol"

Shurr, *The Mystery of Iniquity*, 23-25.

"The Little Good Fellows"

William Bysshe Stein, "Melville's Poetry: Two Rising Notes," *ESQ*, no. 27 (Second Quarter 1962): 12-13.

Stein, *The Poetry of Melville's Late Years*, 159-60.

"The Loiterer"

Stein, *The Poetry of Melville's Late Years*, 154-56.

"Madcaps"

Stein, *The Poetry of Melville's Late Years*, 164-65.

"Magian Wine"

Stein, *The Poetry of Melville's Late Years*, 80-82.

"The Maldive Shark"

Lawrence H. Martin, Jr., "Melville and Christianity: The Late Poems," *MSE* 2 (Spring 1969): 14.

Robert Penn Warren, "Melville the Poet," *KR* 8 (Spring 1946): 218, et passim.

Shurr, *The Mystery of Iniquity*, 137-39.

Stein, *The Poetry of Melville's Late Years*, 54-56.

"Malvern Hills"

Ronald K. Giles, *Expl* 45 (Winter 1987): 27.

"The Man-of-War Hawk"

Stein, *The Poetry of Melville's Late Years*, 58-59.

"The March into Virginia"

Adler, *War in Melville's Imagination*, 141-43.

"The Margrave's Birthnight"

Stein, *The Poetry of Melville's Late Years*, 78-80.

"Marquis de Grandvin"

Aaron Kramer, *Melville's Poetry: Toward the Enlarged Heart* (Rutherford: Fairleigh Dickinson University Press, 1972), 31-42.

"Milan Cathedral"

Stein, *The Poetry of Melville's Late Years*, 117-18.

"Misgivings"

Adler, *War in Melville's Imagination*, 137-39.

Shurr, *The Mystery of Iniquity*, 25-27.

"Monody"

Shurr, *The Mystery of Iniquity*, 166-68.

Charles N. Watson, Jr., "The Estrangement of Hawthorne and Melville," *NEQ* 46 (Sept. 1973): 380-402.

"Naples in the Time of Bomba"

Aaron Kramer, *Melville's Poetry: Toward the Enlarged Heart* (Rutherford: Fairleigh Dickinson University Press, 1972), 42-46.

Shurr, *The Mystery of Iniquity*, 214-23.

Stein, *The Poetry of Melville's Late Years*, 247-70.

"The New Zealot to the Sun"

Stein, *The Poetry of Melville's Late Years*, 88-90.

"The Night March"

Laurence Perrine, "The Nature of Proof in the Interpretation of Poetry," *EJ* 51 (Sept. 1962): 396-97. Reprinted in Perrine, *The Art of Total Relevance*, 14-15.

Stein, *The Poetry of Melville's Late Years*, 77-78.

"Pausilippo"

Stein, *The Poetry of Melville's Late Years*, 137-41.

149

"Pebbles"

Richard Harter Fogle, "The Themes of Melville's Later Poetry," *TSE* 11 (1961): 73-74.

Shurr, *The Mystery of Iniquity*, 145-48.

Stein, *The Poetry of Melville's Late Years*, 20-21, 65-69.

"The Portent"

Adler, *War in Melville's Imagination*, 135-37.

Jerry Herndon, "Parallels in Melville and Whitman," *WWR* 24 (Sept. 1978): 95-108.

Shurr, *The Mystery of Iniquity*, 16-18.

Stein, *The Poetry of Melville's Late Years*, 7-9.

"Profundity and Levity"

Stein, *The Poetry of Melville's Late Years*, 183-84.

"Puzzlement"

Stein, *The Poetry of Melville's Late Years*, 131-32.

"A Rail Road Cutting Near Alexandria in 1855"

Thomas O. Mabbott, *Expl* 9 (June 1951): 55. Reprinted in *The Explicator Cyclopedia* 2:210.

"Rip Van Winkle's Lilac"

Shurr, *The Mystery of Iniquity*, 193-94.

"The Rose Farmer"

Martin Pops, *The Melville Archetype* (Kent: Kent State University Press, 1970), 226-27.

Stein, *The Poetry of Melville's Late Years*, 216-23.

"Rose Window"

Stein, *The Poetry of Melville's Late Years*, 209-12.

"The Scout toward Aldie"

Aaron Kramer, *Melville's Poetry: Toward the Enlarged Heart* (Rutherford: Fairleigh Dickinson University Press, 1972), 20-31.

Ronald Mason, *The Spirit above the Dust: A Study of Herman Melville* (Mamaroneck: Paul P. Appell, 1972), 215-17.

Stein, *The Poetry of Melville's Late Years*, 6-7.

"Shelley's Vision"

Stein, *The Poetry of Melville's Late Years*, 93-94.

"Shiloh"

Adler, *War in Melville's Imagination*, 147.

Richard Chase, *Herman Melville: A Critical Study* (New York: Macmillian, 1949), 238-40.

"Stockings in the Farm-House Chimney"

Stein, *The Poetry of Melville's Late Years*, 173-74.

"Suggested by the Ruins of a Mountain-Temple in Arcadia, One Built by the Architect of the Parthenon"

Stein, *The Poetry of Melville's Late Years*, 121-24.

"Syra"

Stein, *The Poetry of Melville's Late Years*, 141-44.

"Thy Aim, Thy Aim"

Shurr, *The Mystery of Iniquity*, 229-31.

"Time's Betrayal"

Stein, *The Poetry of Melville's Late Years*, 179-82.

"Timoleon"

Martin Pops, *The Melville Archetype* (Kent: Kent State University Press, 1970), 218-22.

Shurr, *The Mystery of Iniquity*, 151-55.

Stein, *The Poetry of Melville's Late Years*, 73-77.

Lawrance Thompson, *Melville's Quarrel with God* (Princeton: Princeton University Press, 1952), 338-41.

"Trophies of Peace

Stein, *The Poetry of Melville's Late Years*, 167-69.

"Under the Ground"

Faye M. Lenarcic, *Expl* 43 (Fall 1984): 38.

Stein, *The Poetry of Melville's Late Years*, 204-6.

"A Utilitarian View of the Monitor's Fight"

Adler, *War in Melville's Imagination*, 147-48.

Andrew Hook, "Melville's Poetry," in *Herman Melville: Reassessments*, ed. A. Robert Lee (London and Totowa: Vision Press; Barnes & Noble, 1984), 180-81.

"The Vial of Attar"

Stein, *The Poetry of Melville's Late Years*, 208-9.

"The Weaver"

Stein, *The Poetry of Melville's Late Years*, 87-88.

"When Forth the Shepherd Leads the Flock"

Stein, *The Poetry of Melville's Late Years*, 156-59.

MOODY, WILLIAM VAUGHN

"Ode in Time of Hesitation"

R.P. Blackmur, "Moody in Retrospect," *Poetry* 38 (Sept. 1931): 334-35.

MORTON, THOMAS

"The Authors Prologue"

Donald Connors, *Thomas Morton* (New York: Twayne, 1969), 76-78.

"Rise Oedipus"

Robert D. Arner, "Mythology and the Maypole of Merrymount: Some Notes on Thomas Morton's 'Rise Oedipus,'" *EAL* 6 (Fall 1971): 156-64.

O'REILLY, JOHN BOYLE

"A White Rose"

Laurence Perrine, "The Untranslatable Language," *EJ* 60 (Jan. 1971): 60. Reprinted in Perrine, *The Art of Total Relevance*, 45.

PAYNE, JOHN HOWARD

"Home Sweet Home"

J.S. Bratton, *The Victorian Popular Ballad* (London: Macmillian, 1975), 90-91.

POE, EDGAR ALLAN

"Al Aaraaf"

Michael Bell, *The Development of American Romance: The Sacrifice of Relation* (Chicago: University of Chicago Press, 1980): 113-14.

Vincent Buranelli, *Edgar Allan Poe* (New York: Twayne, 1961), 96-98.

Edward Davidson, *Poe: A Critical Study* (Cambridge: Harvard University Press, 1957), 15-22.

John Fruit, *The Mind and Art of Poe's Poetry* (New York: AMS Press, 1966), 23-33.

Sharon Furrow, "Psyche and Setting: Poe's Picturesque Landscapes," *Criticism* 15 (Winter 1973): 23-24.

Halliburton, *Edgar Allan Poe*, 75-83.

Daniel Hoffman, *Poe, Poe, Poe, Poe, Poe, Poe, Poe* (Garden City: Doubleday, 1972), 38-43.

David Ketterer, *The Rationale of Deception in Poe* (Baton Rouge and London: Louisiana State University Press, 1979), 161-67.

Knapp, *Edgar Allan Poe*, 60-67.

David Murray, "'A Strange Sound, as of a Harp-string Broken': The Poetry of Edgar Allan Poe," in *Edgar Allan Poe: The Design of Order*, ed. A. Robert Lee (London: Vision; Totowa, N.J.: Barnes & Noble, 1987), 138-40.

R.C. and M.M. Pettigrew, "A Reply to Floyd Stovall's Interpretation of 'Al Aaraaf,'" *AL* 8 (Jan. 1937): 439-45.

Elizabeth Phillips, *Edgar Allan Poe: An American Imagination* (Port Washington and London: Kennikat Press, 1979), 55-60.

Stovall, *Edgar Poe the Poet*, 28-32, 198-202.

Floyd Stovall, "An Interpretation of Poe's 'Al Aaraaf,'" in *Studies in English* (Austin: University of Texas Press, 1929), 9, 106-33.

"Annabell Lee"

Bradford Booth, "The Identity of Annabell Lee," *CE* 7 (Oct. 1945): 17-19.

Wallace C. Brown, "The English Professor's Dilemma," *CE* 5 (Apr. 1944): 380-82.

Richard Fletcher, *The Stylistic Development of Edgar Allan Poe* (The Hague: Mouton, 1973), 155-68.

Halliburton, *Edgar Allan Poe*, 172-74.

J. Gerald Kennedy, *Poe, Death, and the Life of Writing* (New Haven and London: Yale University Press, 1987), 70-72.

Knapp, *Edgar Allan Poe*, 96-99.

Stovall, *Edgar Poe the Poet*, 225.

"The Bells"

Arthur E. Du Bois, "The Jazz Bells of Poe," *CE* 2 (Dec. 1940): 230-44.

Knapp, *Edgar Allan Poe*, 95-96.

"The City in the Sea"

Richard E. Amacher, *Expl* 19 (May 1961): 60. Reprinted in *The Explicator Cyclopedia* 2:235-37.

Roy P. Basler, *Expl* 4 (Feb. 1946): 30. Reprinted in *The Explicator Cyclopedia* 2:235.

Basler, *Sex, Symbolism, and Psychology in Literature*, 192-95.

Michael Bell, *The Development of American Romance: The Sacrifice of Relation* (Chicago: University of Chicago Press, 1980): 107-8.

Bowra, *The Romantic Imagination*, 183-84.

Wilson O. Clough, "Poe's 'The City in the Sea' Revisited," in Gohdes, *Essays on American Literature*, 81-89.

Halliburton, *Edgar Allan Poe*, 97-102.

Daniel Hoffman, *Poe, Poe, Poe, Poe, Poe, Poe, Poe* (Garden City: Doubleday, 1972), 56-60.

T. Frederick Keefer, "'The City in the Sea': A Re-Examination," *CE* 25 (Mar. 1964): 436-39.

Knapp, *Edgar Allan Poe*, 75-78.

Douglas Norvich Leonard, *Expl* 43 (Fall 1984): 30.

T.O. Mabbott, *Expl* 4 (Oct. 1945): 1. Reprinted in *The Explicator Cyclopedia* 2:233-35.

Eric W. Stockton, "Celestial Inferno: Poe's 'The City in the Sun,'" *TSL* 8 (1963): 99-105.

Dwayne Thorpe, "Poe's 'The City in the Sea': Source and Interpretation," *AL* 51 (Nov. 1979): 394-99.

"The Coliseum"

Halliburton, *Edgar Allan Poe*, 102-8.

Elizabeth Phillips, *Edgar Allan Poe: An American Imagination* (Port Washington and London: Kennikat Press, 1979), 65-73.

"The Conqueror Worm"

Halliburton, *Edgar Allan Poe*, 119-22.

Klaus Lubbers, "Poe's 'The Conqueror Worm,'" *AL* 39 (Nov. 1967): 375-79.

Burton R. Pollin, *Expl* 40 (Spring 1982): 25.

Donald R. Swanson, *Expl* 19 (Apr. 1961): 52. Reprinted in *The Explicator Cyclopedia* 2:237-38.

"A Dream"

Arthur Lerner, *Psychoanalytically Oriented Criticism of Three American Poets* (Rutherford: Fairleigh Dickinson University Press, 1970), 50-52.

"Dream-Land"

J.O. Bailey, "The Geography of Poe's 'Dream-Land' and 'Ulalume,'" *SP* 45 (July 1948): 517-18.

Elizabeth Phillips, *Edgar Allan Poe: An American Imagination* (Port Washington and London: Kennikat Press, 1979), 74-82.

"Eldorado"

Eric W. Carlson, "Poe's 'Eldorado,'" *MLN* 76 (Mar. 1961): 232-34.

O.S. Coad, "The Meaning of Poe's Eldorado," *MLN* 59 (Jan. 1944): 59-61.

T.O. Mabbot, "The Sources of Poe's 'Eldorado,'" *MLN* 60 (June 1945): 312-14.

Burton R. Pollin, "Poe's 'Eldorado' Viewed as a Song of the West," *PrS* 46 (Fall 1972): 228-35.

W. Stephen Sanderlin, Jr., "Poe's 'Eldorado' Again," *MLN* 71 (Mar. 1956): 189-92.

"An Enigma"

W.T. Bandy, *Expl* 20 (Dec. 1961): 35. Reprinted in *The Explicator Cyclopedia* 2:238.

"Evening Star"

Patrick E. Kilburn, *Expl* 28 (May 1970): 76.

"For Annie"

Katrina Bachinger 43 (Fall 1984): 33.

Bowra, *The Romantic Imagination*, 188-89.

Halliburton, *Edgar Allan Poe*, 170-72.

"The Happiest Day, The Happiest Hour"

John Fruit, *The Mind and Art of Poe's Poetry* (New York: AMS Press, 1966), 6-8.

"The Haunted Palace"

Halliburton, *Edgar Allan Poe*, 109-16.

Brian Harding, *American Literature in Context*. Vol. 2, *1830-1865* (London: Mentheun, 1982), 49-52.

Richard Wilbur, "The House of Poe," in *Anniversary Lectures 1959* (Washington: Reference Department, Library of Congress, 1959), 26-28. Reprinted in *Poe: A Collection of Critical Essays*, ed. Robert Regan (Englewood Cliffs: Prentice Hall, 1967), 104-6; in *The Recognition of Edgar Allan Poe*, ed. Eric Carlson (Ann Arbor: University of Michigan Press, 1966), 260-64.

"Helen"

Edward Davidson, *Poe: A Critical Study* (Cambridge: Harvard University Press, 1957), 34-36.

"Introduction"

David M. Rein, *Expl* 29 (Sept. 1961): 8. Reprinted in *The Explicator Cyclopedia* 2:238-39.

"Irene"

Halliburton, *Edgar Allan Poe*, 88-92.

"Israfel"

T.O. Mabbot, *Expl* 2 (June 1944): 57. Reprinted in *The Explicator Cyclopedia* 2:239-40.

Halliburton, *Edgar Allan Poe*, 84-88.

Knapp, *Edgar Allan Poe*, 67-69.

Barton Levi St. Armand, "Poe's Unnecessary Angel: 'Israfel' Reconsidered," in *Ruined Eden of the Present: Hawthorne, Melville, and Poe*, ed. G.R. Thompson and Virgil Lokke (West Lafayette: Purdue University Press, 1981), 283-302.

W.L. Werner, *Expl* 2 (Apr. 1944): 44. Reprinted in *The Explicator Cyclopedia* 2:239.

"The Lake: To ____"

Robert Morrison, *Expl* 7 (Dec. 1948): 22. Reprinted in *The Explicator Cyclopedia* 2:240-41.

"Lenore"

J.C. Broderick, "Poe's Revisions of 'Lenore,'" *AL* 35 (Jan. 1964): 504-9.

Halliburton, *Edgar Allan Poe*, 157-61.

Knapp, *Edgar Allan Poe*, 78-80.

"Musiad"

Stovall, *Edgar Poe the Poet*, 68-90.

"The Raven"

Blasing, *American Poetry*, 27-33.

Vincent Buranelli, *Edgar Allan Poe* (New York: Twayne, 1961), 99-103.

Edward Davidson, *Poe: A Critical Study* (Cambridge: Harvard University Press, 1957), 84-92. Reprinted in *Critics on Poe*, ed. David Kesterson (Coral Gables: University of Miami Press, 1973), 115-20.

John Fruit, *The Mind and Art of Poe's Poetry* (New York: AMS Press, 1966), 114-26.

Halliburton, *Edgar Allan Poe*, 122-42.

Roman Jakobson, "Linguistics and Poetics," in *Essays on the Language of Literature*, ed. Seymour Chatman and Samuel R. Levin (Boston: Houghton Mifflin Co., 1967), 316-17.

Howard Mumford Jones, "Poe, 'The Raven,' and the Anonymous Young Man," *WHR* 9 (Spring 1955): 132-38.

Knapp, *Edgar Allan Poe*, 80-89.

Barton Levi St. Armand, "Poe's Emblematic Raven: A Pictorial Approach," *ESQ*, no. 22 (Fourth Quarter): 191-210.

John J. Teunissen and Evelyn J. Hinz, "'Quaint and Curious': Backgrounds for Poe's 'Raven,'" *SHR* 7 (Fall 1973): 411-19.

"Romance"

Edward Davidson, *Poe: A Critical Study* (Cambridge: Harvard University Press, 1957), 27-30.

Daniel Hoffman, *Poe, Poe, Poe, Poe, Poe, Poe, Poe* (Garden City: Doubleday, 1972), 51-53.

"The Sleeper"

W.B. Hunter, Jr., "Poe's 'The Sleeper' and *Macbeth*," *AL* 20 (Mar. 1948): 55-57.

Knapp, *Edgar Allan Poe*, 72-74.

T.O. Mabbot, "Poe's 'The Sleeper' Again," *AL* 21 (Nov. 1949): 339-40.

"Sonnet to Science"

Daniel Hoffman, *Poe, Poe, Poe, Poe, Poe, Poe, Poe* (Garden City: Doubleday, 1972), 49-51.

"Sonnet to Zante"

Burton Pollin, *Discoveries in Poe* (Notre Dame: University of Notre Dame Press, 1970), 91-106.

"Stanzas"

Halliburton, *Edgar Allan Poe*, 70-73.

Michael Hinden, "Poe's Debt to Wordsworth: A Reading of 'Stanzas,'" *SIR* 8 (Winter 1969): 109-20.

"Tamerlane"

Edward Davidson, *Poe: A Critical Study* (Cambridge: Harvard University Press, 1957), 5-10.

John Fruit, *The Mind and Art of Poe's Poetry* (New York: AMS Press, 1966), 8-15.

Halliburton, *Edgar Allan Poe*, 50-57.

David Ketterer, *The Rationale of Deception in Poe* (Baton Rouge and London: Louisiana State University Press, 1979), 154-60.

Knapp, *Edgar Allan Poe*, 55-60.

"To Helen"

Bowra, *The Romantic Imagination*, 185-86, 192.

Wallace C. Brown, "The English Professor's Dilemma," *CE* 5 (Apr. 1944): 382-85.

Alice Moser Claudel, "Poe as Voyager in 'To Helen,'" *ESQ*, no. 60 Supplement (Fall 1970): 33-37.

Cohen, *Writing About Literature*, 3-7, 95-97.

Robert A. Colby, "Poe's Philosophy of Composition," *University of Kansas City Review* 20 (Spring 1954): 211-14.

Edward Davidson, *Poe: A Critical Study* (Cambridge: Harvard University Press, 1957), 32-34.

Drew, *Poetry: A Modern Guide*, 208.

Halliburton, *Edgar Allan Poe*, 152-57.

Knapp, *Edgar Allan Poe*, 69-72.

T.O. Mabbot, *Expl* 1 (June 1943): 60. Reprinted in *The Explicator Cyclopedia* 2:241; in Locke, Gibson, and Arms, *Readings for Liberal Education*, 209-10.

Rosenthal and Smith, *Exploring Poetry*, 603-4.

Satin, *Reading Poetry*, 1080-81.

"To Lake - To ____"

David Murray, "'A Strange Sound, as of a Harp-string Broken': The Poetry of Edgar Allan Poe," in *Edgar Allan Poe: The Design of Order*, ed. A. Robert Lee (London: Vision; Totowa, N.J.: Barnes & Noble, 1987), 136-38.

Stovall, *Edgar Poe the Poet*, 206-7.

"To One in Paradise"

R.P. Basler, "Bryonism in Poe's 'To One in Paradise,'" *AL* 9 (May 1937): 232-36.

Richard Fletcher, *The Stylistic Development of Edgar Allan Poe* (The Hague: Mouton, 1973), 34-36.

"Ulalume"

J.O. Bailey, "The Geography of Poe's 'Dream-Land' and 'Ulalume,'" *SP* 45 (July 1948): 518-23.

Roy P. Basler, *Expl* 2 (May 1944): 49. Reprinted in *The Explicator Cyclopedia* 2:243-44.

Basler, *Sex, Symbolism, and Psychology in Literature*, 184-87. Reprinted in Stallman and Watters, *The Creative Reader*, 861-62.

J.M. Blumenfield, "Poe's 'Ulalume,' Line 43," *N&Q* 197 (29 Mar. 1952): 147.

Brooks and Warren, *Understanding Poetry*, rev. ed., 197-201.

Eric W. Carlson, *Expl* 11 (June 1953): 56. Reprinted in *The Explicator Cyclopedia* 2:245.

Eric W. Carlson, "Symbol and Sense in Poe's 'Ulalume,'" *AL* 35 (Mar. 1963): 22-37.

Thomas E. Connolly, *Expl* 22 (Sept. 1963): 4.

Edward Davidson, *Poe: A Critical Study* (Cambridge: Harvard University Press, 1957), 92-97.

Richard Fletcher, *The Stylistic Development of Edgar Allan Poe* (The Hague: Mouton, 1973), 60-62, 179-84.

John Fruit, *The Mind and Art of Poe's Poetry* (New York: AMS Press, 1966), 76-78, 130-32.

Halliburton, *Edgar Allan Poe*, 142-52.

Daniel Hoffman, *Poe, Poe, Poe, Poe, Poe, Poe, Poe* (Garden City: Doubleday, 1972), 72-76.

J. Gerald Kennedy, *Poe, Death, and the Life of Writing* (New Haven and London: Yale University Press, 1987), 71-77.

David Ketterer, *The Rationale of Deception in Poe* (Baton Rouge and London: Louisiana State University Press, 1979), 177-80.

J.P. Kirby, *Expl* 1 (Oct. 1942): 8. Reprinted in *The Explicator Cyclopedia* 2:241-42.

Knapp, *Edgar Allan Poe*, 89-94.

Lou Ann Kriegisch, "'Ulalume'--A Platonic Profanation of Beauty and Love," *Poe Studies* 11 (Dec. 1978): 29-31.

Lewis Leary, *Expl* 6 (Feb. 1948): 25. Reprinted in *The Explicator Cyclopedia* 2:244.

T.O. Mabbot, *Expl* 1 (Feb. 1943): 25. Reprinted in *The Explicator Cyclopedia* 2:242-43.

T.O. Mabbot, *Expl* 6 (June 1948): 57. Reprinted in *The Explicator Cyclopedia* 2:244-45; in Stallman and Watters, *The Creative Reader*, 860-61.

James E. Miller, Jr., "'Ulalume' Resurrected," *PQ* 34 (Apr. 1955): 197-205.

Edward Shanks, *Edgar Allan Poe* (New York: Macmillian, 1937), 97-100.

Stovall, *Edgar Poe the Poet*, 230-31.

Edward Strickland, *Expl* 34 (Nov. 1975): 19.

Unger and O'Connor, *Poems for Study*, 468-72.

Yvor Winters, "A Crisis in the History of American Obscurantism," *AL* 8 (Jan. 1937): 394-95. Reprinted in Winters, *Maule's Curse*, 112-13; in Winters, *In Defense of Reason*, 252-53.

"The Valley of Unrest"

Basler, *Sex, Symbolism, and Psychology in Literature*, 197-200. Reprinted in Locke, Gibson, and Arms, *Readings for Liberal Education,* 3d ed., 121-22; 4th ed., 210-21; 5th ed., 111-12.

Roy P. Basler, *Expl* 5 (Dec. 1946): 25. Reprinted in *The Explicator Cyclopedia* 2:245-46.

Halliburton, *Edgar Allan Poe*, 92-95.

RILEY, JAMES W.

"Armazindy"

Peter Revell, *James Whitcomb Riley* (New York: Twayne, 1970), 100-101.

"The Flying Islands of the Night"

Peter Revell, *James Whitcomb Riley* (New York: Twayne, 1970), 50-56.

"Out to Old Aunt Mary's"

Peter Revell, *James Whitcomb Riley* (New York: Twayne, 1970), 126-29.

"What Christmas Fetched the Wigginses"

Peter Revell, *James Whitcomb Riley* (New York: Twayne, 1970), 97-99.

ROBINSON, EDWIN A.

"Amaranth"

Hoyt Franchere, *Edwin Arlington Robinson* (New York: Twayne, 1968), 95-100.

Kaplan, *Philosophy in the Poetry of Edwin Arlington Robinson*, 71-85.

Winters, *Edwin Arlington Robinson*, 120-24.

"Amaryllis"

William C. Childers, *Expl* 14 (Feb. 1956), 34. Reprinted in *The Explicator Cyclopedia* 1:245-46.

"Aunt Imogen"

H.R. Wolf, "E.A. Robinson and the Integration of Self," in *Modern American Poetry: Essays in Criticism*, ed. Jerome Mazzaro (New York: McKay, 1970), 47-49.

"Avon's Harvest"

Winters, *Edwin Arlington Robinson*, 100-103.

"Battle after War"

Dean Sherman, *Expl* 27 (Apr. 1969): 64.

"Ben Jonson Entertains a Man from Stratford"

Cestre, *An Introduction to Edwin Arlington Robinson*, 132-35.

"Calverly's"

James Dickey, "Edwin Arlington Robinson: The Many Truths," in *Edwin Arlington Robinson*, ed. Francis Murphy (Englewood Cliffs: Prentice-Hall, 1970), 78-81.

"Captain Craig"

Cestre, *An Introduction to Edwin Arlington Robinson*, 173-84.

Hoyt Franchere, *Edwin Arlington Robinson* (New York: Twayne, 1968), 89-92.

William Free, "The Strategy of 'Flammonde,'" in *Edwin Arlington Robinson*, ed. Ellsworth Barnard (Athens: University of Georgia Press, 1969), 21-24.

Kaplan, *Philosophy in the Poetry of Edwin Arlington Robinson*, 43-55.

Emery Neff, *Edwin Arlington Robinson* (New York: William Sloane Associates, 1948), 114-19.

Redman, *Edwin Arlington Robinson*, 44-52.

W.R. Robinson, "The Alienated Self," in *Edwin Arlington Robinson*, ed. Francis Murphy (Englewood Cliffs: Prentice-Hall, 1970), 129-31.

"Cassandra"

Yvor Winters, "Religious and Social Ideas in the Didactic Work of E.A. Robinson," *ArQ* 1 (Spring 1945): 79-80.

"Cavender's House"

Kaplan, *Philosophy in the Poetry of Edwin Arlington Robinson*, 96-102.

Emery Neff, *Edwin Arlington Robinson* (New York: William Sloane Associates, 1948), 229-31.

"The Clerks"

Louis O. Coxe, "E.A. Robinson: The Lost Tradition," *SR* 62 (Spring 1954): 259-61.

Louis Coxe, *E. A. Robinson* (Minneapolis: University of Minnesota Press, 1962), 32-33.

"Cliff Klingenhangen"

William J. Free, "E.A. Robinson's Use of Emerson," *AL* 38 (Mar. 1966): 79.

"Cortege"

Hoyt Franchere, *Edwin Arlington Robinson* (New York: Twayne, 1968), 63-66.

"Credo"

Richard Adams, "The Failure of Edwin Arlington Robinson," *TSE* 11 (1961): 107-9.

Richard Landini, "Metaphor and Imagery in E.A. Robinson's 'Credo,'" *CLQ* 8 (Mar. 1968: 20-22.

"The Dark Hills"

Perrine and Reid, *100 American Poems*, 22-23.

G. Thomas Tanselle, "Robinson's 'Dark Hills,'" *CEA* 26 (Feb. 1964): 8-10.

"Demos"

Yvor Winters, "Religious and Social Ideas in the Didactic Work of E. A. Robinson," *ArQ* 1 (Spring 1945): 80-81.

"Dionysus in Doubt"

Kaplan, *Philosophy in the Poetry of Edwin Arlington Robinson*, 123-28.

Redman, *Edwin Arlington Robinson*, 86-88.

Winters, *Edwin Arlington Robinson*, 55-57.

Yvor Winters, "Religious and Social Ideas in the Didactic Work of E. A. Robinson," *ArQ* 1 (Spring 1945): 82-84.

"En Passant"

Bernice Slote, *Expl* 15 (Feb. 1957): 27. Reprinted in *The Explicator Cyclopedia* 1:246-47.

"Eros Turannos"

Richard P. Adams, "The Failure of Edwin Arlington Robinson," *TSE* 11 (1961): 145-51.

R. Meredith Bedell, "Perception, Action, and Life in *The Man Against the Sky*," *CLQ* 12 (Mar. 1976): 35-36.

Louis Coxe, "E.A. Robinson: The Lost Tradition," *SR* 62 (Spring 1954): 252-59. Reprinted in *Edwin Arlington Robinson*, ed. Francis Murphy (Englewood Cliffs: Prentice-Hall, 1970), 65-72.

Louis Coxe, *E.A. Robinson* (Minneapolis: University of Minnesota Press, 1962), 24-30.

Richard Gray, *American Poetry of the Twentieth Century* (London: Cambridge University Press, 1976), 149-50.

Joan Manheimer, "Edwin Arlington Robinson's 'Eros Turannos': Narrative Reconsidered," *LitR* 20 (Spring 1977): 253-69.

Pearce, *The Continuity of American Poetry*, 261-64.

Laurence Perrine, *Expl* 8 (Dec. 1949): 20. Reprinted in *The Explicator Cyclopedia* 1:247-48.

"The Field of Glory"

Richard Crowder, *Expl* 8 (Feb. 1950: 31. Reprinted in *The Explicator Cyclopedia* 1:248-49.

"Firelight

James D. Barry, *Expl* 22 (Nov. 1963): 21.

"Flammonde"

Hilton Anderson, "Robinson's 'Flammonde,'" *SoQ* 7 (Jan. 1969): 179-81.

William Free, "The Strategy of 'Flammonde,'" in *Edwin Arlington Robinson*, ed. Ellsworth Barnard (Athens: University of Georgia Press, 1969), 15-30.

Millett, *Reading Poetry*, 64.

Winters, *Edwin Arlington Robinson*, 51-52.

"For a Dead Lady"

Richard P. Adams, "The Failure of Edwin Arlington Robinson," *TSE* 11 (1961): 141-44.

Richard Crowder, *Expl* 5 (Dec. 1946): 19. Reprinted in *The Explicator Cyclopedia* 1:249.

E.S. Fussell, *Expl* 9 (Mar. 1951): 33. Reprinted in *The Explicator Cyclopedia* 1:250.

Clyde L. Grimm, "Robinson's 'For a Dead Lady': An Exercise in Evaluation," *CLQ* 7 (Dec. 1967): 535-47. Reprinted in *Appreciation of Edwin Arlington Robinson*, ed. Richard Cary (Waterville: Colby College Press, 1969), 243-52.

Sylvia Hart and Estelle Paige, *Expl* 10 (May 1952): 51. Reprinted in *The Explicator Cyclopedia* 1:250.

R.H. Super, *Expl* 3 (June 1945): 60. Reprinted in *The Explicator Cyclopedia* 1:249.

R.H. Super, *Expl* 3 (June 1947): 60. Reprinted in *The Explicator Cyclopedia* 1:249-50.

"The Gift of God"

R. Meredith Bedell, "Perception, Action, and Life in *The Man Against the Sky*," *CLQ* 12 (Mar. 1976): 33-35.

Louis Coxe, "E.A. Robinson: The Lost Tradition," *SR* 62 (Spring 1954): 261-65. Reprinted in *Edwin Arlington Robinson*, ed. Francis Murphy (Englewood Cliffs: Prentice-Hall, 1970), 73-76.

Louis Coxe, *E.A. Robinson* (Minneapolis: University of Minnesota Press, 1962), 33-38.

"The Glory of the Nightingales"

Kaplan, *Philosophy in the Poetry of Edwin Arlington Robinson*, 103-110.

Emery Neff, *Edwin Arlington Robinson* (New York: William Sloane Associates, 1948), 231-35.

"The Growth of 'Lorraine'"

Ronald Moran, "Lorraine and the Sirens: Courtesans in Two Poems by E.A. Robinson," in Kirby and Olive, *Essays in Honor of Esmond Linworth Marilla*, 312-15.

"The House on the Hill"

James G. Hepburn, "E.A. Robinson System of Opposites," *PMLA* 80 (June 1965): 269-70.

"How Annandale Went Out"

Charles V. Genthe, "E.A. Robinson's 'Annandale' Poems," *CLQ* 7 (Mar. 1967): 395-7.

Richard Gray, *American Poetry of the Twentieth Century* (London: Cambridge University Press, 1976), 147-48.

David Nivison, "Does It Matter How Annandale Went Out?" in *Appreciation of Edwin Arlington Robinson*, ed. Richard Cary (Waterville: Colby College Press, 1969), 183-90.

"Isaac and Archibald"

James Dickey, "Edwin Arlington Robinson: The Many Truths," in *Edwin Arlington Robinson*, ed. Francis Murphy (Englewood Cliffs: Prentice-Hall, 1970), 88-91.

Edwin Fussell, *Edwin Arlington Robinson* (Berkeley: University of California Press, 1954), 12-16.

J.C. Levenson, "Robinson's Modernity," in *Edwin Arlington Robinson*, ed. Francis Murphy (Englewood Cliffs: Prentice-Hall, 1970), 178-81. Reprinted in *Edwin Arlington Robinson*, ed. Ellsworth Barnard (Athens: University of Georgia Press, 1969), 172-74.

Perrine and Reid, *100 American Poems*, 20-22.

Redman, *Edwin Arlington Robinson*, 52-53.

"Karma"

Brown and Milstead, *Patterns in Poetry*, 143.

"King Jasper"

Kaplan, *Philosophy in the Poetry of Edwin Arlington Robinson*, 128-44.

Emery Neff, *Edwin Arlington Robinson* (New York: William Sloane Associates, 1948), 245-47.

Winters, *Edwin Arlington Robinson*, 124-28.

"Lancelot"

Christopher Brookhouse, "Imagery and Theme in 'Lancelot,'" in *Edwin Arlington Robinson*, ed. Ellsworth Barnard (Athens: University of Georgia Press, 1969), 120-29.

Cestre, *An Introduction to Edwin Arlington Robinson*, 89-98.

Winters, *Edwin Arlington Robinson*, 71-85.

"Lost Anchor"

S.A. Cowan, *Expl* 24 (Apr. 1966), 68.

James Grimshaw, *Expl* 30 (Dec. 1971): 36.

Ralph E. Jenkins, *Expl* 23 (Apr. 1965): 64

Richard Tuerk, *Expl* 32 (Jan. 1974): 37.

Celeste Turner Wright, *Expl* 11 (June 1953): 57. Reprinted in *The Explicator Cyclopedia* 1:250-51.

"Luke Havergal"

Richard P. Adams, "The Failure of Edwin Arlington Robinson," *TSE* 11 (1961): 129-36.

Cestre, *An Introduction to Edwin Arlington Robinson*, 46-49.

Richard Crowder, *Expl* 7 (Nov. 1948): 15. Reprinted in *The Explicator Cyclopedia* 1:254.

N.E. Dunn, "Riddling Leaves: Robinson's 'Luke Havergal,'" *CLQ* 10 (Mar. 1973): 17-25.

Walter Gierasch, *Expl* 3 (Oct. 1944): 8. Abridged in Gwynn, Condee, and Lewis, *The Case for Poetry*, 297. Reprinted in *The Explicator Cyclopedia* 1:251-52.

James G. Hepburn, "E.A. Robinson's System of Opposites," *PMLA* 80 (June 1965): 270-72.

Ronald McFarland, "Robinson's 'Luke Havergal,'" *CLQ* 10 (June 1974): 365-72.

Ronald Moran, "Meaning and Value in 'Luke Havergal,'" *CLQ* 7 (Mar. 1967): 385-92.

Mathilde M. Parlett, *Expl* 3 (June 1945): 57. Reprinted in *The Explicator Cyclopedia* 1:253-54.

A.A. Raven, *Expl* 3 (Dec. 1944): 24 Reprinted in *The Explicator Cyclopedia* 1:252-53.

Bertrand F. Richards, "No, There Is Not a Dawn . . . ," *CLQ* 9 (Sept. 1971): 367-74.

"The Man against the Sky"

Richard P. Adams, "The Failure of Edwin Arlington Robinson," *TSE* 11 (1961): 136-41.

R. Meredith Bedell, "Perception, Action, and Life in 'The Man Against the Sky,'" *CLQ* 12 (Mar. 1976): 36-37.

Cestre, *An Introduction to Edwin Arlington Robinson*, 60-66.

Richard Crowder, "'Man Against the Sky'" *CE* 14 (Feb. 1953): 269-76.

James Dickey, "Edwin Arlington Robinson: The Many Truths," in *Edwin Arlington Robinson*, ed. Francis Murphy (Englewood Cliffs: Prentice-Hall, 1970), 91-93.

Robert S. Fish, "The Tempering of Faith in E.A. Robinson's 'The Man Against the Sky,'" *CLQ* 9 (Mar. 1972): 456-68.

Edwin Fussell, *Edwin Arlington Robinson* (Berkeley: University of California Press, 1954), 95-97.

Richard Gray, *American Poetry of the Twentieth Century* (London: Cambridge University Press, 1976), 150-52.

David Hirsch, "'The Man Against the Sky' and the Problem of Faith," in *Edwin Arlington Robinson*, ed. Ellsworth Barnard (Athens: University of Georgia Press, 1969), 31-42.

Kaplan, *Philosophy in the Poetry of Edwin Arlington Robinson*, 55-63.

Emery Neff, *Edwin Arlington Robinson* (New York: William Sloane Associates, 1948), 182-86.

Pearce, *The Continuity of American Poetry*, 265-67.

Arthur M. Read, II, *Expl* 26 (Feb. 1968): 49.

Redman, *Edwin Arlington Robinson*, 61-64.

John Newell Sanborn, "Juxtaposition as Structure in 'The Man Against the Sky,'" *CLQ* 10 (Dec. 1974): 486-94.

Winfield Townley Scott, "To See Robinson," *New Mexico Quarterly Review* 26 (Summer 1956): 169.

Hyatt Howe Waggoner, *The Heel of Elohim: Science and Values in Modern American Poetry* (Norman: University of Oklahoma Press, 1950), 29-36. Reprinted in *Edwin Arlington Robinson*, ed. Francis Murphy (Englewood Cliffs: Prentice-Hall, 1970), 136-61.

Yvor Winters, "Religious and Social Ideas in the Didactic Work of E. A. Robinson," *ArQ* 1 (Spring 1945): 74-75.

"The Man Who Died Twice"

Cestre, *An Introduction to Edwin Arlington Robinson*, 217-23.

Richard Crowder, "E.A. Robinson's Symphony: 'The Man Who Died Twice,'" *CE* 11 (Dec. 1949): 141-44.

Kaplan, *Philosophy in the Poetry of Edwin Arlington Robinson*, 63-71.

Emery Neff, *Edwin Arlington Robinson* (New York: William Sloane Associates, 1948), 217-19.

"Matthias at the Door"

Hoyt Franchere, *Edwin Arlington Robinson* (New York: Twayne, 1968), 110-12.

Kaplan, *Philosophy in the Poetry of Edwin Arlington Robinson*, 110-17.

W.R. Robinson, *Edwin Arlington Robinson: A Poetry of the Act* (Cleveland: Press of Case Western Reserve University, 1967), 104-6.

Floyd Stovall, "The Optimism Behind Robinson's Tragedies," in *Appreciation of Edwin Arlington Robinson*, ed. Richard Cary (Waterville: Colby College Press, 1969), 66-68.

Winters, *Edwin Arlington Robinson*, 114-19.

"Merlin"

Cestre, *An Introduction to Edwin Arlington Robinson*, 69-88.

Kaplan, *Philosophy in the Poetry of Edwin Arlington Robinson*, 86-95.

Redman, *Edwin Arlington Robinson*, 73-81.

Nathan Starr, "The Transformation of Merlin," in *Edwin Arlington Robinson*, ed. Ellsworth Barnard (Athens: University of Georgia Press, 1969), 106-19.

Winters, *Edwin Arlington Robinson*, 62-71.

"The Mill"

Redman, *Edwin Arlington Robinson*, 40-42.

"Miniver Cheevy"

Abad, *A Formal Approach to Lyric Poetry*, 166-67, 174-75.

Michael G. Miller, "Miniver Grows Lean," *CLQ* 12 (Sept. 1976): 149-50.

Perrine and Reid, *100 American Poems*, 4-5.

Laurence Perrine, "A Reading of 'Miniver Cheevy,'" *CLQ* 6 (June 1962): 65-74. Reprinted in Perrine, *The Art of Total Relevance*, 89-96.

"Mr. Flood's Party"

James L. Allen, Jr. "Symbol and Theme in 'Mr. Flood's Party,'" *MissQ* 15 (Fall 1962): 139-43.

John Ciardi, *How Does a Poem Mean?* (Boston: Houghton Mifflin Co., 1959), 712.

Richard Allan Davidson, *Expl* 29 (Feb. 1971): 45.

Richard Gray, *American Poetry of the Twentieth Century* (London: Cambridge University Press, 1976), 152-53.

Willis D. Jacobs, "E.A. Robinson 'Mr. Flood's Party,'" *CE* 12 (Nov. 1950): 110.

E. Sydnor Ownbey, *Expl* 8 (Apr. 1950): 47. Reprinted in *The Explicator Cyclopedia* 1:254-55.

John E. Parish, "The Rehabilitation of Eben Flood," *EJ* 55 (Sept. 1966): 696-99.

Perrine and Reid, *100 American Poems*, 7-8.

Walsh, *Doors of Perception*, 136-39.

Wheeler, *The Design of Poetry*, 99-102.

H.R. Wolf, "E.A. Robinson and the Integration of Self," in *Modern American Poetry: Essays in Criticism*, ed. Jerome Mazzaro (New York: McKay, 1970), 47-49.

"New England"

Richard E. Amacher, *Expl* 10 (Mar. 1952): 33. Reprinted in *The Explicator Cyclopedia* 1:256.

W.R. Robinson, "E.A. Robinson's Yankee Conscience," *CLQ* 8 (Sept. 1969): 371-76.

H.H. Waggoner, *Expl* 10 (Mar. 1952): 33. Reprinted in *The Explicator Cyclopedia* 1:256-57.

"The Night Before"

J. Vail Fox, "Robinson's Impulse for Narrative," in *Appreciation of Edwin Arlington Robinson*, ed. Richard Cary (Waterville: Colby College Press, 1969), 256-62.

"Octaves"

Ronald Moran, "The 'Octaves' of E.A. Robinson," in *Appreciation of Edwin Arlington Robinson*, ed. Richard Cary (Waterville: Colby College Press, 1969), 315-21.

Winters, *Edwin Arlington Robinson*, 49-51.

"An Old Story"

Richard Crowder, *Expl* 4 (Dec. 1945): 22. Reprinted in *The Explicator Cyclopedia* 1:256-57.

"On the Way"

Yvor Winters, "Religious and Social Ideas in the Didactic Work of E. A. Robinson," *ArQ* 1 (Spring 1945): 81-82.

ROBINSON, EDWIN A.

"The Poor Relation"

Scott Donaldson, "The Book of Scattered Lives," in *Edwin Arlington Robinson*, ed. Ellsworth Barnard (Athens: University of Georgia Press, 1969), 51-53.

"Rembrandt to Rembrandt"

Redman, *Edwin Arlington Robinson*, 90-94.

"Richard Cory"

Ellsworth Barnard, *Edwin Arlington Robinson: A Critical Study* (New York: Macmillan, 1952), 98-100.

Charles Burkhart, *Expl* 19 (Nov. 1960): 9. Reprinted in *The Explicator Cyclopedia* 1:257-58.

William J. Free, "E.A. Robinson's Use of Emerson," *AL* 38 (Mar. 1966): 77-79.

Harry R. Garvin, "Poems Pickled in Anthological Brine," *CEA* 20 (Oct. 1958): 4.

L. Kart, "Richard Cory: Artist without Art," *CLQ* 11 (Sept. 1975): 160-61.

J. Kavka, "Richard Cory's Suicide: A Psychoanalysts's View," *CLQ* 11 (Sept. 1975): 150-59.

Charles R. Morris, *Expl* 23 (Mar. 1965): 52.

Laurence Perrine, "Interpreting Poetry--Two Ways of Going Wrong," *CEJ* 1 (Winter 1965): 47-49. Reprinted in Perrine, *The Art of Total Relevance*, 97-99.

Perrine and Reid, *100 American Poems*, 1-2.

Redman, *Edwin Arlington Robinson*, 36-38.

Stageberg and Anderson, *Poetry as Experience*, 189-92.

Charles A. Sweet, Jr., "A Re-examination of 'Richard Cory,'" *CLQ* 9 (Sept. 1972): 579-82.

Steven Turner, *Expl* 28 (May 1970): 73.

"Roman Bartholow"

Cestre, *An Introduction to Edwin Arlington Robinson*, 209-14.

Emery Neff, *Edwin Arlington Robinson* (New York: William Sloane Associates, 1948), 210-15.

Winters, *Edwin Arlington Robinson*, 103-6.

"The Sheaves"

Richard Crowder, *Expl* 4 (Mar. 1946): 38. Reprinted in *The Explicator Cyclopedia* 1:258.

M.S. Mattfield, "Edwin Arlington Robinson's 'The Sheaves,'" *CEA* 21 (Nov. 1968): 10.

"Sonnet: Oh for a Poet"

M.N.O., *Expl* 5 (May 1947), 21.

"The Three Taverns"

Edwin Fussell, *Edwin Arlington Robinson* (Berkeley: University of California Press, 1954), 162-64.

Winters, *Edwin Arlington Robinson*, 134-36.

"The Town Down the River"

Ellsworth Barnard, *Edwin Arlington Robinson: A Critical Study* (New York: Macmillan, 1952), 75-77.

"The Tree in Pamela's Garden"

Brian M. Barbour, *Expl* 28 (Nov. 1969): 20.

Marvin Klotz, *Expl* 20 (Jan. 1962): 42. Reprinted in *The Explicator Cyclopedia* 1:258.

Laurence Perrine, *Expl* 30 (Nov. 1971): 18.

Elizabeth Wright, *Expl* 21 (Feb. 1963): 47.

"Tristam"

Frederic Carpenter, "Tristam the Transcendent" in *Appreciation of Edwin Arlington Robinson*, ed. Richard Cary (Waterville: Colby College Press, 1969), 75-90.

Cestre, *An Introduction to Edwin Arlington Robinson*, 98-118.

Hoyt Franchere, *Edwin Arlington Robinson* (New York: Twayne, 1968), 127-33.

Winters, *Edwin Arlington Robinson*, 86-96.

"Veteran Sirens"

Scott Donaldson, "The Book of Scattered Lives," in *Edwin Arlington Robinson*, ed. Ellsworth Barnard (Athens: University of Georgia Press, 1969), 49-51.

Ronald Moran, "Lorainne and the Sirens: Courtesans in Two Poems by E. A. Robinson," in Kirby and Olive, *Essays in Honor of Esmond Linworth Marilla*, 315-19.

Laurence Perrine, *Expl* 6 (Nov. 1947): 13. Reprinted in *The Explicator Cyclopedia* 1:260-61.

"The Wandering Jew"

Donald Stanford, "Edwin Arlington Robinson's 'The Wandering Jew,'" *TSE* 23 (1978): 95-108.

Winters, *Edwin Arlington Robinson*, 36-39.

"The Whip"

Henry Pettit, *Expl* 1 (Apr. 1943): 50. Reprinted in *The Explicator Cyclopedia* 1:261-62.

SMITH, WILLIAM JAY

"American Primitive"

C.F. Burgess, "William Jay Smith's 'American Primitive': Toward a Reading," *ArQ* 26 (Spring 1970): 71-75.

TAYLOR, EDWARD

"The Accusation of the Inward Man"
(From *God's Determinations*)

Sidney E. Lind, "Edward Taylor: A Revaluation," *NEQ* 21 (Dec. 1948):525-27.

"An Address to the Soul Occasioned by a Rain"

Willie T. Weathers, "Edward Taylor, Hellenistic Puritan," *AL* 18 (Mar. 1946): 24-25.

"The Ebb and Flow"

Raymond J. Jordan, *Expl* 20 (Apr. 1962): 67. Reprinted in *The Explicator Cyclopedia* 2:327-28.

"The Experience"

W.C. Brown, "Edward Taylor: An American 'Metaphysical,'" *AL* 16 (Nov. 1944): 191, 196-97.

"The Glory of and Grace in the Church Set Out"

G. Giovannini, *Expl* 6 (Feb. 1948): 26. Reprinted in *The Explicator Cyclopedia* 2:328-29.

"God's Determinations"

Michael J. Colacurcio, "God's Determinations Touching Half-Way Membership: Occasion and Audience in Edward Taylor," *AL* 39 (Nov. 1967): 298-314.

Norman Grabo, *Edward Taylor* (New York: Twayne, 1961), 159-68.

Keller, *The Example of Edward Taylor*, 129-38.

J. Daniel Patterson, "'God's Determinations': The Occasion, the Audience, and Taylor's Hope for New England," *EAL* (Spring 1987): 63-81

Evan Prosser, "Edward Taylor's Poetry," *NEQ* 40 (Sept. 1967): 392-98.

William Scheick, "The Jawbones Schema in Edward Taylor's 'God's Determinations,'" in *Puritan Influences in American Literature*, ed. Emory Elliot (Urbana: University of Illinois Press, 1979), 38-54.

Jean L. Thomas, "Drama and Doctrine in 'God's Determinations,'" *AL* 36 (Jan. 1965): 452-62.

Austin Warren, "Edward Taylor's Poetry: Colonial Baroque," *KR* 3 (Summer 1941): 362-65.

Warren, *Rage for Order*, 8-12.

"Huswifery"

Norman S. Grabo, "Edward Taylor's Spiritual Huswifery," *PMLA* 89 (Dec. 1964): 554-60.

John Higby, *Expl* 30 (Mar. 1972): 60.

"*More Than Enough There*," *TLS*, 6 Nov. 1959, xiv.

"Meditation 1.1: What Love Is This of Thine,
That Cannot Be"

W.C. Brown, "Edward Taylor: An American 'Metaphysical,'" *AL* 16 (Nov. 1944): 194-95.

Allen Richard Penner, "Edward Taylor's 'Meditation One,'" *AL* 39 (May 1967): 193-99.

"Meditation 1.3: How Sweet a Lord Is Mine"

Joel R. Kehler, "Physiology and Metaphor in Edward Taylor's 'Meditation. Can. 1.3,'" *EAL* 9 (Winter 1975): 315-20.

Barbara Lewalski, *Protestant Poetics and the Seventeenth-Century Religious Lyric* (Princeton: Princeton University Press, 1979), 418.

"Meditation 1.6: Am I Thy Gold?
Or Purse, Lord, for Thy Wealth"

Kent Bates and William J. Aull, "Touching Taylor Overly: A Note on 'Meditation Six,'" *EAL* 5 (Fall 1970): 57-59.

William K. Bottorff, "Edward Taylor, an Explication: Another Meditation at the Same Time," *EAL* 3 (Spring 1968): 17-21.

Norman S. Grabo, *Expl* 18 (Apr. 1960): 40. Reprinted in *The Explicator Cyclopedia* 2:331-32.

Anne Marie McNamara, *Expl* 17 (Oct. 1958): 3. Reprinted in *The Explicator Cyclopedia* 2:330-31.

Michael North, "Edward Taylor's Metaphors of Promise," *AL* 51 (Mar. 1979): 6-7.

Roy Harvey Pearce, "Edward Taylor: The Poet as Puritan," *NEQ* 23 (Mar. 1950): 34-35.

Donald E. Stanford, "Edward Taylor," in *Major Writers of Early American Literature*, ed. Everett Emerson (Madison: University of Wisconsin Press, 1972), 77-79.

"Meditation 1.8: I Kenning Through Astronomy Divine"

Gerhard T. Alexis, *Expl* 24 (May 1966): 77.

Keller, *The Example of Edward Taylor*, 253.

Barbara Lewalski, *Protestant Poetics and the Seventeenth-Century Religious Lyric* (Princeton: Princeton University Press, 1979), 401-3.

George Monteiro, *Expl* 27 (Feb. 1969): 45.

Roy Harvey Pearce, "Edward Taylor: The Poet as Puritan," *NEQ* 23 (Mar. 1950): 44-45.

Austin Warren, "Edward Taylor's Poetry: Colonial Baroque," *KR* 3 (Summer 1941): 365-68.

Warren, *Rage for Order*, 12-16.

"Meditation 1.20"

Donald Stanford, *Edward Taylor* (Minneapolis: University of Minnesota Press, 1965), 23-25.

"Meditation 1.22: When Thy Bright Beams, My Lord, Do Strike Mine Eye"

Barbara Lewalski, *Protestant Poetics and the Seventeenth-Century Religious Lyric* (Princeton: Princeton University Press, 1979), 410-11.

"Meditation 1.28: When I, Lord, Send Some Bits of Glory Home"

W.C. Brown, "Edward Taylor: An American 'Metaphysical,'" *AL* 16 (Nov. 1944): 192-93.

"Meditation 1.29: My Shattred Phancy Stole Away From Mee"

Ursula Brumm, "The 'Tree of Life' in Edward Taylor's Meditations," *EAL* 3 (Fall 1968): 74-80.

Cecilia L. Halbert, "Tree of Life Imagery in the Poetry of Edward Taylor," *AL* 38 (Mar. 1966): 25-27.

"Meditation 1.30: The Daintiest Draught Thy Pensill Ever Drew"

Cecilia L. Halbert, "Tree of Life Imagery in the Poetry of Edward Taylor," *AL* 38 (Mar. 1966): 31-52.

"Meditation 1.32: Thy Grace, Deare Lord's My Golden Wrack."

Martz, *The Poem of the Mind*, 60-62.

"Meditation 1.33: My Lord, My Life, Can Envy Ever Be"

W.C. Brown, "Edward Taylor: An American 'Metaphysical,'" *AL* 16 (Nov. 1944): 193.

"Meditation 1.34: My Lord I Fain Would
Praise Thee Well But Finde"

P.H. Johnson, "Poetry and Praise in Edward Taylor's *Preparatory Meditations,*" *AL* 52 (Mar. 1979): 89-90.

Barbara Lewalski, *Protestant Poetics and the Seventeenth-Century Religious Lyric* (Princeton: Princeton University Press, 1979), 412.

Evan Prosser, "Edward Taylor's Poetry," *NEQ* 40 (Sept. 1967): 387-88.

"Meditation 1.39: My Sin! My Sin, My God,
These Cursed Dregs"

P.H. Johnson, "Poetry and Praise in Edward Taylor's *Preparatory Meditations,*" *AL* 52 (Mar. 1979): 90-91.

Keller, *The Example of Edward Taylor*, 106-11.

William J. Scheick, "'The Inward Tacles and the Outward Traces': Edward Taylor's Elusive Transitions," *EAL* 12 (Fall 1977): 164-69.

"Meditation 1.40: Still I Complain; I Am Complaining Still"

Robert D. Arner, "Folk Metaphors in Edward Taylor's 'Meditation 1.40,'" *SCN* 31 (Spring 1973): 6-9.

Barbara Lewalski, *Protestant Poetics and the Seventeenth-Century Religious Lyric* (Princeton: Princeton University Press, 1979), 404-6.

"Meditation 1.42: Apples of Gold,
in Silver Pictures Shrin'de"

Sr. M. Laurentia, C.J.S., *Expl* 8 (Dec. 1949): 19. Reprinted in *The Explicator Cyclopedia* 2:329.

"Meditation 1.49: Lord, Do Away My Motes:
and Mountains Great"

Michael Schuldiner, "Edward Taylor's 'Problematic' Imagery," *EAL* 13
(Spring 1978): 94-98.

"Meditation 2.1: Oh Leaden Hell.
Lord, Give, Forgie I Pray"

J. Daniel Patterson, *Expl* 43 (Fall 1984): 22.

Robert E. Reiter, "Edward Taylor's *Preparatory Meditations,* Second Series,
Numbers 10-30," *EAL* 5 (Spring 1970): 113-14.

Rowe, *Saint and Singer*, 38-39.

"Meditation 2.3: Like to the Marigold, I Blushing Close"

Robert E. Reiter, "Edward Taylor's *Preparatory Meditations,* Second Series,
Numbers 10-30," *EAL* 5 (Spring 1970): 115-16.

William J. Scheick, "'The Inward Tacles and the Outward Traces': Edward
Taylor's Elusive Transitions," *EAL* 12 (Fall 1977): 169-73.

"Meditation 2.7: All Dull, My Lord,
My Spirits Flat, and Dead"

P.H. Johnson, "Poetry and Praise in Edward Taylor's *Preparatory
Meditations*," *AL* 52 (Mar. 1979): 93-94.

Robert E. Reiter, "Edward Taylor's *Preparatory Meditations,* Second Series,
Numbers 10-30," *EAL* 5 (Spring 1970): 116-18.

Rowe, *Saint and Singer*, 41-42.

"Meditation 2.9: Lord, Let Thy Dazzling
Shine Refracted Fan'de"

Ira Clark, *Christ Revealed: The History of the Neotypological Lyric in the
English Renaissance* (Gainesville: University Presses of Florida, 1982), 173-
74.

Rowe, *Saint and Singer*, 49-51.

"Meditation 2.10: Moses Farewell.
I With a Mournfull Teare"

Ira Clark, *Christ Revealed: The History of the Neotypological Lyric in the English Renaissance* (Gainesville: University Presses of Florida, 1982), 181-82.

William J. Scheick, "'That Blazing Star in Joshua': Edward Taylor's 'Meditation 2.10' and Increase Mather's *Kometographia*," *SCN* 34 (Summer-Fall 1976): 36-37.

"Meditation 2.11: Eternall Love Burnisht In Glory Thick"

Rowe, *Saint and Singer*, 80-84.

"Meditation 2.14: In Whom Are Hid All the
Treasures of Wisdom and Knowledge"

Ira Clark, *Christ Revealed: The History of the Neotypological Lyric in the English Renaissance* (Gainesville: University Presses of Florida, 1982), 169-70.

"Meditation 2.17: Thou Greate Supream,
Thou Infinite First One"

Rowe, *Saint and Singer*, 107-9.

"Meditation 2.20: Didst Thou, Lord,
Cast Mee In a Worship-mould"

Rowe, *Saint and Singer*, 116-19.

"Meditation 2.22: I From the New Moon
of the First Month High"

Rowe, *Saint and Singer*, 199-202.

"Meditation 2.23: Greate Lord, Yea
Greatest Lords of Lords Thou Art"

Ira Clark, *Christ Revealed: The History of the Neotypological Lyric in the English Renaissance* (Gainesville: University Presses of Florida, 1982), 180-81.

Rowe, *Saint and Singer*, 125-27.

William J. Scheick, "Typology and Allegory: A Comparative Study of George Herbert and Edward Taylor," *ELWIU* 2 (Spring 1975): 79-82.

"Meditation 2.25: Guilty, My Lord, What More Can I Declare"

Jeffrey Hammond, "Reading Taylor Exegetically: The *Preparatory Meditations* and the Commentary Tradition," *TSLL* 24 (Winter 1982): 348-57.

"Meditation 2.26: Unclean, Unclean:
My Lord, Undone, All Vile"

Robert E. Reiter, "Edward Taylor's *Preparatory Meditations*, Second Series, Numbers 10-30," *EAL* 5 (Spring 1970): 119-21.

"Meditation 2.27: My Mentall Eye,
Spying Thy Sparkling Fold"

Karen E. Rowe, "A Biblical Illumination of Taylorian Art," *AL* 40 (Nov. 1968): 370-74.

Rowe, *Saint and Singer*, 135-42.

"Meditation 2.43: When, Lord,
I Seeke to Shew Thy Praises, Then"

Robert M. Benton, "Edward Taylor's Use of His Text," *AL* 39 (Mar. 1967): 39-40.

Ira Clark, *Christ Revealed: The History of the Neotypological Lyric in the English Renaissance* (Gainesville: University Presses of Florida, 1982), 174-75.

P.H. Johnson, "Poetry and Praise in Edward Taylor's *Preparatory Meditations,*" *AL* 52 (Mar. 1979): 88-89.

"Meditation 2.47: No Mervaile If My Mite Amaized Bee"

Robert M. Benton, "Edward Taylor's Use of His Text," *AL* 39 (Mar. 1967): 33-38.

"Meditation 2.48: O! What a Thing Is Might Right Mannag'd"

Ira Clark, *Christ Revealed: The History of the Neotypological Lyric in the English Renaissance* (Gainesville: University Presses of Florida, 1982), 117-78.

"Meditation 2.50: The Artist Hand More Gloriously Bright"

Ira Clark, *Christ Revealed: The History of the Neotypological Lyric in the English Renaissance* (Gainesville: University Presses of Florida, 1982), 170-71.

Rowe, *Saint and Singer*, 46-49.

"Meditation 2.56: Should I with Silver Tooles Delve Through the Hill"

Robert R. Hodges, "Edward Taylor's 'Artificiall Man,'" *AL* 31 (Mar. 1959): 76-77.

"Meditation 2.59: Wilt Thou Enoculate within Mine Eye"

Ira Clark, *Christ Revealed: The History of the Neotypological Lyric in the English Renaissance* (Gainesville: University Presses of Florida, 1982), 161-62.

"Meditation 2.62: Oh! Thou, My Lord, Thou King of Saints, Here Mak'st"

Sr. M. Theresa Clare, O.S.F., *Expl* 19 (Dec. 1960): 16. Reprinted in *The Explicator Cyclopedia* 2:329-30.

"Meditation 2.78: Mine Eyes, That at the
Beautious Sight of Fruite"

Donald E. Stanford, "Edward Taylor," in *Major Writers of Early American Literature*, ed. Everett Emerson (Madison: University of Wisconsin Press, 1972), 74-77.

"Meditation 2.103: The Deity Did Call a Parliament"

James W. Barbour, "The Prose Context of Edward Taylor's Anti-Stoddard Meditations," *EAL* 10 (Fall 1975): 149-51.

Ira Clark, *Christ Revealed: The History of the Neotypological Lyric in the English Renaissance* (Gainesville: University Presses of Florida, 1982), 165-66.

Rowe, *Saint and Singer*, 191-94.

"Meditation 2.106: I Fain Would Prize,
and Praise Thee, Lord, But Finde"

James W. Barbour, "The Prose Context of Edward Taylor's Anti-Stoddard Meditations," *EAL* 10 (Fall 1975): 151-55.

"Meditation 2.108: What Royall Feast Magnificent Is This"

James W. Barbour, "The Prose Context of Edward Taylor's Anti-Stoddard Meditations," *EAL* 10 (Fall 1975): 146-48.

"Meditation 2.109: A Feast Is Said to Be For Laughter Made"

Rowe, *Saint and Singer*, 223-27.

"Meditation 2.112: Oh! Good, Good, Good,
My Lord. What More Love Yet"

Edward M. Griffin, "The Structure and Language of Taylor's 'Meditation 2.112,'" *EAL* 3 (Winter 1968/1969): 205-8.

"Meditation 2.138"

Karen E. Rowe, "Sacred or Profane?: Edward Taylor's Meditations on Canticles," *MP* 72 (Nov. 1974): 134-36.

"Meditations 2.149: My Blessed-Glorious Lord,
Thy Spouse I Spie"

Jeffrey Hammond, "Reading Taylor Exegetically: The *Preparatory Meditations* and the Commentary Tradition," *TSLL* 24 (Winter 1982): 357-64.

Karen E. Rowe, "Sacred or Profane?: Edward Taylor's Meditations on Canticles," *MP* 72 (Nov. 1974): 134-36.

"Meditation 2.163"

Barbara Lewalski, *Protestant Poetics and the Seventeenth-Century Religious Lyric* (Princeton: Princeton University Press, 1979), 424-25.

"A Metrical History of Christianity"

Keller, *The Example of Edward Taylor*, 141-59.

"Preface" to "God's Determinations"

Donald Stanford, *Edward Taylor* (Minneapolis: University of Minnesota Press, 1965), 29-31.

"Prologue" to "God's Determinations"

W.C. Brown, "Edward Taylor: An American 'Metaphysical,'" *AL* 16 (Nov. 1944): 195-96.

"The Reflection"

John Clendenning, "Piety and Imagery in Edward Taylor's 'The Reflection,'" *AQ* 16 (Summer 1964): 203-10.

Joseph M. Garrison, Jr., "Teaching Early American Literature: Some Suggestions," *CE* 31 (Feb. 1970): 492-94.

Austin Warren, "Edward Taylor's Poetry: Colonial Baroque," *KR* 3 (Summer 1941): 368-70.

Warren, *Rage for Order*, 16-17.

"Upon a Spider Catching a Fly"

Judson Boyce Allen, "Edward Taylor's Catholic Wasp: Exegetical Convention in 'Upon a Spider Catching a Fly,'" *ELN* 7 (June 1970): 257-60.

Robert Secor, *Expl* 26 (Jan. 1968): 42.

"Upon the Death of My Endeared, and Tender Wife"

Daly, *God's Altar*, 166-69.

"Upon the Death of That Holy and Reverend Man of God, Mr. Samuel Hooker"

Norman Grabo, *Edward Taylor* (New York: Twayne, 1961), 130-34.

"Upon the Sweeping Flood"

Sanford Pinsker, "Carnal Love/Excremental Skies: A Reading of Edward Taylor's 'Upon the Sweeping Flood,'" *CP* 8 (Spring 1975): 53-54.

"Upon Wedlock, and Death of Children"

C.R.B. Combellack, *Expl* 29 (Oct. 1970): 12.

Daly, *God's Altar*, 163-66.

Norman Grabo, *Edward Taylor* (New York: Twayne, 1961), 128-30.

Cecilia L. Halbert, "Tree of Life Imagery in the Poetry of Edward Taylor," *AL* 38 (Mar. 1966): 22-25.

Keller, *The Example of Edward Taylor*, 46-47.

Gene Russell, *Expl* 27 (May 1969): 71.

Jes Simmons, *Expl* 42 (Fall 1983): 17.

THOREAU, HENRY DAVID

"All Things Are Current Found"

Carl Dennis, "Correspondence in Thoreau's Nature Poetry," *ESQ*, no. 58 (Part 3 1970): 105.

"The Cliffs & Springs"

Arthur L. Ford, "The Poetry of Henry David Thoreau," *ESQ*, no. 61 (1970): 18-19.

"The Fisher's Son"

Williard Bonner, *Harp on the Shore: Thoreau and the Sea* (Albany: State University of New York Press, 1985), 62-64.

"It Is No Dream of Mine"

Carl Dennis, "Correspondence in Thoreau's Nature Poetry," *ESQ*, no. 58 (Part 3 1970): 107.

"I Was Born upon They Bank River"

Carl Dennis, "Correspondence in Thoreau's Nature Poetry," *ESQ*, no. 58 (Part 3 1970): 107.

"Light-winged Smoke"

Carl Dennis, "Correspondence in Thoreau's Nature Poetry," *ESQ*, no. 58 (Part 3 1970): 108.

"May Morning"

Douglas V. Noverr, "Thoreau's 'May Morning': Nature, Poetic Vision, and the Poet's Publication of His Truth," *Thoreau Quarterly* 2 (15 July 1970), 7-10

"My Boots"

Arthur L. Ford, "The Poetry of Henry David Thoreau," *ESQ*, no. 61 (1970): 19.

"Poem, No. 189"

Mary S. Mattfield, "Thoreau's Poem #189: An Emended Reading," *CEA* 33 (Nov. 1970): 10-12.

"The Sluggish Smoke"

Arthur L. Ford, "The Poetry of Henry David Thoreau," *ESQ* no. 61 (1970): 16-18.

"Smoke"

Delmer Rodabaugh, *Expl* 17 (Apr. 1959): 47. Reprinted in *The Explicator Cyclopedia* 2:343-44.

"Smoke in the Winter"

Matthiessen, *The American Renaissance*, 165-66.

"With Frontier Strength Ye Stand Your Ground"

Williard Bonner, *Harp on the Shore: Thoreau and the Sea* (Albany: State University of New York Press, 1985), 46-48.

TRUMBULL, JOHN

"Epithalamium"

Alexander Cowie, *John Trumbull: Connecticut Wit* (Chapel Hill: University of North Carolina Press, 1936), 49-52.

"M'Fingal"

Alexander Cowie, *John Trumbull: Connecticut Wit* (Chapel Hill: University of North Carolina Press, 1936), 145-206.

Victor Gimmestad, *John Trumbull* (New York: Twayne, 1974), 77-106.

Leon Howard, *The Connecticut Wits* (Chicago: University of Chicago Press, 1943), 71-77.

"The Progress of Dullness"

Alexander Cowie, *John Trumbull: Connecticut Wit* (Chapel Hill: University of North Carolina Press, 1936), 94-124.

Victor Gimmestad, *John Trumbull* (New York: Twayne, 1974), 59-76.

Leon Howard, *The Connecticut Wits* (Chicago: University of Chicago Press, 1943), 58-66.

TUCKERMAN, FREDERICK GODDARD

"Coralie"

Samuel Golden, *Frederick Goddard Tuckerman* (New York: Twayne, 1966), 118-19.

"The Cricket"

Samuel Golden, *Frederick Goddard Tuckerman* (New York: Twayne, 1966), 108-16.

N. Scott Momaday, "The Heretical Cricket," *SoR* 3 (1967): 43-50.

David Seed, "Alone with God and Nature: The Poetry of John Very and Frederick Goddard Tuckerman," in Lee, *Nineteenth-Century American Poetry*, 188-90.

Winters, *Forms of Discovery*, 259-62.

"Margites"

Samuel Golden, *Frederick Goddard Tuckerman* (New York: Twayne, 1966), 119-21.

"Rhotruda"

Samuel Golden, *Frederick Goddard Tuckerman* (New York: Twayne, 1966), 123-25.

"Sonnet II.23"

David Seed, "Alone with God and Nature: The Poetry of John Very and Frederick Goddard Tuckerman," in Lee, *Nineteenth-Century American Poetry*, 183-84.

"Sonnet IV, Part V"

Samuel Golden, *Frederick Goddard Tuckerman* (New York: Twayne, 1966), 94-95.

"Sonnet XXXVII, Part II: As Eponina Brought, to Move the King"

Edwin H. Cady, "Frederick Goddard Tuckerman," in Godhes, *Essays on American Literature*, 147-48.

Samuel Golden, *Frederick Goddard Tuckerman* (New York: Twayne, 1966), 80-82.

"Under the Locust Blossom"

Samuel Golden, *Frederick Goddard Tuckerman* (New York: Twayne, 1966), 117-18.

"An Upper Chamber in a Darkened House"

Edwin H. Cady, "Frederick Goddard Tuckerman," in Godhes, *Essays on American Literature*, 149-51.

Eugene England, "Tuckerman's Sonnet I:10: The First Post-Symbolist Poem," *SoR* 12 (Apr. 1976): 323-47.

VERY, JONES

"The Autumn Leaf"

Edwin Gittleman, *Jones Very: The Effective Years, 1833-40* (New York and London: Columbia University Press, 1967), 140-41.

"The Baker's Island Lights"

Carl Dennis, "Correspondence in Very's Nature Poetry," *NEQ* 43 (June 1970): 265-66.

"Beauty"

Edwin Gittleman, *Jones Very: The Effective Years, 1833-40* (New York and London: Columbia University Press, 1967), 153-55.

"The Columbine"

Carl Dennis, "Correspondence in Very's Nature Poetry," *NEQ* 43 (June 1970): 263-65.

"The Hand and Foot"

Yvor Winters, "Jones Very: A New England Mystic," *American Review* 7 (May 1936): 161-63.

Winters, *Maule's Curse*, 127-29. Reprinted in Winters, *In Defense of Reason*, 264-66.

"Hast Thou Ever Heard the Voice of Nature"

Edwin Gittleman, *Jones Very: The Effective Years, 1833-40* (New York and London: Columbia University Press, 1967), 28-32.

"The Holy of Holies"

David Seed, "Alone with God and Nature: The Poetry of Jones Very and Frederick Goddard Tuckerman," in Lee, *Nineteenth-Century American Poetry*, 176-77.

"The Lost"

Carl Dennis, "Correspondence in Very's Nature Poetry," *NEQ* 43 (June 1970): 268-70.

Yvor Winters, "Jones Very: A New England Mystic," *American Review* 7 (May 1936): 171-72.

Winters, *Maule's Curse*, 138-39. Reprinted in Winters, *In Defense of Reason*, 274-76.

"Man in Harmony with Nature"

Carl Dennis, "Correspondence in Very's Nature Poetry," *NEQ* 43 (June 1970): 257-58.

"Nature"

Edwin Gittleman, *Jones Very: The Effective Years, 1833-40* (New York and London: Columbia University Press, 1967), 173-75.

"The New Birth"

Carl Dennis, "Correspondence in Very's Nature Poetry," *NEQ* 43 (June 1970): 259.

"The Puritans"

David Seed, "Alone with God and Nature: The Poetry of Jones Very and Frederick Goddard Tuckerman," in Lee, *Nineteenth-Century American Poetry*, 171-73.

"The Revelation of the Spirit Through the Material World"

Carl Dennis, "Correspondence in Very's Nature Poetry," *NEQ* 43 (June 1970): 259-60.

"The Son"

David Seed, "Alone with God and Nature: The Poetry of Jones Very and Frederick Goddard Tuckerman," in Lee, *Nineteenth-Century American Poetry*, 178-79.

"The Song"

Edwin Gittleman, *Jones Very: The Effective Years, 1833-40* (New York and London: Columbia University Press, 1967), 175-77.

"To the Canary Bird"

Carl Dennis, "Correspondence in Very's Nature Poetry," *NEQ* 43 (June 1970): 261-62.

Edwin Gittleman, *Jones Very: The Effective Years, 1833-40* (New York and London: Columbia University Press, 1967), 143-45.

"The Tree" (*Poems and Essays*, 1886, 70)

Carl Dennis, "Correspondence in Very's Nature Poetry," *NEQ* 43 (June 1970): 262-63.

"The Tree" (*Poems and Essays*, 1886, 121)

Carl Dennis, "Correspondence in Very's Nature Poetry," *NEQ* 43 (June 1970): 267-68.

"The True Light"

Carl Dennis, "Correspondence in Very's Nature Poetry," *NEQ* 43 (June 1970): 258-59.

WHEATLEY, PHILLIS

"America"

Sondra O'Neale, "A Slave's Subtle War: Phillis Wheatley's Use of Biblical Myth and Symbol," *EAL* (Fall 1986), 153-54.

"An Elegy on Leaving --"

M.A. Isani, "'An Elegy on Leaving --': A New Poem by Phillis Wheatley," *AL* 58 (Dec. 1986): 609-13.

"On Being Brought from Africa"

James A. Levernier, *Expl* 40 (Fall 1981): 25.

Sondra O'Neale, "A Slave's Subtle War: Phillis Wheatley's Use of Biblical Myth and Symbol," *EAL* (Fall 1986), 147-48.

"On Liberty and Peace"

Angelene Jamison, "Analysis of Selected Poetry of Phillis Wheatley," in *Critical Essays on Phillis Wheatley*, ed. William Robinson (Boston: G.K. Hall, 1982), 132-33.

"On the Death of Rev. George Whitefield"

William Robinson, *Phillis Wheatley in the Black American Beginnings* (Detroit: Broadside Press, 1975), 39-40.

"To Maecenas"

Terrence Collins, "Phillis Wheatley: The Dark Side of the Poetry," in *Critical Essays on Phillis Wheatley*, ed. William Robinson (Boston: G.K. Hall, 1982), 150-51.

"To the Right Honourable William, Earl of Dartmouth"

Terrence Collins, "Phillis Wheatley: The Dark Side of the Poetry," in *Critical Essays on Phillis Wheatley*, ed. William Robinson (Boston: G.K. Hall, 1982), 152-54.

Angelene Jamison, "Analysis of Selected Poetry of Phillis Wheatley," in *Critical Essays on Phillis Wheatley*, ed. William Robinson (Boston: G.K. Hall, 1982), 133-34.

Sondra O'Neale, "A Slave's Subtle War: Phillis Wheatley's Use of Biblical Myth and Symbol," *EAL* (Fall 1986), 156-57.

"To the University of Cambridge in New England"

Terrence Collins, "Phillis Wheatley: The Dark Side of the Poetry," in *Critical Essays on Phillis Wheatley*, ed. William Robinson (Boston: G.K. Hall, 1982), 151-52.

WHITMAN, WALT

"Aboard at a Ship's Helm"

Robert LaRue, "Whitman's Sea: Large Enough for Moby Dick," *WWR* 12 (Sept. 1966): 57.

Douglas A. Noverr, "'Aboard as a Ship's Helm: A Minor Sea Drama, The Poet, and The Soul," *WWR* 17 (Mar. 1971): 23-25.

"An Army Corp on the March"

Waskow, *Whitman*, 112-13.

"As I Ebb'd with the Ocean of Life"

Gay Wilson Allen, *Solitary Singer: A Critical Biography of Walt Whitman* (New York: New York University Press, 1967), 246-48.

Melvin W. Askew, "Whitman's 'As I Ebb'd with the Ocean of Life,'" *WWR* 10 (Dec. 1964): 87-92.

Stephen A. Black, "Radical Utterances from the Soul's Abysms: Toward a New Sense of Whitman," *PMLA* 88 (Jan. 1973): 103-4.

Black, *Whitman's Journeys into Chaos*, 55-61.

Harold Bloom, "The Central Man: Emerson, Whitman, Wallace Stevens," *MR* 7 (Winter 1966): 34-36.

Bloom, *A Map of Misreading*, 178-84.

Carlisle, *The Uncertain Self*, 83-87.

Cavitch, *My Soul and I*, 139-45.

David Cavitch, "Whitman's Mystery," *SIR* 17 (Spring 1978): 105-6.

Chase, *Walt Whitman Reconsidered*, 124-27.

Lawrence Kramer, "Ocean and Vision: Imaginative Dilemma in Wordsworth, Whitman, and Stevens," *JEGP* 79 (Apr. 1980): 219-24.

Robert LaRue, "Whitman's Sea: Large Enough for Moby Dick," *WWR* 12 (Sept. 1966): 52-54.

Miller, *Walt Whitman's Poetry*, 44-48.

Jon Rosenblatt, "Whitman's Body, Whitman's Language," in *Whitman Here and Now*, ed. Joann Krieg (Westport: Greenwood Press, 1985), 106-113.

Salska, *Walt Whitman and Emily Dickinson*, 72-76.

Schyberg, *Walt Whitman*, 149-51.

Waskow, *Whitman*, 202-10.

Larzer Ziff, "Whitman and the Crowd," *CritI* 10 (June 1984): 588-89.

"The Base of All Metaphysics"

Joan Berbrich, *Three Voices from Paumanok* (Port Washington: Ira J. Friedman, 1969), 140-41.

R. Galen Hanson, "A Critical Reflection on Whitman's 'The Base of All Metaphysics,'" *WWR* 18 (June 1972): 67-70.

"A Boston Ballad (1854)"

Stephen D. Malin, "'A Boston Ballad' and the Boston Riot," *WWR* 9 (Sept. 1963) 51-57.

Edward A. Martin, "Whitman's 'A Boston Ballad (1854),'" *WWR* 11 (Sept. 1965): 61-69.

"A Broadway Pageant"

Richard P. Sugg, "Whitman's Symbolic Circle and 'A Broadway Pageant," *WWR* 16 (June 1970): 35-40.

"By Blue Ontario's Shore"

Harold Aspiz, "Walt Whitman: The Spermatic Imagination," *AL* 56 (Oct. 1984): 388-89.

Black, *Whitman's Journeys into Chaos*, 143-50.

Cavitch, *My Soul and I*, 104-5.

Gary A. Culbert, "Whitman's Revisions of 'By Blue Ontario's Shore,'" *WWR* 23 (Mar. 1977): 35-45.

Myrth J. Killingsworth, "Whitman's Love-Spendings," *WWR* 26 (Dec. 1980): 145-53.

James E. Miller, Jr., *Walt Whitman* (New York: Twayne, 1962), 105-6.

Miller, *Walt Whitman's Poetry*, 63-65.

Jeffrey Steinbrink, "'To Span Vast Realms of Space and Time': Whitman's Vision of History," *WWR* 24 (June 1978): 46, 50, 56.

M. Wynn Thomas, *The Lunar Light of Whitman's Poetry* (Cambridge and London: Harvard University Press, 1987), 260-63.

Cecelia Tichi, *New World, New Earth: Environmental Reform in American Literature From the Puritans Through Whitman* (New Haven: Yale University Press, 1979), 225-26.

Waskow, *Whitman*, 98-100.

Willie T. Weathers, "Whitman's Poetic Translations of His 1855 Preface," *AL* 19 (Mar. 1947): 24-27.

"Calamus"

Gay Wilson Allen, *Solitary Singer: A Critical Biography of Walt Whitman* (New York: New York University Press, 1967), 250-57.

Black, *Whitman's Journeys into Chaos*, 197-212.

Lawrence Buell, "Transcendental Catalogue Rhetoric: Vision Versus Form," *AL* 40 (Nov. 1968): 326-28.

Carlisle, *The Uncertain Self*, 121-31.

Cavitch, *My Soul and I*, 126-28, 133-34.

Chase, *Walt Whitman Reconsidered*, 116-17.

Russell A. Hunt, "Whitman's Poetics and the Unity of 'Calamus,'" *AL* 46 (Jan. 1975): 482-94.

Jerome Loving, *Emerson, Whitman, and the American Muse* (Chapel Hill: University of North Carolina Press, 1982), 162-65.

Minor W. Major, "A New Interpretation of Whitman's Calamus Poems," *WWR* 13 (June 1967): 51-54.

Robert Martin, "Conversion and Identity: The 'Calamus' Poems," *WWR* 25 (June 1979): 59-66.

James E. Miller, Jr., "Whitman's 'Calamus': The Leaf and the Root," *PMLA* 72 (Mar. 1957): 249-71.

M. Wynn Thomas, "Whitman's Achievement in the Personal Style in 'Calamus,'" *WWR* 1 (Dec. 1983): 36-47.

"Calamus ," No. 9

R. Galen Hanson, "Anxiety as Human Predicament: Whitman's 'Calamus', no. 9," *WWR* 21 (June 1975): 73-75.

Schyberg, *Walt Whitman*, 163-66.

"Cavalry Crossing a Ford"

Richard Allan Davison, "Mixed Tone in 'Cavalry Crossing a Ford,'" *WWR* 16 (Dec. 1970): 114-17.

Dale Doepke, "Whitman's Theme in 'Cavalry Crossing a Ford,'" *WWR* 18 (Dec. 1972): 132-36.

"Chanting the Square Deific"

Alfred H. Marks, "Whitman's Triadic Imagery," *AL* 23 (Mar. 1951): 112-18.

G.L. Sixbey, "'Chanting the Square Deific'--A Study in Whitman's Religion," *AL* 9 (May 1937): 171-95.

"Children of Adam"

Evie Allen, *Walt Whitman as Man, Poet, and Legend* (Carbondale: Southern Illinois University Press, 1961), 59-62.

Harold Aspiz, "Walt Whitman: The Spermatic Imagination," *AL* 56 (Oct. 1984): 390-94.

Black, *Whitman's Journeys into Chaos*, 212-20.

Carlisle, *The Uncertain Self*, 113-21.

Marilyn Teichert, "Children of Adam: Whitman's Gospel of Sexuality," *WWR* 28 (Mar. 1982): 29.

"A Clear Midnight"

Stephen Mainville and Ronald Schleifer, "Whitman's Printed Leaves: The Literal and Metaphorical in *Leaves of Grass*," *ArQ* 37 (Spring 1981): 26-27.

"Clef Poem"

Stephen A. Black, "Radical Utterances from the Soul's Abysms: Toward a New Sense of Whitman," *PLMA* 88 (Jan. 1973): 101-2.

Black, *Whitman's Journeys into Chaos*, 49-53.

"Crossing Brooklyn Ferry"

Richard P. Adams, "Whitman: A Brief Revaluation," *TSE* 5 (1955): 135-38.

Gay Wilson Allen, *A Reader's Guide to Walt Whitman* (New York: Farrar, Straus & Giroux, 1970), 186-91.

Black, *Whitman's Journeys into Chaos*, 157-67.

John E. Byron, "Significance of T, I, and O in 'Crossing Brooklyn Ferry,'" *WWR* 9 (Dec. 1963): 89-90.

Carlisle, *The Uncertain Self*, 59-72.

Cavitch, *My Soul and I*, 106-13.

Chase, *Walt Whitman Reconsidered*, 107-9.

Stanley Coffman, "Crossing Brooklyn Ferry: A Note on Whitman's Catalogue Technique," in *Walt Whitman: A Collection of Criticism*, ed. Arthur Golden (New York: McGraw-Hill, 1974), 61-71.

F.C. Cronin, "Modern Sensibility in Stanza 2 of 'Crossing Brooklyn Ferry,'" *WWR* 15 (Mar. 1969): 56-57.

Wilson F. Engel, III, "Two Biblical Echoes in 'Crossing Brooklyn Ferry,'" *WWR* 23 (June 1977): 88-90.

Marvin Felheim, "The Problem of Structure in Some Poems by Whitman," in Ludwig, *Aspects of American Poetry*, 91-94.

James W. Gargano, "Technique in 'Crossing Brooklyn Ferry': The Everlasting Moment," *JEGP* 62 (Apr. 1963): 262-69.

Eugene R. Kanjo, "Time and Eternity in 'Crossing Brooklyn Ferry,'" *WWR* 18 (Sept. 1972): 82-90.

Mark Kinkead-Weekes, "Walt Whitman Passes the Full-Stop by. . . . ," in Lee, *Nineteenth-Century American Poetry*, 56-59.

Barbara Kroll, "The 'Confession' in 'Crossing Brooklyn Ferry' and the Jewish Day of Atonement Prayers," *WWR* 23 (Sept. 1977): 125-29.

James Machor, "Pastoralism and the American Urban Ideal: Hawthorne, Whitman, and the Literary Pattern," *AL* 54 (Oct. 1982): 336-40.

James E. Miller, Jr., *Walt Whitman* (New York: Twayne, 1962), 97-98.

Miller, *Walt Whitman's Poetry*, 199-208.

Tenney Nathanson, "Whitman's Tropes of Light and Flood: Language and Representation in the Early Editions of *Leaves of Grass*," *ESQ* 31 (Second Quarter 1985): 115-20, 123-24.

Richard Pascal, "What Is It Then Between Us?: 'Crossing Brooklyn Ferry' As Dramatic Meditation," *WWR* 26 Supplement (1980): 59-70.

Robert Pincus, "On Time and Form in Whitman's 'Crossing Brooklyn Ferry,'" *WWR* 2 (Summer 1984): 12-21.

Susan Strom, "'Face to Face': Whitman's Biblical References," *WWR* 24 (Mar. 1978): 7-16.

Walter Sutton, *American Free Verse: The Modern Revolution in Poetry* (New York: New Directions, 1973), 15-16.

M. Wynn Thomas, *The Lunar Light of Whitman's Poetry* (Cambridge and London: Harvard University Press, 1987), 92-116.

Hyatt H. Waggoner, *American Visionary Poetry* (Baton Rouge: Louisiana State University Press, 1982), 51-53.

Waskow, *Whitman*, 215-222.

Larzer Ziff, "Whitman and the Crowd," *CritI* 10 (June 1984): 587-88.

"Darest Thou Now O Soul"

Jannacone, *Walt Whitman's Poetry*, 41-44.

"The Dismantled Ship"

Walter Sutton, *American Free Verse: The Modern Revolution in Poetry* (New York: New Directions, 1973), 22-23.

"Eidolons"

Lois A. Cudy, "Exploration of Whitman's 'Eidolons,'" *WWR* 19 (Dec. 1973): 153-57.

Phillipa P. Harrison, "'Eidolons': An Entrance-Song," *WWR* 17 (June 1971): 35-45.

Jannacone, *Walt Whitman's Poetry*, 40-41.

"Ethiopia Saluting the Colors"

Jannacone, *Walt Whitman's Poetry*, 23-24.

J.R. LeMasters, "Some Traditional Poems from *Leaves of Grass*," *WWR* 13 (June 1967): 44-51.

"Europe"

Gay Wilson Allen, *A Reader's Guide to Walt Whitman* (New York: Farrar, Straus & Giroux, 1970), 161-64.

"Excelsior"

Thomas W. Ford, "Whitman's 'Excelsior': The Poem as Microcosm," *TSLL* 17 (Winter 1976): 778-85.

"Faces"

Harold Aspiz, "A Reading of Whitman's 'Faces,'" *WWR* 19 (June 1973): 37-48.

Ivan Marki, "The Last Eleven Poems in the 1885 *Leaves of Grass*," *AL* 54 (May 1982): 233-34.

Hyatt H. Waggoner, *American Visionary Poetry* (Baton Rouge: Louisiana State University Press, 1982), 36-38.

"The First Dandelion"

Marilyn De Eulis, "Whitman's 'The First Dandelion' and Emily Dickinson's 'The Dandelion's Pallid Tube,'" *WWR* 25 (Mar. 1979): 29-32.

"A Font of Type"

Stephen Mainville and Ronald Schleifer, "Whitman's Printed Leaves: The Literal and Metaphorical in *Leaves of Grass*," *ArQ* 37 (Spring 1981): 18-19.

"From Pent-up Aching Rivers"

Cavitch, *My Soul and I*, 121-24.

Waskow, *Whitman*, 82-84.

"Give Me the Splendid Silent Sun"

J. Thomas Chaffin, Jr., "Give Me Faces and Streets: Walt Whitman and the City," *WWR* 23 (Sept. 1977): 114-16.

James Machor, "Pastoralism and the American Urban Ideal: Hawthorne, Whitman, and the Literary Pattern," *AL* 54 (Oct. 1982): 332-35.

"Good-bye My Fancy!"

Rose Cherie Reissman, "Recurrent Motifs in 'Good-bye My Fancy,'" *WWR* 21 (Mar. 1975): 29-30, 33.

"Great Are the Myths"

Eric Mottram, "Law and the Open Road: Whitman's America," in Lee, *Nineteenth-Century American Poetry*, 19-20.

"Halcyon Days"

Donald Stauffer, "Walt Whitman and Old Age," *WWR* 24 (Dec. 1978): 144-46.

"I Hear It Was Charged Against Me"

J. Thomas Chaffin, Jr., "Give Me Faces and Streets: Walt Whitman and the City," *WWR* 23 (Sept. 1977): 116.

"In Cabin'd Ships at Sea"

Stephen Mainville and Ronald Schleifer, "Whitman's Printed Leaves: The Literal and Metaphorical in *Leaves of Grass*," *ArQ* 37 (Spring 1981): 22-23.

"In Paths Untrodden"

Cavitch, *My Soul and I*, 126-27.

Stephen Mainville and Ronald Schleifer, "Whitman's Printed Leaves: The Literal and Metaphorical in *Leaves of Grass*," *ArQ* 37 (Spring 1981): 23-24.

Waskow, *Whitman*, 88-91.

"I Saw in Louisiana a Live-Oak Growing"

Cavitch, *My Soul and I*, 131-32.

Waskow, *Whitman*, 78-80.

"I Sing the Body Electric"

David Cavitch, "Whitman's Mystery," *SIR* 17 (Spring 1978): 106-7.

Robert Coskren, "A Reading of Whitman's 'I Sing the Body Electric,'" *WWR* 22 (Sept. 1976): 125-32.

John H. Matle, "The Body Acclaimed," *WWR* 16 (Dec. 1970): 110-14.

Waskow, *Whitman*, 84-88.

"I Thought That Knowledge Alone Would Suffice"

Cavitch, *My Soul and I*, 134-36.

"The Last Invocation"

Jannacone, *Walt Whitman's Poetry*, 181-85.

"Lingering Last Drops"

Rose Cherie Reissman, "Recurrent Motifs in 'Good-bye My Fancy,'" *WWR* 21 (Mar. 1975): 32-33.

"A March in the Ranks Hard-Prest, and the Road Unknown"

Harold Aspiz, *Walt Whitman and the Body Beautiful* (Urbana: University of Illinois Press, 1980), 88-89.

Dominick A. Labianca and William J. Reeves, "'A March in the Ranks Hard-Prest, and the Road Unknown': A Chemical Analysis," *AN&Q* 15 (Apr. 1977): 110-11.

"Myself and Mine"

Eric Mottram, "Law and the Open Road: Whitman's America," in Lee, *Nineteenth-Century American Poetry*, 17-19.

"The Mystic Trumpeter"

Jannacone, *Walt Whitman's Poetry*, 177-79.

W.L. Werner, "Whitman's 'The Mystic Trumpeter' as Autobiography," *AL* 7 (Jan. 1936): 455-60.

"Native Moments"

Waskow, *Whitman*, 77-78.

"A Noiseless Patient Spider"

Bert Case Diltz, *Sense or Nonsense: Contemporary Education at the Crossroads* (Toronto: McCelland & Stewart, 1972), 100-101.

Wilton Eckley, *Expl* 22 (Nov. 1963): 20.

Stephen Mainville and Ronald Schleifer, "Whitman's Printed Leaves: The Literal and Metaphorical in *Leaves of Grass*," *ArQ* 37 (Spring 1981): 27-28.

Arnold Mersch, "Teilhard de Chardin and Whitman's 'A Noiseless, Patient Spider,'" *WWR* 17 (Sept. 1971): 99-100.

Van Doren, *Introduction to Poetry*, 43-45.

Fred D. White, "Whitman's Cosmic Spider," *WWR* 23 (June 1977): 85-88.

"O Captain, My Captain"

Jannacone, *Walt Whitman's Poetry*, 24-29.

"One Hour to Madness and Joy"

Deborah Barrett, "The Desire for Freedom: Whitman's 'One Hour to Madness and Joy,'" *WWR* 25 (1979): 26-28.

Cavitch, *My Soul and I*, 124-25.

"On Journeys Through the States"

B.J. Leggett, "The Structure of Whitman's 'On Journeys Through the States,'" *WWR* 14 (June 1968): 58-59.

"On the Beach at Night"

Matthiessen, *American Renaissance*, 575-77.

"Our Old Feuillage"

Robert J. Griffin, "Notes on Structural Devices in Whitman's Poetry," *TSL* 6 (1961): 18-19.

Robin P. Hoople, "'Chants Democratic and Native American': A Neglected Sequence in the Growth of *Leaves of Grass*," *AL* 42 (May 1970): 188-89.

Douglas A. Noverr, "Poetic Vision and Locus in Whitman's 'Our Old Feuillage,'" *WWR* 22 (Sept. 1976): 118-22.

M. Wynn Thomas, *The Lunar Light of Whitman's Poetry* (Cambridge and London: Harvard University Press, 1987), 133-36.

"Out of the Cradle"

Richard P. Adams, "Whitman: A Brief Revaluation," *TSE* 5 (1955): 138-40, 146-49.

Evie Allen, *Walt Whitman as Man, Poet, and Legend* (Carbondale: Southern Illinois University Press, 1961), 54-55.

Gay Wilson Allen, *A Reader's Guide to Walt Whitman* (New York: Farrar, Straus & Giroux, 1970), 192-95.

Roy P. Basler, *Expl* 5 (June 1947): 59. Reprinted in *The Explicator Cyclopedia* 2:352.

Stephen A. Black, "Radical Utterances from the Soul's Abysms: Toward a New Sense of Whitman," *PLMA* 88 (Jan. 1973): 107-10.

Black, *Whitman's Journeys into Chaos*, 66-77.

Brooks, Lewis, and Warren, *American Literature*, 941-42.

Carlisle, *The Uncertain Self*, 151-57.

Cavitch, *My Soul and I*, 145-53.

Richard Chase, "'Out of the Cradle' as a Romance," in *The Presence of Walt Whitman: Selected Papers from the English Institute*, ed. R.W.B. Lewis (New York: Columbia University Press, 1962), 52-71.

Richard Chase, *Walt Whitman* (Minneapolis: University of Minnesota Press, 1961), 27-32.

Chase, *Walt Whitman Reconsidered*, 121-24.

Cornelius C. Cunningham, *Literature as a Fine Art: Analysis and Interpretation* (New York: Thomas Nelson and Sons, 1941), 176-85.

Dickinson, *Suggestions for Teachers of "Introduction to Literature,"* 32.

Susan G. Feinberg, *Expl* 37 (Fall 1978): 35.

Marvin Felheim, "The Problem of Structure in Some Poems by Whitman," in Ludwig, *Aspects of American Poetry*, 84-87.

Paul Fussell, Jr., "Whitman's Curious Warble: Reminiscence and Reconciliation," in *The Presence of Walt Whitman: Selected Papers from the English Institute*, ed. R.W.B. Lewis (New York: Columbia University Press, 1962), 28-51.

Hutchinson, *The Ecstatic Whitman*, 122-30.

Neil D. Isaacs, "The Autoerotic Metaphor," *L&P* 15 (Spring 1965): 104-6.

C.W.M. Johnson, *Expl* 5 (May 1947): 52. Reprinted in *The Explicator Cyclopedia* 2:351-52.

Mark Kinkead-Weekes, "Walt Whitman Passes the Full-Stop by. . . . ," in Lee, *Nineteenth-Century American Poetry*, 51-56.

Robert LaRue, "Whitman's Sea: Large Enough for Moby Dick," *WWR* 12 (Sept. 1966): 54-56.

Arthur Lerner, *Psychoanalytically Oriented Criticism of Three American Poets* (Rutherford: Fairleigh Dickinson University Press, 1970), 73-75.

Alfred H. Marks, "Whitman's Triadic Imagery," *AL* 23 (Mar. 1951): 120-26.

Edwin H. Miller, *Walt Whitman's Poetry*, 175-86.

James E. Miller, Jr., *Walt Whitman* (New York: Twayne, 1962), 98-100.

Tracey R. Miller, "The Boy, the Bird, and the Sea: An Archetypal Reading of 'Out of the Cradle,'" *WWR* 19 (Sept. 1973) :93-103.

Char Mollison and Charles Walcutt, "The Emersonian Key to Whitman's 'Out of the Cradle Endlessly Rocking,'" *ArQ* 37 (Spring 1981): 5-16.

Pearce, *The Continuity of American Poetry*, 170-72.

Louise Pound, "Note on Walt Whitman and Bird Poetry," *EJ* 19 (Jan. 1930): 34-36.

Joseph N. Riddel, "Walt Whitman and Wallace Stevens: Functions of a 'Literatus,'" *SAQ* 61 (Autumn 1962): 515-17.

Rosenthal and Smith, *Exploring Poetry*, 695-96.

Salska, *Walt Whitman and Emily Dickinson*, 70-72.

B. Schapiro, "Shelley's 'Alastor' and Whitman's 'Out of the Cradle': The Ambivalent Mother," *AI* 36 (Fall 1979): 245-59.

Schyberg, *Walt Whitman*, 145-49.

Leo Spitzer, "'Explication de Texte' Applied to Whitman's 'Out of the Cradle Endlessly Rocking,'" *ELH* 16 (Sept. 1949): 229-49. Reprinted in *Essays on English and American Literature by Leo Spitzer*, ed. Anna Hatcher (Princeton: Princeton University Press, 1962), 14-36; in *Critical Essays on Walt Whitman*, ed. James Woodress (Boston: G.K. Hall, 1983), 218-27.

Floyd Stovall, "Main Drifts in Whitman's Poetry," *AL* 4 (Mar. 1932): 8-10.

Beverly Luzietti Strohl, "An Interpretation of 'Out of the Cradle,'" *WWR* 10 (Dec. 1964): 83-87.

Walter Sutton, *American Free Verse: The Modern Revolution in Poetry* (New York: New Directions, 1973), 16-19.

Walter Sutton, "Whitman's Poetic Ensembles," in *Whitman: A Collection of Essays*, ed. Roy Harvey Pearce (Englewood Cliffs: Prentice-Hall, 1962), 124-27.

Charles C. Walcutt, "Whitman's 'Out of the Cradle Endlessly Rocking,'" *CE* 10 (Feb. 1949): 277-79.

Harry R. Warfel, "'Out of the Cradle Endlessly Rocking,'" *TSL* 3 (1958): 83-87.

Waskow, *Whitman*, 115-29.

S.E. Whicher, *Expl* 5 (Feb. 1947): 28. Reprinted in *The Explicator Cyclopedia* 2:350-51.

Stephen Whicher, "Whitman's Awakening to Death: Toward a Biographical Reading of 'Out of the Cradle Endlessly Rocking,'" in *The Presence of Walt Whitman: Selected Papers from the English Institute*, ed. R.W.B. Lewis (New York: Columbia University Press, 1962), 1-27. Reprinted in *Walt Whitman: A Collection of Criticism*, ed. Arthur Golden (New York: McGraw-Hill, 1974), 77-96.

"Passage to India"

Richard P. Adams, "Whitman: A Brief Revaluation," *TSE* 5 (1955): 138-40, 141-43.

Harsharam S. Ahluwalia, "A Reading of Whitman's 'Passage to India,'" *WWR* 1 (June 1983): 9-17.

Gay Wilson Allen, *A Reader's Guide to Walt Whitman* (New York: Farrar, Straus & Giroux, 1970), 202-211.

Richard E. Amacher, *Expl* 9 (Dec. 1950): 2. Reprinted in *The Explicator Cyclopedia* 2:352-53.

Blair, Hornberger, and Stewart, *The Literature of the United States*, 2:217.

Carlisle, *The Uncertain Self*, 170-76.

Cavitch, *My Soul and I*, 179-81.

S.K. Coffman, Jr., "Form and Meaning in Whitman's 'Passage to India,'" *PMLA* 70 (June 1955): 337-49.

David Daiches, "Walt Whitman: Impressionist Poet," in Hindus, *Leaves of Grass: One Hundred Years After*, 120-22.

Marvin Felheim, "The Problem of Structure in Some Poems by Whitman," in Ludwig, *Aspects of American Poetry*, 94-97.

Arthur Golden, "Passage to Less than India: Structure and Meaning in Whitman's 'Passage to India,'" *PMLA* 88 (Oct. 1973): 1095-1103.

Clare R. Goldfarb, "The Poet's Role in 'Passage to India,'" *WWR* 8 (Dec. 1962): 75-79.

Emory Holloway, *Free and Lonesome Heart: The Secret of Walt Whitman* (New York: Vantage Press, 1960): 125-26.

Hutchinson, *The Ecstatic Whitman*, 176-82.

Jannacone, *Walt Whitman's Poetry*, 173-74.

Joel R. Kehler, "A Typological Reading of 'Passage to India,'" *ESQ* 23 (Second Quarter 1977): 123-29.

James S. Leonard, *Expl* 39 (Summer 1981): 15.

Stephen Mainville and Ronald Schleifer, "Whitman's Printed Leaves: The Literal and Metaphorical in *Leaves of Grass*," *ArQ* 37 (Spring 1981): 24-26.

Edwin H. Miller, *Walt Whitman's Poetry*, 212-22.

James E. Miller, Jr., *A Critical Guide to Leaves of Grass* (Chicago: University of Chicago Press, 1957), 120-29.

Richardson, *Myth and Literature*, 147-49.

Judge M. Schonfeld, "No Exit in 'Passage to India': Existence Precedes Essence in Section 5," *WWR* 19 (Dec. 1973): 147-51.

Schyberg, *Walt Whitman*, 228-32.

Som P. Sharma, "Self, Soul, and God in 'Passage to India,'" *CE* 27 (Feb. 1966): 394-99.

Ruth Slonim, "Walt Whitman's 'Open Road,'" *RS* 25 (Mar. 1957): 72-74.

Ruth Stauffer, *Expl* 9 (May 1951): 50. Reprinted in *The Explicator Cyclopedia* 2:353.

Jeffrey Steinbrink, "'To Span Vast Realms of Space and Time': Whitman's Vision of History," *WWR* 24 (June 1978): 51, 58.

Floyd Stovall, "Main Drifts in Whitman's Poetry," *AL* 4 (Mar. 1932): 1-21.

Charles Stubblefield, "The Great Circle: Whitman's 'Passage to India,'" *PrS* 49 (Spring 1975): 19-30.

"Patroling Barnegat"

Gregory Haynes, "Running around in Barnegat Bay: Whitman's Symbols and Their Rhetorical Intentionalities," in *Whitman Here and Now*, ed. Joann Krieg (Westport: Greenwood Press, 1985), 116-22.

Raymond G. Malbone, "Organic Language in 'Patroling Barnegat," *WWR* 13 (Dec. 1967): 125-27.

"Pictures"

George H. Soule, Jr., "Walt Whitman's 'Pictures': An Alternative to Tennyson's 'Palace of Art,'" *ESQ*, no. 22 (First Quarter 1976): 29-47.

"Pioneers! O Pioneers!"

Gay Wilson Allen, "On the Trochaic Meter of 'Pioneers! O Pioneers!'" *AL* 20 (Jan. 1949): 449-51.

Edward G. Fletcher, "Pioneers! O Pioneers!" *AL* 19 (Nov. 1947): 259-61.

Jannacone, *Walt Whitman's Poetry*, 30-36.

Schyberg, *Walt Whitman*, 204-6.

Jeffrey Steinbrink, "'To Span Vast Realms of Space and Time': Whitman's Vision of History," *WWR* 24 (June 1978): 56.

"Poem of the Many in One"

Cavitch, *My Soul and I*, 104.

"Poem of Wonder at the Resurrection of the Wheat"

Cavitch, *My Soul and I*, 88-90.

"A Prairie Sunset"

R. Galen Hanson, "Whitman as Hymnwriter: Notes on 'A Prairie Sunset,'" *WWR* 27 (Sept. 1981): 135-36.

"Prayer of Columbus"

Carlisle, *The Uncertain Self*, 88-91.

"Proto-leaf"

Hutchinson, *The Ecstatic Whitman*, 110-22.

"Proud Music of the Storm"

Sydney J. Krause, "Whitman, Music, and *Proud Music of the Storm*," *PMLA* 72 (Sept. 1957): 707-16.

James C. McCullagh, "'Proud Music of the Storm': A Study in Dynamics," *WWR* 21 (June 1975): 66-73.

Tenney Nathanson, "Whitman's Tropes of Light and Flood: Language and Representation in the Early Editions of *Leaves of Grass*," *ESQ* 31 (Second Quarter 1985): 122-23.

"A Riddle Song"

Louise Kawada, "The Truth about 'A Riddle Song,'" *WWR* 27 (June 1981): 78-81.

C. Scott Pugh, "The End as Means in 'A Riddle Song,'" *WWR* 23 (June 1977): 82-85.

"Respondez"

Eric Mottram, "Law and the Open Road: Whitman's America," in Lee, *Nineteenth-Century American Poetry*, 23-25.

Waskow, *Whitman*, 213-15.

"Sail Out for Good, Eidolon Yacht!"

Rose Cheris Reissman, "Recurrent Motifs in *Good-bye My Fancy*," *WWR* 21 (Mar. 1975):29, 32-33.

"Salut au Monde"

David Daiches, "Walt Whitman: Impressionist Poet," in Hindus, *Leaves of Grass: One Hundred Years After*, 114-16.

Alvin Rosenfeld, "The Poem as Dialogical Process: A New Reading of 'Salut au Monde,'" *WWR* 10 (June 1964): 34-40.

William Vance, "Whitman's Lonely Orbit: 'Salut au Monde,'" *WWR* 25 (Mar. 1979): 3-13.

"Scented Herbage of My Breast"

Chase, *Walt Whitman Reconsidered*, 117-20.

Philip V. Coleman, "Walt Whitman's Ambiguities of 'I,'" *PLL* 5 Supplement (Summer 1969): 41-42.

Roberts French, "Whitman in Crisis: A Reading of 'Scented Herbage of My Breast,'" *WWR* 24 (1978): 29-32.

Miller, *Walt Whitman's Poetry*, 151-53.

Waskow, *Whitman*, 91-94.

"Sea Drift"

Cavitch, *My Soul and I*, 139-53.

"A Sight in the Camp in the Daybreak Gray and Dim"

Walter Sutton, *American Free Verse: The Modern Revolution in Poetry* (New York: New Directions, 1973), 21-22.

Robert B. Sweet, "A Writer Looks at Whitman's 'A Sight in the Camp in the Daybreak Gray and Dim,'" *WWR* 17 (June 1971): 58-62.

James T.F. Tanner, "A Note on Whitman's 'A Sight in Camp,'" *ESQ*, no. 58 (Part Four, 1970): 123-24.

William A. Wortman, "Spiritual Progression in 'A Sight in Camp,'" *WWR* 14 (Mar. 1968): 24-26.

"The Singer in the Prison"

Jannacone, *Walt Whitman's Poetry*, 20-22.

"The Sleepers"

Robert E. Abrams, "The Function of Dreams and Dream-Logic in Whitman's Poetry," *TSLL* 17 (Fall 1975): 605-11.

Gay Wilson Allen, *A Reader's Guide to Walt Whitman* (New York: Farrar, Straus & Giroux, 1970), 180-86.

Black, *Whitman's Journeys into Chaos*, 125-37.

Mutlu Blasing, "'The Sleepers': The Problem of the Self in Whitman," *WWR* 21 (Sept. 1975): 111-19.

Carlisle, *The Uncertain Self*, 165-70.

Cavitch, *My Soul and I*, 74-81.

Harry James Cook, "The Individualization of a Poet: The Process of Becoming in Whitman's 'The Sleepers,'" *WWR* 21 (Sept. 1975): 101-11.

Sr. Eva Mary, "Shades of Darkness in 'The Sleepers,'" *WWR* 15 (Sept. 1969): 187-90.

Hutchinson, *The Ecstatic Whitman*, 59-67.

George Hutchinson, "Parallels to Shamanism in 'The Sleepers,'" *WWR* 26 (June 1980): 43-52.

Joyce Kornblatt, "Whitman's Vision of the Past in 'The Sleepers,'" *WWR* 16 (Sept. 1970): 86-89.

Ivan Marki, "The Last Eleven Poems in the 1885 *Leaves of Grass*," *AL* 54 (May 1982): 234-35.

Ivan Marki, *The Trial of the Poet: An Interpretation of the First Edition of 'Leaves of Grass*,'" (New York: Columbia University Press, 1974), 235-39.

Robert K. Martin, *Expl* 33 (Oct. 1974): 13.

Matthiessen, *American Renaissance*, 572-73.

Edwin H. Miller, *Walt Whitman's Poetry*, 72-84.

James E. Miller, Jr., *Walt Whitman* (New York: Twayne, 1962), 106-8.

Pearce, *The Continuity of American Poetry*, 168-70.

Francis E. Skipp, "Whitman's Lucifer: A Footnote to 'The Sleepers,'" *WWR* 11 (June 1965): 52-53.

R.W. Vince, "A Reading of 'The Sleepers,'" *WWR* 18 (Mar. 1972): 17-28.

James Perrin Warren, "Rhetoric in 'The Sleepers,'" *WWR* 5 (Fall 1987): 16-34.

Waskow, *Whitman*, 136-57.

"So Long"

Hutchinson, *The Ecstatic Whitman*, 130-35.

"Song for Occupations"

Hollis, *Language and Style in "Leaves of Grass*," 108-14.

Robin P. Hoople, "'Chants Democratic and Native American': A Neglected Sequence in the Growth of *Leaves of Grass*," *AL* 42 (May 1970): 187-88.

Ivan Marki, *The Trial of the Poet: An Interpretation of the First Edition of 'Leaves of Grass*,'" (New York: Columbia University Press, 1974), 232-33.

M. Wynn Thomas, *The Lunar Light of Whitman's Poetry* (Cambridge and London: Harvard University Press, 1987), 12-21.

"A Song of Joys"

Roger Asselineau, *The Evolution of Walt Whitman* (Cambridge: Belknap Press, Harvard University Press, 1960), 190-91.

Joan Berbrich, *Three Voices from Paumanok* (Port Washington: Ira J. Friedman, 1969), 129-50.

Carlisle, *The Uncertain Self*, 79-83.

Donald Stauffer, "Walt Whitman and Old Age," *WWR* 24 (Dec. 1978): 143.

"Song of Myself"

Richard P. Adams, "Whitman: A Brief Revaluation," *TSE* 5 (1955): 144-45.

Richard R. Adicks, "The Sea-Fight Episode in 'Song of Myself,'" *WWR* 13 (Mar. 1967): 16-21.

Gay Wilson Allen, *A Reader's Guide to Walt Whitman* (New York: Farrar, Straus & Giroux, 1970), 131-48, 170-80.

Gay Wilson Allen, *Solitary Singer: A Critical Biography of Walt Whitman* (New York: New York University Press, 1967), 157-64.

Harold Aspiz, "'The Body Electric': Science, Sex, and Metaphor," *WWR* 24 (Dec. 1978): 137-42.

Harold Aspiz, "Walt Whitman: The Spermatic Imagination," *AL* 56 (Oct. 1984): 379-88.

Harold Aspiz, *Walt Whitman and the Body Beautiful* (Urbana: University of Illinois Press, 1980), 56-61.

Roger Asselineau, *The Evolution of Walt Whitman* (Cambridge: Belknap Press, Harvard University Press, 1960), 67-70.

Sally Ann Batchelor, "Whitman's Yawp and How He Yawped It," *WWR* 18 (Sept. 1972): 97-101.

Adrianne Baytop, "'Song of Myself' 52: Motion as Vehicle for Meaning," *WWR* 18 (Sept. 1972): 101-3.

Joel Jay Belson, "Whitman's 'Overstaid Fraction,'" *WWR* 17 (June 1971): 63-65.

Joan Berbrich, *Three Voices from Paumanok* (Port Washington: Ira J. Friedman, 1969), 166-67.

Black, *Whitman's Journeys into Chaos*, 88-118.

Blasing, *American Poetry*, 121-26, 130-31.

Bloom, *Poetry and Repression*, 248-66.

Carlisle, *The Uncertain Self*, 177-204.

Eric W. Carlson, *Expl* 18 (Nov. 1959): 13. Reprinted in *The Explicator Cyclopedia* 2:353-54.

Cavitch, *My Soul and I*, 45-71.

David Cavitch, "Whitman's Mystery," *SIR* 17 (Spring 1978): 105-28.

Richard Chase, "One's Self I Sing," in Feidelson and Brodtkorb, *Interpretations of American Literature*, 176-185.

Chase, *Walt Whitman Reconsidered*, 58-98.

Ann Cleary, "The Prism and Night Vision: Walt Whitman's Use of Color in 'Song of Myself,'" *WWR* 26 (Sept. 1980): 92-100.

Philip Y. Coleman, "Walt Whitman's Ambiguities of 'I,'" *PLL* 5 Supplement (Summer 1969): 45-59.

Malcolm Cowley, "An Analysis of 'Song of Myself,'" in *Critical Essays on Walt Whitman*, ed. James Woodress (Boston: G.K. Hall, 1983), 258-70.

Malcolm Cowley, "Walt Whitman's Buried Masterpiece," *Saturday Review* 42 (31 Oct. 1959): 11-13, 32-34.

David Daiches, "Walt Whitman: Impressionist Poet," in Hindus, *Leaves of Grass: One Hundred Years After*, 110-13.

Joseph M. DeFalco, "The Narrative Shift in Whitman's 'Song of Myself,'" *WWR* 9 (Dec. 1963): 82-84.

Griffith Dudding, "The Function of Whitman's Imagery in 'Song of Myself,'1885," *WWR* 13 (Mar. 1967): 3-11.

Massud Farzan, "Whitman and Sufism: Toward 'A Persian Lesson,'" *AL* 47 (Jan. 1976): 574-81.

Ida Fasel, "'Song of Myself' as Prayer," *WWR* 17 (Mar. 1971): 19-22.

Hugh Fausset, *Walt Whitman: Poet of Democracy* (New Haven: Yale University Press, 1942), 116-34.

Richard J. Fein, "Whitman and the Emancipated Self," *CentR* 20 (Winter 1976): 36-49.

Robert Fredrickson, "Public Onanism: Whitman's Song of Himself," *MLQ* 46 (June 1985): 143-60.

Albert Gelpi, *The Tenth Muse: The Psyche of the American Poet* (Cambridge: Harvard University Press, 1975), 169-209.

Sam B. Girgus, "Culture and Post-Culture in Walt Whitman," *CentR* 18 (Fall 1974): 398-400.

Clarence Gohdes, "Section 50 of Whitman's 'Song of Myself,'" *MLN* 75 (Dec. 1960): 654-56.

Robert J. Griffin, *Expl* 21 (Oct. 1962): 16.

Robert J. Griffin, "Notes on Structural Devices in Whitman's Poetry," *TSL* 6 (1961): 15-16.

Brian Harding, *American Literature in Context*. Vol. 2, *1830-1865* (London: Mentheun, 1982), 202-14.

Hollis, *Language and Style in "Leaves of Grass"*, 36-64.

Emory Holloway, *Free and Lonesome Heart: The Secret of Walt Whitman* (New York: Vantage Press, 1960): 78-79.

Chaviva Hosek, "The Rhetoric of Whitman's 1855 'Song of Myself,'" *CentR* 20 (Summer 1976): 263-77.

Hutchinson, *The Ecstatic Whitman*, 67-94.

Jannacone, *Walt Whitman's Poetry*, 61-64, 171-72.

D.R. Jarvis, "Whitman and Speech-based Prosody, " *WWR* 27 (June 1981): 51-60.

David J. Johnson, "The Effect of Suspension Dots, Parentheses, and Italics on Lyricism of 'Song of Myself,'" *WWR* 21 (June 1975): 47-58.

Kenneth G. Johnston and John O. Rees, Jr., *WWR* 17 (Mar. 1971): 3-10.

Dwight Kalita, "Walt Whitman: Ecstatic Sea-Voyager," *WWR* 21 (Mar. 1975): 14-21.

T.J. Kallsen, "The Improbabilities of Section 11 of 'Song of Myself,'" *WWR* 15 (Sept. 1967): 87-92.

T.J. Kallsen, "'Song of Myself': Logical Unity through Analogy," *WVUPP* 9 (June 1953): 33-40.

Karl Keller, "Alephs, Zahirs, and the Triumph of Ambiguity: Typology in Nineteenth-Century American Literature," in Miner, *Literary Uses of Typology from the Late Middle Ages to the Present*, 290-91.

Karl Keller, "Walt Whitman Camping," 26 (Dec. 1980): 138-44.

Anetta Kelley, *Expl* 46 (Fall 1987): 22-23.

Diane Kepner, "From Spears to Leaves: Walt Whitman's Theory of Nature in 'Song of Myself,'" *AL* 51 (May 1979): 179-204.

James A. Kilby, "Walt Whitman's 'Trippers and Askers,'" *AN&Q* 4 (Nov. 1965): 37-39.

Mark Kinkead-Weekes, "Walt Whitman Passes the Full-Stop by. . . . ," in Lee, *Nineteenth-Century American Poetry*, 43-60.

John Kinnaird, "The Paradox of American 'Identity,'" *PR* 25 (Summer 1958): 385-94.

Donald D. Kummings, "The Vernacular Hero in Whitman's 'Song of Myself,'" *WWR* 23 (Mar. 1977): 23-24.

David Charles Leonard, "Lamarckian Evolution in Whitman's 'Song of Myself,'" *WWR* 24 (1978): 21-28.

Herbert Levine, "Union and Disunion in 'Song of Myself,'" *AL* 59 (Dec. 1987): 570-89.

T.O. Mabbott, *Expl* 5 (Apr. 1947): 43. Reprinted in *The Explicator Cyclopedia* 2:354.

T.O. Mabbott, *Expl* 11 (Mar. 1953): 34. Reprinted in *The Explicator Cyclopedia* 2:354-55.

Robin Magowan, "The Horse of Gods: Possession in 'Song of Myself,'" *WWR* 15 (June 1969): 67-76.

Ivan Marki, *The Trial of the Poet: An Interpretation of the First Edition of 'Leaves of Grass,'* (New York: Columbia University Press, 1974), 91-227.

John B. Mason, "Walt Whitman's Catalogues: Rhetorical Means for Two Journeys in 'Song of Myself,'" *AL* 45 (Mar. 1973): 34-49.

Matthiessen, *American Renaissance*, 535, 547-49.

Edwin H. Miller, *Walt Whitman's Poetry*, 19-22, 86-114.

James E. Miller, Jr., "'Song of Myself' as Inverted Mystical Experience," *PMLA* 70 (Sept. 1955): 636-61.

James E. Miller, Jr., *Walt Whitman* (New York: Twayne, 1962), 92-97.

James E. Miller, Jr., "Whitman and Eliot: The Poetry of Mysticism," *SWR* 73 (Spring 1958): 114-23.

J. Middleton Murry, "Walt Whitman: The Prophet of Democracy," in Hindus, *Leaves of Grass: One Hundred Years After*, 129-37.

Eric Mottram, "Law and the Open Road: Whitman's America," in Lee, *Nineteenth-Century American Poetry*, 29-32.

James E. Mulqueen, "'Song of Myself': Whitman's Hymn to Eros," *WWR* 20 (June 1974): 60-66.

J.M. Nagle, "Toward Theory of Structure in 'Song of Myself,'" *WWR* 15 (Sept. 1969): 162-71.

Tenney Nathanson, "Whitman's Tropes of Light and Flood: Language and Representation in the Early Editions of *Leaves of Grass*," *ESQ* 31 (Second Quarter 1985): 119, 122, 129.

Raymond Nelson, *Kenneth Patchen and American Mysticism* (Chapel Hill: University of North Carolina, 1984), 86-91.

Mary A. Neuman, "'Song of Myself,' Section 21: An Explication," *WWR* 13 (Sept. 1967): 98-99.

Michael Orth, "Walt Whitman, Metaphysical Teapot: The Structure of 'Song of Myself,'" *WWR* 14 (Mar. 1968): 16-24.

Pearce, *The Continuity of American Poetry*, 72-83, 167-68.

Roy Harvey Pearce, "Toward an American Epic," *HudR* 12 (Autumn 1959): 366-70.

Elizabeth Phillips, "'Song of Myself': The Numbers of the Poem in Relation to Its Form," *WWR* 16 (Sept. 1970): 67-81.

Michael D. Reed, "First Person Persona and the Catalogue in 'Song of Myself,'" *WWR* 23 (Dec. 1977): 147-55.

Alfred S. Reid, "The Structure of 'Song of Myself' Reconsidered," *SHR* 7 (Fall 1973): 507-14.

Dennis Renner, "The Conscious Whitman: Allegorical Manifest Destiny in 'Song of Myself,'" *WWR* 24 (Dec. 1978): 149-55.

Richardson, *Myth and Literature*, 144-45.

A.H. Rose, "Destructive Vision in the First and Last Versions of 'Song of Myself,'" *WWR* 15 (Dec. 1969): 215-22.

P.Z. Rosenthal, "'Dilation' in Whitman's Early Writing," *WWR* 20 (Mar. 1974): 3-14.

Thomas J. Roundtree, "Whitman's Indirect Expression and Its Application to 'Song of Myself,'" *PMLA* 73 (Dec. 1958): 549-55.

Salska, *Walt Whitman and Emily Dickinson*, 43-46, 66-69, 105-6.

Schyberg, *Walt Whitman*, 83-98.

Carl F. Strauch, "The Structure of Walt Whitman's 'Song of Myself,'" *EJ* 27, College ed. (Sept. 1938): 597-607.

Jeffrey Steele, *The Representation of the Self in the American Renaissance* (Chapel Hill: University of North Carolina Press, 1987), 67-99.

Walter Sutton, *American Free Verse: The Modern Revolution in Poetry* (New York: New Directions, 1973), 12-15.

Stephen Tapscott, "Leaves of Myself: Whitman's Egypt in 'Song of Myself,'" *AL* 50 (Mar. 1978): 49-73.

M. Wynn Thomas, *The Lunar Light of Whitman's Poetry* (Cambridge and London: Harvard University Press, 1987), 40-71.

George Y. Trail, "'Song of Myself': Events in Micro-structure," *WWR* 25 (Sept. 1979): 106-13.

George Y. Trail, "Whitman's Spear of Summer Grass: Epic Invocations in 'Song of Myself,'" *WWR* 23 (Sept. 1977): 120-25.

Hyatt H. Waggoner, *American Visionary Poetry* (Baton Rouge: Louisiana State University Press, 1982), 48-51.

Wallace, *God Be with the Clown*, 53-75.

James Perrin Warren, "The 'Real Grammar': Deverbal Style in 'Song of Myself,'" *AL* 56 (Mar. 1984): 1-16.

Waskow, *Whitman*, 158-89.

Ward Welty, "The Persona as Kosmos in 'Song of Myself,'" *WWR* 25 (1979): 98-105.

Donez Xiques, "Whitman's Catalogues and the Preface of *Leaves of Grass*, 1855," *WWR* 23 (June 1977): 70.

Paul Zweig, *Walt Whitman: The Making of the Poet* (New York: Basic Books, 1984), 248-75.

"Song of the Banner at Day-Break"

Schyberg, *Walt Whitman*, 193-95.

"Song of the Broad-Axe"

Black, *Whitman's Journeys into Chaos*, 151-57.

David Cavitch, "The Lament in 'Song of the Broad-Axe," in *Whitman Here and Now*, ed. Joann Krieg (Westport: Greenwood Press, 1985), 125-35.

Cavitch, *My Soul and I*, 90-96.

Stanley Coffman, Jr., *Expl* 12 (Apr. 1954): 39.

Robin P. Hoople, "'Chants Democratic and Native American': A Neglected Sequence in the Growth of *Leaves of Grass*," *AL* 42 (May 1970): 185-87.

James E. Miller, Jr., *Walt Whitman* (New York: Twayne, 1962), 103-5.

Linda S. Peavy, "'Wooded Flesh and Metal Bone': A Look at the Riddle of the Broad-Axe," *WWR* 20 (Dec. 1974): 152-54.

Cecelia Tichi, *New World, New Earth: Environmental Reform in American Literature From the Puritans Through Whitman* (New Haven: Yale University Press, 1979), 228-44.

"Song of the Open Road"

Paul Bove, *Destructive Poetics* (New York: Columbia University Press, 1980), 168-70.

Carlisle, *The Uncertain Self*, 1-15.

Cavitch, *My Soul and I*, 83-87.

Chase, *Walt Whitman Reconsidered*, 103-6.

David Daiches, "Walt Whitman: Impressionist Poet," in Hindus, *Leaves of Grass: One Hundred Years After*, 116-17.

Hollis, *Language and Style in "Leaves of Grass,"* 116-20.

James E. Miller, Jr., *Walt Whitman* (New York: Twayne, 1962), 102-3.

Salska, *Walt Whitman and Emily Dickinson*, 117-19.

Schyberg, *Walt Whitman*, 132-33.

Waskow, *Whitman*, 189-202.

"Song of the Redwood Tree"

Richardson, *Myth and Literature*, 145-47.

Cecelia Tichi, *New World, New Earth: Environmental Reform in American Literature from the Puritans through Whitman* (New Haven: Yale University Press, 1979), 244-49.

"A Song of the Rolling Earth"

Eugene Chesnick, "Whitman and the Poetry of the Trillions," *WWR* 22 (Mar. 1976): 18-21.

James Griffin, "The Pregnant Muse: Language and Birth in 'A Song of the Rolling Earth,'" *WWR* 1 (June 1983): 1-8.

Hollis, *Language and Style in "Leaves of Grass*," 142-46.

Jannacone, *Walt Whitman's Poetry*, 174-77.

Jerome Loving, *Emerson, Whitman, and the American Muse* (Chapel Hill: University of North Carolina Press, 1982), 158-59.

Suzanne Poirier, "'A Song of the Rolling Earth' as Transcendental and Poetic Theory," *WWR* 22 (June 1976): 67-74.

Salska, *Walt Whitman and Emily Dickinson*, 170-72.

Schyberg, *Walt Whitman*, 133-34.

"Sparkles from the Wheel"

Richard Pascal, "Whitman's 'Sparkles from the Wheel,'" *WWR* 28 (Mar. 1982): 20-24.

M. Wynn Thomas, *The Lunar Light of Whitman's Poetry* (Cambridge and London: Harvard University Press, 1987), 172-75.

"Spirit That Form'd This Scene"

Harold Aspiz, *Expl* 28 (Nov. 1969): 25.

"Spontaneous Me"

Harold Aspiz, "Walt Whitman: The Spermatic Imagination," *AL* 56 (Oct. 1984): 394-95.

Cavitch, *My Soul and I*, 37-43.

Shirley Chosy, "Whitman's 'Spontaneous Me': Sex as Symbol," *WWR* 25 (Sept. 1979): 113-17.

Robert J. Griffin, "Notes on Structural Devices in Whitman's Poetry," *TSL* 6 (1961): 17.

Douglas Leonard, *Expl* 45 (Winter 1987): 29.

Harry R. Warfel, "Whitman's Structural Principles in 'Spontaneous Me,'" *CE* 18 (Jan. 1957): 191-95.

Waskow, *Whitman*, 80-82.

"Starting from Poumanok"

Gay Wilson Allen, *A Reader's Guide to Walt Whitman* (New York: Farrar, Straus & Giroux, 1970), 122-25.

Frances H. Bennett, "'Starting from Poumanok' as Functional Poetry," *WWR* 15 (June 1969): 117-20.

Kenneth Burke, "Policy Made Personal: Whitman's Verse and Prose-Salient Traits," in Hindus, *Leaves of Grass: One Hundred Years After*, 93-95.

Robert J. Griffin, "Notes on Structural Devices in Whitman's Poetry," *TSL* 6 (1961): 17.

Miller, *Walt Whitman's Poetry*, 135-37.

Schyberg, *Walt Whitman*, 152-55.

Cecelia Tichi, *New World, New Earth: Environmental Reform in American Literature from the Puritans through Whitman* (New Haven: Yale University Press, 1979), 227-28.

"Sun-Down Poem"

Cavitch, *My Soul and I*, 106-8.

"There Was a Child Went Forth"

Stephen A. Black, "Radical Utterances from the Soul's Abysms: Toward a New Sense of Whitman," *PMLA* 88 (Jan. 1973): 105-6.

Black, *Whitman's Journeys into Chaos*, 61-66.

Cavitch, *My Soul and I*, 32-35, 37-42.

Richard Chase, "Go-Befores and Embryons: A Biographical Reprise," in Hindus, *Leaves of Grass: One Hundred Years After*, 35-36.

Hollis, *Language and Style in "Leaves of Grass,"* 186-95.

Arthur Lerner, *Psychoanalytically Oriented Criticism of Three American Poets* (Rutherford: Fairleigh Dickinson University Press, 1970), 69-71.

Ivan Marki, "The Last Eleven Poems in the 1885 *Leaves of Grass*," *AL* 54 (May 1982): 237-38.

Ivan Marki, *The Trial of the Poet: An Interpretation of the First Edition of 'Leaves of Grass,'* (New York: Columbia University Press, 1974), 243-45.

Miller, *Walt Whitman' Poetry*, 24-40. Reprinted in *Critical Essays on Walt Whitman*, ed. James Woodress (Boston: G.K. Hall, 1983), 271-80; in *Walt Whitman: A Collection of Criticism*, ed. Arthur Golden (New York: McGraw-Hill, 1974), 72-76.

Sr. M.P. Slattery, "Patterns of Imagery in Whitman's 'There Was a Child Went Forth,'" *WWR* 15 (June 1969): 112-14.

Waskow, *Whitman*, 129-35.

"This Compost"

Cavitch, *My Soul and I*, 87-88.

Robert J. Griffin, *Expl* 21 (Apr. 1963): 68.

"Thou Mother with Thy Equal Brood"

Jeffrey Steinbrink, "'To Span Vast Realms of Space and Time': Whitman's Vision of History," *WWR* 24 (June 1978): 57-58.

"To a Locomotive in Winter"

George Arms, *Expl* 5 (Nov. 1946): 14. Reprinted in Stageberg and Anderson, *Poetry as Experience*, 491; in *The Explicator Cyclopedia* 2:356.

Dickinson, *Suggestions for Teachers of "Introduction to Literature*," 32-33.

Roberts French, "Music for a Mad Scene: A Reading of 'To a Locomotive in Winter,'" *WWR* 27 (Mar. 1981): 32-39.

F.J. Hoffman, "The Technological Fallacy in Contemporary Poetry," *AL* 21 (Mar. 1949): 98. Reprinted in Stageberg and Anderson, *Poetry as Experience*, 491.

Walsh, *Doors into Poetry*, 18-20.

"To the Sunset Breeze"

Dwight Kalita, "Whitman and the Correspondent Breeze," *WWR* 21 (Sept. 1975): 125-30.

"To Think of Time"

Black, *Whitman's Journeys into Chaos*, 120-25.

Carlisle, *The Uncertain Self*, 54-59.

Cavitch, *My Soul and I*, 72-74.

Ivan Marki, "The Last Eleven Poems in the 1885 *Leaves of Grass*," *AL* 54 (May 1982): 235-36.

Ivan Marki, *The Trial of the Poet: An Interpretation of the First Edition of 'Leaves of Grass*,'" (New York: Columbia University Press, 1974), 233-35.

Matthiessen, *American Renaissance*, 610-12.

Estelle W. Taylor, "Analysis and Comparison of the 1855 and 1891 Versions of Whitman's 'To Think of Time,'" *WWR* 13 (Dec. 1967): 107-22.

M. Wynn Thomas, *The Lunar Light of Whitman's Poetry* (Cambridge and London: Harvard University Press, 1987), 34-36.

Hyatt H. Waggoner, *American Visionary Poetry* (Baton Rouge: Louisiana State University Press, 1982), 38-40.

"To You"

Waskow, *Whitman*, 101-5.

"Transpositions"

Robin P. Hoople, "'Chants Democratic and Native American': A Neglected Sequence in the Growth of *Leaves of Grass*," *AL* 42 (May 1970): 189-90.

"Twenty-eight Young Men"

James Davidson, "Whitman's 'Twenty-eight Young Men,'" *WWR* 12 (Dec. 1966): 100-101.

"Two Rivulets"

Alfred H. Marks, "Whitman's Triadic Imagery," *AL* 23 (Mar. 1951): 105-6.

"Unfolded out of the Folds"

Harold Aspiz, "Unfolding the Folds," *WWR* 12 (Dec. 1966): 81-87.

"Unnamed Lands"

Jeffrey Steinbrink, "'To Span Vast Realms of Space and Time': Whitman's Vision of History," *WWR* 24 (June 1978): 48-49.

"Unseen Buds"

Donald Stauffer, "Walt Whitman and Old Age," *WWR* 24 (Dec. 1978): 147.

"Vigil Strange I Kept on the Field One Night"

Cavitch, *My Soul and I*, 160-62.

"A Voice from Death"

Rose Cherie Reissman, "Recurrent Motifs in *Good-bye My Fancy*," *WWR* 21 (Mar. 1975): 32.

"Weave in, Weave in, My Hardy Life"

Jannacone, *Walt Whitman's Poetry*, 50-53.

"We Two, How Long We Were Fool'd"

Cavitch, *My Soul and I*, 119-21.

"When I Heard the Learn'd Astronomer"

Walter Blair and John Gerber, *Better Reading 2: Literature* (Chicago: Scott, Foresman & Company), 114.

Bernth Lindfors, "Whitman's 'When I Hear'd the Learn'd Astronomer,'" *WWR* 10 (Mar. 1964): 19-21.

"When Lilacs Last in the Dooryard Bloom'd"

Richard P. Adams, "Whitman's 'Lilacs' and the Tradition of Pastoral Elegy," *PMLA* 72 (June 1957): 479-87.

Harsharan Singh Ahluwalia, "The Private Self and the Public Self in Whitman's 'Lilacs,'" *WWR* 23 (Dec. 1977): 166-75.

Gay Wilson Allen, *Expl* 10 (June 1952): 55. Reprinted in *The Explicator Cyclopedia* 2:358-59.

Gay Wilson Allen and Charles Davis, from *Critical Selections with Critical Aids: Walt Whitman's Poems* in Coyle, *Poet and the President*, 260-65.

Mutlu Konuk Blasing, "Whitman's 'Lilacs' and the Grammars of Time," *PMLA* 97 (Jan. 1982): 31-39.

Brooks, Lewis, and Warren, *American Literature*, 942-43.

Calvin S. Brown, "The Musical Development of Symbols: Whitman," in Feidelson and Brodtkorb, *Interpretations of American Literature*, 187-96.

Robert Emerson Carlile, "Leitmotif and Whitman's 'Lilacs,'" *Criticism* 13 (Fall 1971): 329-39.

E. Fred Carlisle, *The Uncertain Self*, 157-64.

Cavitch, *My Soul and I*, 162-69.

Richard Chase, *Walt Whitman* (Minneapolis: University of Minnesota Press, 1961), 34-37.

Chase, *Walt Whitman Reconsidered*, 140-45. Reprinted in *Critical Essays on Walt Whitman*, ed. James Woodress (Boston: G.K. Hall, 1983), 253-57.

Richard A. Davidson, "Ambivalent Imagery in Whitman's 'Lilacs,'" *WWR* 14 (June 1968): 54-56.

Lyle Domina, "Whitman's 'Lilacs': Process of Self-Realization," *ESQ*, no. 58 (Part Four, 1970): 124-27.

Charles C. Doyle, "Poetry and Pastoral: A Dimension of Whitman's 'Lilacs,'" *WWR* 15 (Dec. 1969): 242-45.

W.P. Elledge, "Whitman's 'Lilacs' as Romantic Narrative," *WWR* 12 (Sept. 1966): 59-67.

Charles Feidelson, from *Symbolism and American Literature* in Coyle, *Poet and the President*, 236-39.

Marvin Felheim, "The Problem of Structure in Some Poems by Whitman," in Ludwig, *Aspects of American Poetry*, 88-91.

Evelyn J. Hinz, "Whitman's 'Lilacs': The Power of Elegy," *BuR* 20 (Fall 1972): 35-54.

Andrew Hook, *American Literature in Context*. Vol. 3, *1865-1900* (London: Metheun, 1983), 14-18.

Hutchinson, *The Ecstatic Whitman*, 149-69.

Joseph Jones, *Expl* 9 (Apr. 1951): 42. Reprinted in *The Explicator Cyclopedia* 2:356-58.

T.J. Kallsen, "The World of 'When Lilacs Last in the Dooryard Bloom'd,'" in Coyle, *Poet and the President*, 221-27.

Mark Kinkead-Weekes, "Walt Whitman Passes the Full-Stop by. . . . ," in Lee, *Nineteenth-Century American Poetry*, 46-51.

Oswald LeWinter, "Whitman's 'Lilacs,'" *WWR* 10 (Mar. 1964): 10-14.

Matthiessen, *American Renaissance*, 618-23. Reprinted in Locke, Gibson, and Arms, *Readings for Liberal Education*, 543-47.

Edwin H. Miller, *Walt Whitman's Poetry*, 186-98.

James E. Miller, Jr., from *A Critical Guide to 'Leaves of Grass'* in Coyle, *Poet and the President*, 273-82.

James A. Nelson, "Ecstacy and Transformation in Whitman's 'Lilacs,'" *WWR* 18 (Dec. 1972): 113-23.

Ferner Nuhn, "*Leaves of Grass* Viewed as an Epic," *ArQ* 7 (Winter 1951): 335-36.

Margaret C. Patterson, "'Lilacs,' a Sonata," *WWR* 14 (June 1968): 46-50.

Joseph Pici, "An Editing of Walt Whitman's 'When Lilacs Last in the Dooryard Bloom'd,'" *UDR* 9 (Summer 1972): 35.

Floyd Stovall, "Main Drifts in Whitman's Poetry," *AL* 4 (Mar. 1932): 13-15.

M. Wynn Thomas, *The Lunar Light of Whitman's Poetry* (Cambridge and London: Harvard University Press, 1987), 241-51.

Waskow, *Whitman*, 222-42.

Patricia Lee Yongue, "Violence in Whitman's 'When Lilacs Last in the Dooryard Bloom'd,'" *WWR* 4 (Mar. 1984): 12-20.

"Whispers of Heavenly Death"

J.T. Ledbetter, "Whitman's Power in the Short Poem: A Discussion of 'Whispers of Heavenly Death,'" *WWR* 21 (Dec. 1975): 155-58.

"Whoever You Are Holding Me Now in Hand"

Cavitch, *My Soul and I*, 127-29.

Philip Y. Colemen, "Walt Whitman's Ambiguities of 'I,'" *PLL* 5 Supplement (Summer 1969): 42-45.

Lloyd Frankenberg, *Invitation to Poetry* (New York: Doubleday & Company, 1956), 97-99.

"Who Learns My Lesson Complete?"

Don Bogen, "'I' and 'You' in 'Who Learns My Lesson Complete?': Some Aspects of Whitman's Poetic Evolution," *WWR* 25 (Sept. 1979): 87-98.

Hollis, *Language and Style in "Leaves of Grass,"* 241-48.

"A Woman Waits For Me"

Cavitch, *My Soul and I*, 117-19.

Myrth J. Killingsworth, "Whitman's Love-Spendings," *WWR* 26 (Dec. 1980): 145-53.

"The World Below the Brine"

Ida Fasel, *Expl* 25 (Sept. 1966): 7.

William A. Freedman, *Expl* 23 (Jan. 1965): 39.

"The Wound-Dresser"

Harold Aspiz, *Walt Whitman and the Body Beautiful* (Urbana: University of Illinois Press, 1980), 89-95.

Agnes Dicken Cannon, "Fervid Atmosphere and Typical Events: Autobiography in *Drum-Taps*," *WWR* 20 (Sept. 1974): 86-87.

"Year of Meteors"

Jerry Herndon, "Parallels in Melville and Whitman," *WWR* 24 (Sept. 1978): 95-108.

WHITTIER, JOHN GREENLEAF

"Among the Hills"

Leary, *John Greenleaf Whittier*, 144-46.

"Amy Wentworth"

Pickard, *John Greenleaf Whittier*, 74-75.

"Barbara Frietchie"

Arms, *The Fields Were Green*, 43-44.

Leary, *John Greenleaf Whittier*, 109-10.

"The Barefoot Boy"

Leary, *John Greenleaf Whittier*, 148-50.

"Birchbrook Mill"

Arms, *The Fields Were Green*, 37-38.

Pickard, *John Greenleaf Whittier*, 73-74.

"The Black Fox"

Frances Pray, *A Study of Whittier's Apprenticeship as a Poet* (Bristol: Musgrove Printing House, 1930), 84-89.

"The Bridal of Pennacock"

Leary, *John Greenleaf Whittier*, 125-27.

"Cassandra Southwick"

Pickard, *John Greenleaf Whittier*, 65-66.

"The Cypress-Tree of Ceylon"

Leary, *John Greenleaf Whittier*, 120-22.

"The Eternal Goodness"

Pickard, *John Greenleaf Whittier*, 111-12.

"Ichabod"

Arms, *The Fields Were Green*, 39-40.

Wayne R. Kime, *Expl* 28 (Mar. 1970): 59.

Notley Sinclair Maddox, *Expl* 18 (Apr. 1960): 38. Reprinted in *The Explicator Cyclopedia* 2:359-60.

Notley Sinclair Maddox, *Expl* 30 (Mar. 1972): 59.

Pickard, *John Greenleaf Whittier*,105-7.

"Mabel Martin"

Pickard, *John Greenleaf Whittier*, 36-38.

"Maud Muller"

Arms, *The Fields Were Green*, 41-43.

Leary, *John Greenleaf Whittier*, 150-54.

Pickard, *John Greenleaf Whittier*, 82-84.

"Moll Pitcher"

Frances Pray, *A Study of Whittier's Apprenticeship as a Poet* (Bristol: Musgrove Printing House, 1930), 89-104.

"My Namesake"

Edward Wagenknecht, *John Greenleaf Whittier: A Portrait in Paradox* (New York: Oxford University Press, 1967), 11-13.

"The Panorama"

Leary, *John Greenleaf Whittier*, 113-16.

"The Pennsylvania Pilgrim"

Arms, *The Fields Were Green*, 38-39.

Leary, *John Greenleaf Whittier*, 129-33.

Pickard, *John Greenleaf Whittier*, 88-90.

"The Pipes at Lucknow: An Incident of the Sepoy Mutiny"

Brooks, Lewis, and Warren, *American Literature*, 547-48.

"The Prophecy of Samuel Sewall"

Leary, *John Greenleaf Whittier*, 133-35.

"Skipper's Ireson's Ride"

Arms, *The Fields Were Green*, 40-44.

Leary, *John Greenleaf Whittier*, 137-41.

Pickard, *John Greenleaf Whittier*, 69-73.

"Snow-Bound"

Arms, *The Fields Were Green*, 44-47.

E. Miller Budick, "The Immortalizing Power of Imagination: A Reading of Whittier's 'Snow-Bound,'" *ESQ* 31 (Second Quarter 1985): 89-99.

Leary, *John Greenleaf Whittier*, 157-65.

Lewis H. Miller, Jr., "The Supernaturalism of 'Snow-Bound,'" *NEQ* 79 (Sept. 1980): 291-307.

John P. Pickard, "Imagistic and Structural Unity in 'Snow-Bound,'" *CE* 21 (Mar. 1960): 338-43.

Pickard, *John Greenleaf Whittier*, 90-99.

Donald A. Ringe, "Sound Imagery in Whittier's 'Snow-Bound,'" *PLL* 5 (Spring 1969): 139-44.

Leonard M. Trawick, "Whittier's 'Snow-Bound': A Poem about Imagination," *ELWIU* 1 (Spring 1974): 46-53.

Robert Penn Warren, *John Greenleaf Whittier's Poetry: An Appraisal and a Selection* (Minneapolis: University of Minnesota Press, 1971), 47-54.

"Telling the Bees"

Leary, *John Greenleaf Whittier*, 154-57.

Pickard, *John Greenleaf Whittier*, 56-58.

Sanders, *The Discovery of Poetry*, 282-85.

"To J. P."

Abe C. Ravits, *Expl* 13 (Feb. 1955): 22. Reprinted in *The Explicator Cyclopedia* 2:360-61.

"The Weird Gathering"

Frances Pray, *A Study of Whittier's Apprenticeship as a Poet* (Bristol: Musgrove Printing House, 1930), 72-76.

"The Wreck of Rivermouth"

Pickard, *John Greenleaf Whittier*, 78-79.

WIGGLESWORTH, MICHAEL

"A Conclusion Hortatory"

Richard Crowder, *No Featherbed to Heaven: A Biography of Michael Wigglesworth, 1631-1705* (Lansing: Michigan State University, 1962), 135-36.

"The Day of Doom"

Richard Crowder, *No Featherbed to Heaven: A Biography of Michael Wigglesworth, 1631-1705* (Lansing: Michigan State University, 1962), 107-9.

"God's Controversy with New England"

Richard Crowder, *No Featherbed to Heaven: A Biography of Michael Wigglesworth, 1631-1705* (Lansing: Michigan State University, 1962), 115-19.

"Meditation III"

Richard Crowder, *No Featherbed to Heaven: A Biography of Michael Wigglesworth, 1631-1705* (Lansing: Michigan State University, 1962), 136-7.

"A Postscript unto the Reader"

Richard Crowder, *No Featherbed to Heaven: A Biography of Michael Wigglesworth, 1631-1705* (Lansing: Michigan State University, 1962), 111-12.

"Songs"

Richard Crowder, *No Featherbed to Heaven: A Biography of Michael Wigglesworth, 1631-1705* (Lansing: Michigan State University, 1962), 138-43.

"Vanity of Vanities: A Song of Emptiness"

Daly, *God's Altar*, 133-34.

WILCOX, ELLA WHEELER

"After the Fierce Midsummer All Ablaze"

I.A. Richards, *Principles of Literary Criticism* 2d ed. (London: Kegan Paul, Trench, Trubner & Company, 1926), 200-202.

WILLIAMS, ROGER

"Key into the Language of America"

Daly, *God's Altar*, 154-61.

Main Sources Consulted

ABAD, GEMINO H. *A Formal Approach to Lyric Poetry*. Quezon City, Philippines: University of the Philippines Press, 1978.

ADLER, JOYCE. *War in Melville's Imagination*. New York: New York University Press, 1981.

American Literature: A Journal of Literary History, Criticism, and Bibliography 1 (1929)-59 (December 1987).

ANDERSON, CHARLES. *Emily Dickinson's Poetry: Stairway of Surprise*. New York: Holt, Rinehart & Winston, 1960.

ARMS, GEORGE. *The Fields Were Green: A New View of Bryant, Whittier, Holmes, Lowell, and Longfellow*. Stanford: Stanford University Press, 1953.

ARVIN, NEWTON. *Longfellow: His Life and Works*. Boston: Little, Brown & Co., 1962.

BAKER, WILLIAM E. *Syntax in English Poetry, 1870-1930*. Berkeley: University of California Press, 1967.

BARKER, WENDY. *Lunacy of Light: Emily Dickinson and the Experience of Metaphor*. Carbondale: Southern Illinois University Press, 1987.

241

BASLER, ROY P. *Sex, Symbolism, and Psychology in Literature*. New Brunswick: Rutgers University Press, 1948.

BEATY, JEROME, and WILLIAM H. MATCHETT. *Poetry: From Statement to Meaning*. New York: Oxford University Press, 1965.

BENFEY, CHRISTOPHER. *Emily Dickinson and the Problem of Others*. Amherst: University of Massachusetts Press, 1984.

BLACK, STEPHEN. *Whitman's Journeys into Chaos*. Princeton: Princeton University Press, 1975.

BLACKMUR, R.P. *The Expense of Greatness*. New York: Arrow Editions, 1940.

_____. *Language as Gesture: Essays in Poetry*. New York: Harcourt, Brace & Co., 1952.

BLAIR, WALTER, THEODORE HORNBERGER, and RANDALL STEWART, eds. *The Literature of the United States*. Chicago: Scott, Foresman, & Co., 1947.

BLASING, MUTLU. *American Poetry: The Rhetoric of Its Forms*. New Haven: Yale University Press, 1987.

BLOOM, HAROLD. *A Map of Misreading*. New York: Oxford University Press, 1975.

_____. *Poetry and Repression: Revisionism from Blake to Stevens*. New Haven: Yale University Press, 1976.

BOWRA, C.M. *The Romantic Imagination*. Cambridge: Harvard University Press, 1949.

BROOKS, CLEANTH, Jr., JOHN THIBAUT PURSER, and ROBERT PENN WARREN. *An Approach to Literature*. Rev. ed. New York: F.S. Crofts & Co., 1942. 3d ed., 1952. 4th ed., 1964.

BROOKS, CLEANTH, Jr., and ROBERT PENN WARREN. *Understanding Poetry: An Anthology for College Students*. New York: Henry Holt & Co., 1938. Rev. ed., 1950. 4th ed., 1964.

BROOKS, CLEANTH, Jr., R.W.B. LEWIS, and ROBERT PENN WARREN. *American Literature: The Makers and the Making*. New York: St. Martin's Press, 1973.

BROWN, HARRY, and JOHN MILSTEAD. *Patterns in Poetry: An Introductory Anthology*. Glenview: Scott, Foresman & Co., 1968.

BUDICK, E. MILLER. *Emily Dickinson and the Life of Language: A Study in Symbolic Poetics*. Baton Rouge: Louisiana State University Press, 1985.

CAMERON, SHARON. *Lyric Time: Dickinson and the Limits of Genre*. Baltimore: Johns Hopkins University Press, 1979.

CARLISLE, E. FRED. *The Uncertain Self: Whitman's Drama of Identity*. Lansing: Michigan State University Press, 1973.

CAVITCH, DAVID. *My Soul and I: The Inner Life of Walt Whitman*. Boston: Beacon Press, 1985.

CESTRE, CHARLES. *An Introduction to Edwin Arlington Robinson*. New York: Macmilliam Co., 1930.

CHASE, RICHARD. *Emily Dickinson*. New York: William Sloane Associates, 1951.

_____. *Walt Whitman Reconsidered*. New York: William Sloane Associates, 1955.

CHATMAN, SEYMOUR. *An Introduction to the Language of Poetry*. Boston: Houghton Mifflin, 1968.

CODY, JOHN. *After Great Pain: The Inner Life of Emily Dickinson*. Cambridge: Harvard University Press, 1971.

COHAN, B. BERNARD. *Writing About Literature*. Chicago: Scott, Foresman & Co., 1963.

COHEN, EDWARD. *Ebenezer Cooke: The Sot-Weed Canon*. Athens: University of Georgia Press, 1975.

Colby Library Quarterly 1 (February 1946)-14 (March 1978).

College English 1 (October 1939)-49 (December 1987).

COYLE, WILLIAM. *The Poet and the President: Whitman's Lincoln Poems*. New York: Odyssey Press, 1962.

Criticism: A Quarterly for Literature and the Arts 1 (Winter 1959)-29 (Fall 1987).

DAICHES, DAVID, and WILLIAM CHARVAT. *Poems in English, 1530-1940*. New York: Ronald Press Company, 1950.

DALY, ROBERT. *God's Altar: The World and the Flesh in Puritan Poetry*. Berkeley: University of California Press, 1978.

DANIELS, EARL. *The Art of Reading Poetry*. New York: Farrar & Rinehart, 1941.

DAVIS, THOMAS, ed. *14 by Emily Dickinson*. Chicago: Scott, Foresman & Co., 1964.

DICKINSON, LEON T. *Suggestions for Teachers of "Introduction to Literature,"* 5th ed. Teachers Manual. See Locke, Gibson, and Arms, *Readings for Liberal Education*.

Dickinson Studies [formerly *Emily Dickinson Bulletin*], no. 19 (December 1971)-no. 64 (Second Half 1987).

DIEHL, JOANNE. *Emily Dickinson and The Romantic Imagination*. Princeton: Princeton University Press, 1981.

DREW, ELIZABETH. *Poetry: An Modern Guide to Its Understanding and Enjoyment*. New York: W.W. Norton & Co., 1959.

DUNCAN, DOUGLAS. *Emily Dickinson*. Edinburgh: Oliver & Boyd, 1965

Early American Literature 2 (Spring 1967)-22 (Fall 1987).

EBERWEIN, JANE DONAHUE. *Dickinson: Strategies of Limitation*. Amherst: University of Massachusetts Press, 1985.

ELLIOTT, EMORY. *Revolutionary Writers and Authority in the New Republic*. New York: Oxford University Press, 1982.

English Journal 19 (January 1930)-76 (December 1987).

English Language Notes 1 (September 1963)-25 (December 1987).

ESQ 20 (First Quarter 1973)-33 (First Quarter 1986).

Essays in Criticism 1 (January 1951)-37 (October 1987).

The Explicator 1 (October 1942)-46 (Fall 1987).

The Explicator Cyclopedia. Edited by Charles Child Walcutt and J. Edwin Whitesell. Vol. 1, *Modern Poetry*. Vol. 2, *Traditional Poetry: Medieval to Late Victorian*. Chicago: Quadrangle Books, 1, 1966; 2, 1968.

FEIDELSON, CHARLES, Jr., and PAUL BRODTKORB, Jr. *Interpretations of American Literature*. London: Oxford University Press, 1959.

FERLAZZO, PAUL. *Critical Essays on Emily Dickinson*. Boston: G.K. Hall, 1984.

FLEMING, ROBERT. *James Weldon Johnson*. Boston: Twayne, 1987.

FORD, THOMAS. *Heaven Beguiles the Tired: Death in the Poetry of Emily Dickinson*. University: University of Alabama Press, 1966.

FRIAR, KIMON, and JOHN MALCOLM BRINNIN. *Modern Poetry, American and British*. New York: Appleton-Century-Crofts, 1951.

FRIEDMAN, NORMAN, and CHARLES A. MCLAUGHLIN. *Poetry: An Introduction to Its Form and Art*. New York: Harper & Brothers, 1961.

GILBERT, SANDRA, and SUSAN GUBAR. *The Madwoman in the Attic: The Woman Writer and the Nineteenth-Century Literary Imagination*. New Haven and London: Yale University Press, 1979.

GODHES, CLARENCE, ed. *Essays on American Literature in Honor of Jay B. Hubbell*. Durham: Duke University Press, 1967.

GRIFFITH, CLARK. *The Long Shadow: Emily Dickinson's Tragic Poetry*. Princeton: Princeton University Press, 1964.

GWYNN, FREDERICK, RALPH CONDEE, and ARTHUR LEWIS, eds. *The Case for Poetry*. Englewood Cliffs: Prentice-Hall, 1954.

MAIN SOURCES CONSULTED

HALLIBURTON, DAVID. *Edgar Allan Poe: A Phenomenological View*. Princeton: Princeton University Press, 1973.

HINDUS, MILTON. *Leaves of Grass: One Hundred Years After*. Stanford: Stanford University Press, 1955.

HOFFMAN, DANIEL. *The Poetry of Stephen Crane*. New York: Columbia University Press, 1957.

HOLLIS, C. CARROLL. *Language and Style in "Leaves of Grass."* Baton Rouge and London: Louisiana State University Press, 1983.

HUTCHINSON, GEORGE. *The Ecstatic Whitman: Literary Shamanism & the Crisis of the Union*. Columbus: Ohio State University Press, 1986.

JANNACONE, PASQUALE. *Walt Whitman's Poetry*. Translated by Peter Mitilineos. Washington: NCR/Microcard Editions, 1973.

JEROME, JUDSON. *Poetry: Premeditated Art*. Boston: Houghton Mifflin Co., 1968.

JOHNSON, GREG. *Emily Dickinson: Perception and the Poet's Quest*. University: University of Alabama Press, 1985.

Journal of English Literary History 1 (April 1934)-54 (Winter 1987).

JUHASZ, SUZANNE. *Feminist Critics Read Emily Dickinson*. Bloomington: Indiana University Press, 1983.

_____. *The Undiscovered Continent: Emily Dickinson and the Space of Mind*. Bloomington: Indiana University Press, 1983.

KAPLAN, ESTELLE. *Philosophy in the Poetry of Edwin Arlington Robinson* New York: Columbia University Press, 1940.

KELLER, KARL. *The Example of Edward Taylor*. Amherst: University of Massachusetts, 1975.

KHER, INDER. *The Landscape of Absence: Emily Dickinson's Poetry*. New Haven and London: Yale University Press, 1974.

KIMPEL, BEN. *Emily Dickinson as Philosopher*. New York and Toronto: Edwin Mellen Press, 1981.

KIRBY, THOMAS AUSTIN, and WILLIAM JOHN OLIVE, eds. *Essays in Honor of Esmond Linworth Marilla*. Baton Rouge: Louisiana State University Press, 1970.

KIRK, RICHARD RAY, and ROGER PHILIP MCCUTCHEON. *An Introduction to the Study of Poetry*. New York: American Book Co., 1934.

KNAPP, BETTINA. *Edgar Allan Poe*. New York: Ungar, 1984.

LEARY, LEWIS. *John Greenleaf Whittier*. New York: Twayne Publishers, 1961.

LEE, A. ROBERT, ed. *Nineteenth-Century American Poetry*. London: Vision; N.J.: Barnes & Noble, 1985.

LINDBERG-SEYERSTED, BRITA. *The Voice of the Poet: Aspects of Style in the Poetry of Emily Dickinson*. Cambridge: Harvard University Press, 1968.

LOCKE, LOUIS G., WILLIAM M. GIBSON, and GEORGE ARMS. *Readings for Liberal Education*. Volume 2, *Introduction to Literature*. New York: Rinehart & Co., 1948. 3d ed., 1957. 4th ed., New York: Holt, Rinehart & Winston, 1962. 5th ed., 1967.

LOVING, JEROME. *Emily Dickinson: The Poet on the Second Story*. Cambridge: Cambridge University Press, 1986.

LUCAS, DOLORES. *Emily Dickinson and Riddle*. DeKalb: Northern Illinois University, 1969.

LUDWIG, RICHARD M., ed. *Aspects of American Poetry: Essays Presented to Howard Mumford Jones*. Columbus: Ohio State University Press, 1962.

McLEAN, ALBERT, Jr. *William Cullen Bryant*. New York: Twayne, 1964.

MALLOY, CHARLES. *A Study of Emerson's Major Poems*. Edited by Kenneth Walter Cameron. Hartford: Transcendental Books, 1973.

MARTIN, JAY, ed. *A Singer in the Dawn: Reinterpretations of Paul Laurence Dunbar*. New York: Dodd, Mead & Co., 1975.

MARTIN, WENDY. *An American Triptych: Anne Bradstreet, Emily Dickinson, and Adrienne Rich*. Chapel Hill and London: University of North Carolina Press, 1984.

MARTZ, LOUIS L. *The Poem of the Mind: Essays on Poetry English and American*. New York: Oxford University Press, 1966.

MATTHIESSEN, F.O. *American Renaissance: Art and Expression in the Age of Emerson and Whitman*. New York: Oxford University Press, 1941.

MILLER, CRISTANNE. *Emily Dickinson: A Poet's Grammar*. Cambridge: Harvard University Press, 1987.

MILLER, EDWIN HAVILAND. *Walt Whitman's Poetry: A Psychological Journey*. Boston: Houghton Mifflin Co., 1968.

MILLER, RUTH. *The Poetry of Emily Dickinson*. Middletown: Wesleyan University Press, 1968.

MILLET, FRED B. *Reading Poetry: A Method of Analysis with Selections for Study*. Lincoln: University of Nebraska Press, 1960.

Modern Language Notes 40 (January 1925)-102 (December 1987).

Modern Language Quarterly 1 (March 1940)-47 (September 1986).

MOSSBERG, BARBARA CLARKE. *Emily Dickinson: When a Writer Is a Daughter*. Bloomington: Indiana University Press, 1982.

MUDGE, JEAN. *Emily Dickinson and the Image of Home*. Amherst: University of Massachusetts Press, 1975.

New England Quarterly 1 (1928)-60 (December 1987).

PATTERSON, REBECCA. *Emily Dickinson's Imagery*. Amherst: University of Massachusetts Press, 1979.

PEACH, LINDEN. *British Influence on the Birth of American Literature*. London: Macmillian Press, 1982.

PEARCE, ROY HARVEY. *The Continuity of American Poetry*. Princeton: Princeton University Press, 1961.

PECKHAM, MORSE, and SEYMOUR CHATMAN. *Word, Meaning, Poem*. New York: Thomas Crowell Co., 1961.

PERRINE, LAURENCE. *The Art of Total Relevance*. Rowley: Newbury House Publishers, 1976.

_____. *Sound and Sense: An Introduction to Poetry*. New York: Harcourt, Brace & Co., 1956. 2d ed., 1963.

PERRINE, LAURENCE, and JAMES M. REID. *100 American Poems of the Twentieth Century*. New York: Harcourt, Brace & World, 1966.

PICKARD, JOHN. *John Greenleaf Whittier: An Introduction and Interpretation*. New York: Barnes & Noble, 1961.

PIERCY, JOSEPHINE. *Anne Bradstreet*. New York: Twayne, 1965.

POLLAK, VIVIAN. *Dickinson: The Anxiety of Gender*. Ithaca and London: Cornell University Press, 1984.

PORTER, DAVID. *The Art of Emily Dickinson's Early Poetry*. Cambridge: Harvard University Press, 1966.

_____. *Dickinson: The Modern Idiom*. Cambridge: Harvard University Press, 1981.

_____. *Emerson and Literary Change*. Cambridge and London: Harvard University Press, 1978.

Publications of the Modern Language Association of America 40 (March 1925)-102 (November 1987).

REDMAN, BEN RAY. *Edwin Arlington Robinson*. New York: Robert McBride & Co., 1926.

REVELL, PAUL. *Paul Laurence Dunbar*. Boston: G.K. Hall, 1979.

RICHARDSON, ROBERT D. *Myth and Literature in the American Renaissance*. Bloomington, Ind.: Indiana University Press, 1978.

ROBINSON, JOHN. *Emily Dickinson: Looking to Canaan*. London: Faber & Faber, 1986.

ROSENTHAL, M.L., and A.J.M. SMITH. *Exploring Poetry*. New York: Macmillan Co., 1955.

ROWE, KAREN. *Saint and Singer: Edward Taylor's Typology and the Poetics of Meditation*. Cambridge: Cambridge University Press, 1986.

SALSKA, AGNIESZKA. *Walt Whitman and Emily Dickinson: Poetry of Central Consciousness*. Philadelphia: University of Pennsylvania Press, 1985.

SANDERS, THOMAS E. *The Discovery of Poetry*. Glenview: Scott, Foresman & Co., 1967.

SATIN, JOSEPH. *Reading Poetry* (Part Four of *Reading Literature*). Boston: Houghton Mifflin Co., 1964.

SCHYBERG, FREDRICK. *Walt Whitman*. Translated by Evie Allen. New York: Columbia University Press, 1951.

SEWALL, RICHARD B. *Emily Dickinson: A Collection of Critical Essays*. Englewood Cliffs: Prentice-Hall, 1963.

Sewanee Review 33 (January 1925)-95 (October-December 1987).

SHERWOOD, WILLIAM. *Circumference and Circumstance: Stages in the Mind and Art of Emily Dickinson*. New York: Columbia University Press, 1968.

SHURR, WILLIAM. *The Mystery of Iniquity: Melville as Poet, 1857-1891*. Lexington: University Press of Kentucky, 1972.

The Southern Review 1 (July 1935)-7 (Spring 1942); 1, no. 1, n.s. (January 1965)-23 (Autumn 1987).

STAGEBERG, NORMAN C., and WALLACE ANDERSON. *Poetry as Experience*. New York: American Book Co., 1952.

STALLMAN, R.W., and R.E. WATTERS. *The Creative Reader: An Anthology of Fiction, Drama, and Poetry*. New York: Ronald Press Co., 1954.

STANFORD, ANN. *Anne Bradstreet: The Worldly Puritan*. New York: B. Franklin, 1975.

STEIN, WILLIAM. *The Poetry of Melville's Late Years*. Albany: State University of New York Press, 1970.

Studies in Romanticism 1, no. 1 (Autumn 1961)-26 (Winter 1987).

STOVALL, FLOYD. *Edgar Poe the Poet*. Charlottesville: University of Virginia Press, 1969.

TATE, ALLEN. *On the Limits of Poetry*. New York: Swallow Press; William Morrow & Co., 1948.

_____. *Reactionary Essays on Poetry and Ideas*. New York: Charles Scribner's Sons, 1936.

_____. *Reason in Madness*. New York: G.P. Putnam's Sons, 1941.

Texas Studies in Literature and Language 1 (Spring 1959)-29 (Winter 1987).

Tulane Studies in English 1 (1949)-24 (1983).

UNGER, LEONARD, and WILLIAM VAN O'CONNOR. *Poems for Study*. New York: Rinehart & Co., 1953.

VAN DOREN, MARK. *Introduction to Poetry*. New York: William Sloane Associates, 1951.

VITZTHUM, RICHARD. *Land and Sea: The Lyric Poetry of Philip Freneau*. Minneapolis: University of Minnesota, 1978.

WAGENKNECHT, EDWARD. *Henry Wadsworth Longfellow: His Poetry and Prose*. New York: Ungar, 1986.

WAGGONER, HYATT. *Emerson as Poet*. Princeton: Princeton University Press, 1974.

WAIN, JOHN, ed. *Interpretations: Essays on Twelve English Poems*. London: Routledge & Kegan Paul, 1955

WALLACE, RONALD. *God Be with the Clown: Humor in American Poetry*. Columbia: University of Missouri, 1984.

WALSH, CHAD. *Doors into Poetry*. Englewood Cliffs: Prentice-Hall, 1962.

Walt Whitman Review [formerly the *Walt Whitman Newsletter*] 1 (January 1955)-28 (December 1982). Superseded by *Walt Whitman Quarterly Review* 1 (June 1983)-5 (Fall 1987).

WARREN, AUSTIN. *Rage for Order: Essays in Criticism*. Chicago: University of Chicago Press, 1948.

WASKOW, HOWARD J. *Whitman: Explorations in Form*. Chicago: University of Chicago Press, 1966.

WEISBUCH, ROBERT. *Emily Dickinson's Poetry*. Chicago: University of Chicago Press, 1972.

WHEELER, CHARLES B. *The Design of Poetry*. New York: W.W. Norton & Co., 1966.

WHICHER, GEORGE. *This Was a Poet: A Critical Biography of Emily Dickinson*. New York: Charles Scribner's Sons, 1938. Reprint. Ann Arbor: University of Michigan Press, 1957.

WHITE, ELIZABETH WADE. *Anne Bradstreet: The Tenth Muse*. New York: Oxford University Press, 1971.

WINTERS, YVOR. *Edwin Arlington Robinson*. Norfolk: New Directions Books, 1946. Reprint. New York: New Directions, 1971.

_____. *Forms of Discovery: Critical and Historical Essays on the Forms of the Short Poem in English*. Chicago: Alan Swallow, 1967.

_____. *In Defense of Reason*. New York: Swallow Press; William Morrow & Co., 1947; 3d ed., Denver: Alan Swallow, 1960.

_____. *Maule's Curse*. Norfolk: New Directions, 1938.

WOLOSKY, SHIRA. *Emily Dickinson: A Voice of War*. New Haven: Yale University Press, 1984.

YODER, R.A. *Emerson and the Orphic Poet in America*. Berkeley, Los Angeles, and London: University of California Press, 1978.